D0707681

DESCRIBING
ARCHIVES

A Content Standard

SOCIETY OF
American
Archivists

Chicago

THE SOCIETY OF AMERICAN ARCHIVISTS
www.archivists.org

Printed in the United States of America
Fourth printing 2007 (index added).
Fifth printing September 2008.

Describing Archives: A Content Standard (DACS) was officially adopted as a standard by the Council of the Society of American Archivists in March 2005, following review by the SAA Standards Committee, its Technical Subcommittee for Descriptive Standards, and the general archival community.

The Library of Congress has catalogued the 2004 edition as follows:

Library of Congress Cataloging-in-Publication Data
Society of American Archivists.
 Describing archives : a content standard.
     p. cm.
 Includes bibliographical references.
 ISBN 1-931666-08-3
 1. Cataloging of archival material--Standards. I. Title: DACS. II. Title.

Z695.2.S625 2004
025.3'414--dc22

                                                              2004052584

Contents

Preface   v
Acknowledgements   ix
Statement of Principles   xi
Overview of Archival Description   xvii

Part I—Describing Archival Materials

Introduction to Describing Archival Materials   3

1.   Levels of Description   7

2.   Identity Elements
     2.1 Reference Code   13
     2.2 Name and Location of Repository   16
     2.3 Title   17
     2.4 Date   24
     2.5 Extent   29
     2.6 Name of Creator(s)   33
     2.7 Administrative/Biographical History   34

3.   Content and Structure Elements
     3.1 Scope and Content   35
     3.2 System of Arrangement   40

4.   Conditions of Access and Use Elements
     4.1 Conditions Governing Access   43
     4.2 Physical Access   46
     4.3 Technical Access   48
     4.4 Conditions Governing Reproduction and Use   50
     4.5 Languages and Scripts of the Material   54
     4.6 Finding Aids   56

5.   Acquisition and Appraisal Elements
     5.1 Custodial History   59
     5.2 Immediate Source of Acquisition   61
     5.3 Appraisal, Destruction, and Scheduling Information 63
     5.4 Accruals   66

6. Related Materials Elements
    6.1 Existence and Location of Originals   69
    6.2 Existence and Location of Copies   71
    6.3 Related Archival Materials   73
    6.4 Publication Note   75

7. Note Elements   77

8. Description Control Elements   81

Part II—Describing Creators

Introduction to Describing Creators   85

9. Identifying Creators   89

10. Administrative/Biographical History   93

11. Authority Records   105

Part III—Forms of Names

Introduction to Forms of Names   117

12. Form of Names for Persons and Families   119

13. Form of Geographic Names   153

14. Form of Names for Corporate Bodies   159

Appendices

A. Glossary   201

B. Companion Standards   209

C. Crosswalks   213

D. Full EAD and MARC 21 Examples   225

Index   271

Preface

Archives, Personal Papers, and Manuscripts[1] has served the U.S. archival community as a content standard for catalog records for more than two decades. The advent of new technologies and descriptive tools, including the Web, XML, and EAD, have encouraged archivists to go beyond placing basic catalog records in online systems to putting full descriptions of their holdings, frequently enhanced with digital images, on the Web. Archival descriptions in an online environment, where not only researchers but other archivists can see them, have highlighted differences and similarities in practice between repositories and brought to the fore the need for a content standard for finding aids.

As a descriptive standard of the Society of American Archivists, *APPM* was placed on a review/revision schedule in the early 1990s. By the time EAD was launched in 1996, it was apparent that any revision of *APPM* should incorporate rules for finding aids as well as for catalog records. It was also thought that the two international standards, the *General International Standard Archival Description (ISAD(G))*[2] and the *International Standard Archival Authority Record for Corporate Bodies, Persons, and Families (ISAAR (CPF))*,[3] should be accommodated, and that perhaps a joint Canadian/U.S. standard could be created.

To that end, discussions with descriptive standards experts in Canada began with a week-long Bentley Library Research Fellowship Program project in summer 1996. The results of that project were promising enough that the discussions continued and, in 1999, the Gladys Kreibel Delmas Foundation funded another joint meeting in Toronto, which produced the "Toronto Accord on Descriptive Standards." It seemed that there was enough common ground to pursue a joint project.

The CUSTARD Project

In 2001 the Society of American Archivists received a grant from the National Endowment for the Humanities, which was augmented by the Delmas Foundation, to embark on a joint U.S.-Canadian descriptive standard project called CUSTARD (Canadian-U.S. Task Force on Archival Description). The project as envisioned would produce a content standard that would replace *APPM* and possibly the Canadian *Rules for Archival Description (RAD)*,[4] accommodate all the data elements of *ISAD(G)* and *ISAAR (CPF)*, and be applicable to all types of archival descriptions. To do this, eight Canadian

---

[1] Steven Hensen, comp., *Archives, Personal Papers, and Manuscripts*, 2nd ed. (Chicago: Society of American Archivists, 1989). The first edition was published in 1983.

[2] ICA Committee on Descriptive Standards, *ISAD(G): General International Standard Archival Description*, 2nd ed. (Ottawa: International Council on Archives, 1999). Available online at <http://www.ica.org/biblio/cds/isad_g_2e.pdf>.

[3] ICA Ad Hoc Commission on Descriptive Standards, *ISAAR (CPF): International Standard Archival Authority Record for Corporate Bodies, Persons and Families*, (Ottawa, International Council on Archives, 1996). Available online at <http://www.ica.org/biblio/isaar_eng.pdf>.

[4] *Rules for Archival Description* (Ottawa, Bureau of Canadian Archivists, 1990). Available online at <http://www.cdncouncilarchives.ca/archdescrules.html>.

archivists, seven U.S. archivists, and the project manager[5] met four times over two years to draft a set of rules.

By spring 2003 it had become apparent that there were enough significant differences between Canadian and U.S. practice that a joint content standard was not possible at this time. Consequently, the Canadians are using the CUSTARD project draft as the basis for a new edition of *RAD* (*RAD2*), and the U.S. archivists have distilled the draft into *Describing Archives: A Content Standard* (*DACS*). Despite continued maintenance of two separate national standards, the dialogue between Canadian and U.S. archivists will surely continue.

Relationship to other Standards

DACS is related to three other groups of standards. Descriptions created according to *DACS* may be stored and exchanged electronically using the syntax of data structure and communication protocols like *MARC 21* and *EAD*. Various thesauri and authority files may serve as the basis for indexing *DACS* records as described in the Overview of Archival Description. Most significantly, *DACS* is associated with other descriptive conventions, notably *APPM*, which it supersedes. That relationship is detailed in the following section. There are also close connections to the *Anglo-American Cataloguing Rules* (*AACR2*) and with the two conventions promulgated by the International Council on Archives: *ISAD(G)* and *ISAAR(CPF)*.

Like *APPM*, *DACS* was developed in part as a replacement for the skeletal rules in Chapter 4 of *AACR2*, which itself acknowledges the need for other cataloging codes. Its Rule 0.1 states, "These rules are designed for use in the construction of catalogues and other lists in general libraries of all sizes. They are not specifically intended for specialist and archival libraries, but such libraries are recommended to use the rules as the basis of their cataloguing and to augment their provisions as necessary." In this way, *DACS* provides more specific guidance in the description of contemporary archival materials and eliminates some of the less user-friendly aspects of *AACR2*, including many abbreviations and the coded recording of uncertain dates, conventions necessitated by the space limitations of 3x5 catalog cards but no longer helpful or necessary in modern information systems. It also provides syntax for the recording of names when families have been identified as the creators of archival materials. While not included in *AACR2*, the use of family names as creators in the description of archives was part of previous bibliographic cataloging codes, has a long tradition in archival descriptive practice, and has been officially sanctioned at least since the first edition of *APPM* was published by the Library of Congress in 1983.

All 26 data elements of *ISAD(G)* and *ISAAR(CPF)* are incorporated into *DACS*, in some cases virtually word for word. The exception is the exclusion, for two reasons, of the

---

[5] The group comprised the members of the Canadian Committee on Archival Description (CCAD)— Hélène Cadieux, Tim Hutchinson, Bob Krawczyk, Lucie Pagé, Mario Robert, Gerald Stone, Marlene van Ballegooie, Wendy Duff (who substituted for Kent Haworth), and editor and project manager Jean Dryden; and U.S. members Michael Fox, Steve Hensen, Lynn Holdzkom, Margit Kerwin, Kris Kiesling, Bill Landis, and Lydia Reid.

Level of Description element from *ISAD(G)*. While five levels of arrangement and description are recognized in *ISAD(G)*, experienced archivists understand that complex holdings often include many more levels of hierarchy. At this time, there is no consensus in the U.S. as to how existing terminology might be applied when there are more than five levels of arrangement. There is no benefit in prescribing data that cannot be applied consistently, especially when such uniformity is a primary requirement for the use of the information. Moreover, the simple recording of the level element, even if it could be assigned in a standardized way, is obviously insufficient for linking together information in the various parts of a multilevel description. As a more pragmatic solution, Chapter 1 of *DACS* simply requires that an information system employ some means of linking together the various levels of description. This could involve linked *MARC* records, nested components in *EAD*, associated tables in a relational database, or some other local solution.

Comparison to *APPM*

Those accustomed to using *APPM* will have little difficulty adopting this new standard. Everything that was in the second edition of *APPM* is here, and more. While *APPM* was a content standard intended specifically for the creation of catalog records, *DACS* can be used to create any type or level of description of archival and manuscript materials, including catalog records and full finding aids. In addition, *DACS* moves away from the bibliographic model represented by the *Anglo-American Cataloging Rules*[6] and to a certain extent followed by *APPM*, to reflect a more thoroughly archival approach to description.

Structurally speaking, *APPM* is divided into two parts and *DACS* three: *APPM* comprises Part I. Description, and Part II. Headings and Uniform Titles; *DACS* comprises Part I. Describing Archival Materials, Part II. Describing Creators, and Part III. Forms of Names. The organization of the data elements is different in several instances. Many of the elements in the *APPM* Note Area (1.7) are now rearranged into different conceptual areas or even separate chapters in *DACS*. For example, Biographical/Historical Note (*APPM* 1.7B1) is now Chapter 10 Administrative/Biographical History in Part II of *DACS*. In this, as in many other cases, significantly more guidance as to the content of the data element is provided. In addition, the numbering system has been simplified in *DACS*. Within each data element, only the rules themselves are numbered. The exceptions to this are Chapters 12-14, which, as they are drawn from *AACR2*, follow that standard's numbering system. Further, *DACS* simply omits areas mentioned in *APPM* that have little or no relevance to the description of archival materials, such as bibliographic series, parallel titles, statements of responsibility, etc.

The Statement of Principles, a revision of the principles developed early in the CUSTARD project, provides a concise articulation of the nature of archival materials and how that nature translates into descriptive tools. The statement forms the underpinnings of the rules themselves.

---

[6] *Anglo-American Cataloging Rules*, 2nd ed., 2002 revision (Chicago: American Library Association; Ottawa: Canadian Library Association; London: Chartered Institute of Library and Information Professionals, 2002).

DACS

The Overview of Archival Description discusses various types of descriptive tools and the importance of providing access points or index terms to lead researchers to them. While names of creators and functions are powerful access mechanisms for the context of materials, the importance of topical subjects, documentary forms, geographic names, and other types of index terms are emphasized in this section.

Chapter 1 outlines the *DACS* elements that must be included in different levels of descriptions, "level" referring both to the hierarchy of the materials themselves (i.e., whether a given description encompasses the entirety of an individual's papers or a single letter therein) and to the amount of detail provided in the description. The chapter articulates specific data elements that should be included in descriptions ranging from accession records to full finding aids, from a collection-level MARC 21 record to a fully encoded EAD instance. "Requiredness" of specific data elements was cumbersome to articulate in the context of each rule due to varying needs and practices at different levels of description, so this information has been placed in text boxes on pages 8–11.

DACS also contains a "commentary" for many data elements and occasionally for a specific rule. The commentaries serve to amplify, explain, or provide greater context for the element or rule, particularly in areas where archival practice has been less than uniform in the past.

DACS integrates rules for describing archival and manuscript materials and collections. Gone is the notion of the "artificial" collection. Materials that are gathered together by a person, family, or organization irrespective of their provenance are intentionally and consciously assembled for some purpose. Most repositories in the U.S. have such collections, and they need to be handled and described the same way as materials traditionally considered to be "organic."

DACS contains no specific rules for the description of particular media, e.g., sound recordings, maps, photographs, etc. Standards for the description of such materials are created and maintained by other groups in the library and archival communities, and to reproduce these rules or try to supersede them here would be both presumptuous and a maintenance nightmare. Archivists who need such specialized rules should consult media-specific standards, which are listed in Appendix B.

Finally, while *DACS* is designed to be output neutral, it nevertheless provides examples encoded in both EAD and MARC 21 for each data element in Part I, and for Chapters 9 and 10, as these are the two output systems currently used by most archivists.

KRIS KIESLING
Co-chair, CUSTARD Project Steering Committee

Acknowledgements

The Society of American Archivists gratefully acknowledges the financial support for this project from the National Endowment for the Humanities and the Gladys Kreibel Delmas Foundation.

Projects of this nature are dependent upon significant contributions of time by archivists and the support of the institutions that employ them. Therefore, special thanks are due to the Duke University Rare Book, Manuscript, and Special Collections Library; the Harry Ransom Humanities Research Center at the University of Texas at Austin; the Library of Congress Manuscript Division; the Manuscripts Department, University of North Carolina at Chapel Hill; the Minnesota Historical Society; the National Archives and Records Administration; and the University of California, Irvine, Special Collections and Archives.

Statement of Principles

The following statement of principles forms the basis for the rules in this standard. It is a recapitulation of generally accepted archival principles as derived from theoretical works and a variety of other sources. These include earlier statements about description and descriptive standards found in the reports of working groups commissioned to investigate aspects of archival description,[7] national rules for description,[8] and statements of the ICA Committee on Descriptive Standards.[9] In recognizing the disparate nature of archival holdings, the statement is also grounded in accepted professional practice in the United States.

Holdings of archival repositories represent every possible type of material acquired from a wide variety of sources. How archives manage and describe their holdings is rooted in the nature of the materials, the context of their creation, and 200 years of archival theory. Archival descriptive practices have increasingly been applied to all of the materials held by archives regardless of their provenance or method of acquisition. These principles examine the nature of archival materials and their context, and reflect how those aspects are made apparent in description.

The Nature of Archival Holdings

Archival collections are the natural result of the activities of individuals and organizations and serve as the recorded memory thereof. This distinctive relationship between records and the activities that generated them differentiates archives from other documentary resources.

Principle 1: Records in archives possess unique characteristics.
Archival materials have traditionally been understood to consist of the documents organically created, accumulated, and/or used by a person or organization in the course of the conduct of affairs and preserved because of their continuing value. They most often consist of aggregations of documents (largely unpublished) and are managed as such, though archival institutions frequently hold discrete items that must also be treated

---

[7] Working Group on Standards for Archival Description, "Archival Description Standards: Establishing a Process for their Development and Implementation," *American Archivist* 52, no. 4 (Fall 1989) (hereinafter cited as WGSAD Report), 440–43; *Toward Descriptive Standards: Report and Recommendations of the Canadian Working Group on Archival Descriptive Standards* (Ottawa: Bureau of Canadian Archivists, 1985), 6–9, 55–59, 63–64; Wendy M. Duff and Kent M. Haworth, "Advancing Archival Description: A Model for Rationalizing North American Descriptive Standards," *Archives and Manuscripts* 25, no. 2 (1997) (hereinafter cited as the Bentley Report), 198–99, 203–4.

[8] *Rules for Archival Description* (Ottawa, Bureau of Canadian Archivists, 1990), xi-xvi, rules 0.1, 0.2, 0.22, 1.0A1, 1.0A2 (hereinafter cited as *RAD*); Steven Hensen, comp., *Archives, Personal Papers, and Manuscripts*, 2nd ed. (Chicago: Society of American Archivists, 1989), rules 0.3, 0.9, 0.10, 0.12, 1.0A (hereinafter cited as *APPM*).

[9] ICA Statement of Principles, 8–16; ICA Committee on Descriptive Standards, *ISAD(G) : General International Standard Archival Description*, 2nd ed. (Ottawa: International Council on Archives, 1999), 7–12 (hereinafter cited as *ISAD(G)*).

consistently within the institution's descriptive system. In the course of their regular activities, individuals, archival repositories, and other institutions may also consciously acquire and assemble records that do not share a common provenance or origin but that reflect some common characteristic, such as a particular subject, theme, or form. Such collections are part of the holdings in most institutions and must be described in a way that is consistent with the rest of the holdings. All of these materials may be described using this standard.

Principle 2: The principle of *respect des fonds* is the basis of archival arrangement and description.
The records created, assembled, accumulated, and/or maintained and used by an organization or individual must be kept together (i.e., identified as belonging to the same aggregation) in their original order, if such order exists or has been maintained. They ought not be mixed or combined with the records of another individual or corporate body. This dictum is the natural and logical consequence of the organic nature of archival materials.[10] Inherent in the overarching principle of *respect des fonds* are two sub-principles—provenance and original order. The principle of provenance means that the records that were created, assembled, accumulated, and/or maintained by an organization or individual must be represented together, distinguishable from the records of any other organization or individual. The principle of original order means that the order of the records that was established by the creator should be maintained by physical and/or intellectual means whenever possible to preserve existing relationships between the documents and the evidential value inherent in their order. Together, these principles form the basis of archival arrangement and description.

In the context of this standard, the principle of provenance requires further elaboration. The statement that the records of one creator must be represented together does not mean that it is necessary (or even possible) to keep the records of one creator physically together. It does, however, mean that the provenance of the records must be clearly reflected in the description, that the description must enable retrieval by provenance, and that a descriptive system must be capable of representing together all the records of a single creator held by a single repository.

The Relationship between Arrangement and Description

If the archival functions of arrangement and description are based on the principle of *respect des fonds*, what is the relationship between arrangement and description? While the two are intimately intertwined, it is possible to distinguish between them in the following way. *Arrangement* is the intellectual and/or physical processes of organizing documents in accordance with accepted archival principles, as well as the results of these processes. *Description* is the creation of an accurate representation of the archival material by the process of capturing, collating, analyzing, and organizing information that

---

[10] S. Muller, J.A. Feith, and R. Fruin. *Manual for the arrangement and description of archives.* Translation of the second edition. Chicago, Society of American Archivists, 2002, p19. "An archival collection is an organic whole."

serves to identify archival material and to explain the context and records systems that produced it, as well as the results of these processes.

Principle 3: Arrangement involves the identification of groupings within the material.

Arrangement is the process of identifying the logical groupings of materials within the whole as they were established by the creator, of constructing a new organization when the original ordering has been lost, or of establishing an order when one never existed. The archivist then identifies further sub-groupings within each unit down to the level of granularity that is feasible or desirable, even to the individual item. This process creates hierarchical groupings of material, with each step in the hierarchy described as a level. By custom, archivists have assigned names to some, but not all, levels of arrangement. The most commonly identified are collection, record group, series, file (or filing unit), and item. A large or complex body of material may have many more levels. The archivist must determine for practical reasons which groupings will be treated as a unit for purposes of description. These may be defined as the entire corpus of material of the creator (papers, records, or collection), a convenient administrative grouping (record and manuscript groups), or a reflection of administrative record-keeping systems (series and filing units).

Principle 4: Description reflects arrangement.

Archival repositories must be able to describe holdings ranging from thousands of linear feet to a single item. The amount of description and level of detail will depend on the importance of the material, management needs and resources of the repository, and access requirements of the users. That being the case, an archival description may consist of a multilevel structure that begins with a description of the whole and proceeds through increasingly more detailed descriptions of the parts, or it may consist only of a description of the whole. Within a given body of material, the repository may choose to describe some parts at a greater level of detail than others. A single item may be described in minute detail, whether or not it is part of a larger body of material.

The Nature of Archival Description

Archival holdings are varied in their nature and provenance, and archival description reflects this fact. If archival materials are to be described consistently within an institutional, regional, or national descriptive system, the rules must apply to a variety of forms and media created by, and acquired from, a variety of sources.

Principle 5: The rules of description apply to all archival materials regardless of form or medium.

It is acknowledged that archival materials come in a variety of forms and media, and rules for archival description must therefore accommodate all forms and media (and the relationships between them). Inherent in the principle of provenance—that the records created, assembled, accumulated, and/or maintained and used by an organization or individual must be kept together—is the assumption that no records are excluded from the description because of their particular form or medium. Different media of course require different rules to describe their particular characteristics; for example, sound recordings may require some indication of playing speed, and photographs may require some indication of polarity and color.

Principle 6: The principles of archival description apply equally to records created by corporate bodies, individuals, or families.
The documents that are the product of the functions and activities of organizations may differ in extent, arrangement, subject matter, etc., from those that result from the activities of individuals or families. While there may be valid reasons to distinguish between them in the workflow of a repository, the principles of archival arrangement and description should be applied equally to materials created by individuals, families, or organizations.

Principle 7: Archival descriptions may be presented at varying levels of detail to produce a variety of outputs.
The nature and origins of a body of archival materials may be summarized in their entirety in a single collective description. However, the extent and complexity of archival materials may require a more detailed description of their various components as well. The resulting technique of multilevel description is "the preparation of descriptions that are related to one another in a part-to-whole relationship and that need complete identification of both parts and the comprehensive whole in multiple descriptive records."[11] This requires some elucidation regarding the order in which such information is presented and the relationships between description(s) of the parts and the description of the whole.[12]

Principle 7.1: Levels of description correspond to levels of arrangement.
The levels of arrangement determine the levels of description. However, because not all levels of arrangement are required or possible in all cases, it follows that not all levels of description are required. It is understood that description is an iterative and dynamic process; that is, descriptive information is recorded, reused, and enhanced at many stages in the management of archival holdings. For example, basic information is recorded when incoming material is accessioned, well before the material is arranged. Furthermore, arrangement can change, particularly when a repository receives regular accruals of records from an ongoing organization. In that situation, the arrangement will not be complete until the organization ceases to exist. Thus, it is more appropriate to say that description reflects the current state of arrangement (whatever that may be) and can (and does) change as a result of further arrangement activities.[13]

Principle 7.2: Relationships between levels of description must be clearly indicated.
While the actual work of arrangement and description can proceed in any order that makes sense to the archivist, a descriptive system must be able to represent and maintain the relationships among the various parts of the hierarchy. Depending on the point at

---

[11] *RAD*, p. D-5.

[12] The rules for multilevel description are found in *RAD*, rule 1.0A2 and in ISAD(G), 12.

[13] *ISAD(G)*, Statement I-3, p. 7.

which the descriptive system is entered, an end user must be able to navigate to higher or lower levels of description.

Principle 7.3: Information provided at each level of description must be appropriate to that level.

When a multilevel description is created, the information provided at each level of description must be relevant to the material being described at that level. This means that it is inappropriate to provide detailed information about the contents of files in a description of a higher level. Similarly, archivists should provide administrative or biographical information appropriate to the materials being described at a given level (e.g., a series). This principle also implies that it is undesirable to repeat information recorded at higher levels of description. Information that is common to the component parts should be provided at the highest appropriate level.

The Creators of Archival Material

An important aspect of understanding archival materials is the description of the context in which they were created.

Principle 8: The creators of archival materials, as well as the materials themselves, must be described.

Since the principle of provenance is fundamental to the arrangement and description of archival materials, it follows that the provenance, or the creator(s), of archival materials must be described as well. Except in cases where the creator or collector is truly unknown, this means that the creator or collector of the materials must be identified and included in (or linked to) the description of the materials. Moreover, the functions or activities of the creator(s) that produced the archival materials must be described. Finally, standardized access points must be provided that indicate not just the primary creator but also the relationships between successive creators, for example, the parts of a corporate body that has undergone reorganization(s). *DACS* includes rules for providing all of this information in a consistent way. The repository as collector does not need to be described.

Overview of Archival Description

The principal objective of archival description is the creation of access tools that assist users in discovering desired records. The nature of archival materials, their distribution across many institutions, and the physical requirements of archival repositories necessitate the creation of these descriptive surrogates, which can then be consulted in lieu of directly browsing through quantities of original documents. The archivist must consult other standards and protocols in addition to *DACS* in order to construct a robust system of access. This section describes their roles and that of *DACS* within the larger context of the creation of archival descriptions.

Access Tools

DACS is a standard that is independent of particular forms of output in given information systems, such as manual and electronic catalogs, databases, and other finding aid formats.[14] However, archivists recognize that these rules do not exist as abstractions but will be implemented in actual systems. In practice, *DACS* will be used principally with the two most commonly employed forms of access tools, catalogs and inventories, though it may be useful in the construction of guides and calendars as well. The archivist must recognize that the systems in which these descriptions appear have functionality and requirements that extend beyond simply presenting the descriptions of archival materials based on Part I and information about the creators of archival records created according to the rules in Part II.

When descriptive information is managed in a locally developed database or presented as entries in a card catalog or as a typescript inventory, local decisions must be made about database design and presentation, or the layout of data on the card or printed inventory. When descriptions are recorded in a standard electronic format—MARC 21, EAD, or both—the archivist will have to master the encoding scheme in which the data is stored electronically. Various publications are instructive in the application of these two standards, while the official documentation for each is available in print and online, and is cited in Appendix B.[15]

Beyond the details of their respective encoding protocols, both MARC 21 and EAD require the inclusion of data that supplements the information specified in *DACS*. MARC 21 includes a series of fields of coded information that assist in machine processing of data, such as the dates of the material. The structure of and permissible values for these

---

[14] See Appendix A for definitions of various access tools.

[15] See *MARC 21 Format for Bibliographic Data: Including Guidelines for Content Designation.* Prepared by the Network Development and MARC Standards Office, Library of Congress, in cooperation with Standards and Support, National Library of Canada. Washington, DC: Library of Congress, Cataloging Distribution Service, 1999; and *Encoded Archival Description Tag Library, Version 2002.* Prepared and Maintained by the Encoded Archival Description Working Group of the Society of American Archivists and the Network Development and MARC Standards Office of the Library of Congress. Chicago, IL: Society of American Archivists, 2002.

codes may be found in the MARC 21 documentation. In EAD, the EAD Header element contains information about the electronic file. Its formulation is described in the *EAD Tag Library*.

Access Points

Then there is the matter of "access points." While archival description is narrative, and electronic catalogs and databases typically provide full-text searching of every word in the text, information systems often also identify specific terms, codes, concepts, and names for which specialized indexes are created to permit faster and more precise searching. In a manual environment, these terms appear as entry headings on catalog records. A variety of protocols, both standardized and local, determine which of the names and terms in a description become "access points" for searching in this way, as well as the form in which they appear. For example, the archivist is instructed in section 3.1 of *DACS* to include in the scope and content element information about the "subject matter to which the records pertain, such as topics, events, people, and organizations." The natural language terminology used to describe such a topic in the scope and content statement must be subsequently translated into the formal syntax of a subject heading, as specified by a standardized thesaurus like the *Library of Congress Authorities*.[16] For example, a collection might contain information about railroads in Montana. After consulting the Library of Congress subject headings and reviewing the directions in the *Subject Cataloging Manual. Subject Headings* on the formulation of compound subject terms, the archivist will establish the access point as Railroads--Montana. When embedded in a MARC 21 record, the coding will be

> 650 b0 ‡a Railroads ‡z Montana.

If this data is placed in an EAD finding aid, the resulting encoding will look like this:

> <controlaccess>
>   <subject source="lcsh">Railroads--Montana</subject>
> </controlaccess>

Once rendered in a consistent form and included in electronic indexes or as headings in a card file, such standardized data become a powerful tool for researchers to discover materials related to that topic.

It is a local decision as to which names, terms, and concepts found in a description will be included as formal access points, but repositories should provide them in all types of descriptions. Such indexing becomes increasingly important as archivists make encoded finding aids and digital content available to end users through a variety of repository-based and consortial online resource discovery tools.

---

[16] The *Library of Congress Authorities* online resource combines *the Library of Congress Name Authority File* (LCNAF) and the *Library of Congress Subject Headings* (LCSH).

Access points fall into six broad categories:
- Names
- Places
- Subjects
- Documentary forms
- Occupations
- Functions

Each category is described below and contains a discussion of the parts of the descriptive record in which the concepts that are rendered as access points may be found. The standard format of such terms can be developed locally, but preferably will be taken from standard thesauri such as those in Appendix B, or will be recorded following the rules in Part III.

Names

The names of persons, families, and organizations that are associated with a body of archival materials, either as the creator or the subject of the records, constitute an important pathway by which researchers discover relevant materials. Names that are rendered as *nominal access points* can be found in several areas of the descriptive record:

- Name of Creator(s) Element (2.6, Chapter 9)
- Title Element (2.3)
- Scope and Content Element (3.1)
- Administrative/Biographical History Element (2.7, Chapter 10)
- Custodial History Element (5.1)
- Immediate Source of Acquisition Element (5.2)

At a minimum, an access point should be made for every name included in the Name of Creator(s) Element in a single-level description, or at the highest level in a multilevel description. Names found in other descriptive elements may be utilized as access points in accordance with local or consortial practice.

Part III provides directions on how to render these personal, family, and corporate names in a standardized form. The *Library of Congress Authorities* database should be consulted first to determine whether or not a standardized form of name for a given individual or organization has already been established.

Places

The names of places and geographic features to which the records pertain may be important to researchers. Geographic place names that should be considered for use as access points may be found in the following parts of the descriptive record.

- Name of Creator(s) Element (2.6, Chapter 9)
- Title Element (2.3)
- Scope and Content Element (3.1)
- Administrative/Biographical History Element (2.7, Chapter 10)

Guidance on the formation of geographic names in general is found in Chapter 13 of *DACS*. The form of name for many places has already been established in the *Library of Congress Authorities* database. Another general purpose source is the *Getty Thesaurus of Geographic Names*. For places in the United States not found in these sources, archivists should consult the U.S. Board on Geographic Names *Gazetteer of the United States of America*. For places outside the United States that are not included in the Library of Congress or Getty lists, consult the GEOnet Names Server (GNS).

Topical Subjects

The topical subject matter to which the records pertain is among the most important aspects of the archival materials. Terms suggesting topics that might be employed as access points may be found in the following areas of the descriptive record:

- Title Element (2.3)
- Scope and Content Element (3.1)
- Administrative/Biographical History Element (2.7, Chapter 10)

A variety of general and specialized subject thesauri, including the *Library of Congress Authorities* may be employed as the source for standardized terminology. The most commonly used of these are listed in Appendix B.

Documentary Forms

Terms that indicate the documentary form(s) or intellectual characteristics of the records being described (e.g., minutes, diaries, reports, watercolors, documentaries) provide the user with an indication of the content of the materials based on an understanding of the common properties of particular document types. For example, one can deduce the contents of ledgers because they are a standard form of accounting record, one that typically contains certain types of data. Documentary forms are most often noted in the following areas of the descriptive record:

- Title Element (2.3)
- Extent Element (2.5)
- Scope and Content Element (3.1)

The *Thesaurus for Graphic Materials II: Genre and Physical Characteristics Terms*, the *Art & Architecture Thesaurus*, the *Library of Congress Authorities*, or appropriate media-specific thesauri should be the first sources consulted for terms denoting documentary forms and literary genres.

Occupations

The occupations, avocations, or other life interests of individuals that are documented in a body of archival material may be of significance to users. Such information is most often mentioned in the following areas of the descriptive record:

- Scope and Content Element (3.1)
- Administrative/Biographical History Element (2.7, Chapter 10)

Again, the *Library of Congress Authorities* is a widely used source of terms noting occupations and avocations. The U.S. Department of Labor's *Dictionary of Occupational Titles* provides a structured enumeration of job titles.

Functions and Activities

Terms indicating the function(s), activity(ies), transaction(s), and process(es) that generated the material being described help to define the context in which records were created. Examples of such concepts might be the regulation of hunting and fishing or the conservation of natural resources. Functions and activities are often noted in these areas of the descriptive record:

- Title Element (2.3)
- Scope and Content Element (3.1)
- Administrative/Biographical History Element (2.7, Chapter 10)

The *Art & Architecture Thesaurus* contains a hierarchy of terms denoting functions. The *Library of Congress Authorities* also may be employed.

PART I

Describing Archival Materials

Introduction to
Describing Archival Materials

Purpose and Scope

Part I of *DACS* contains rules to ensure the creation of consistent, appropriate, and self-explanatory descriptions of archival material. The rules may be used for describing archival and manuscript materials at all levels of description, regardless of form or medium. They may also be applied to the description of intentionally assembled collections, and to discrete items.

While the rules apply to all levels of description and forms of material, some repositories may wish to describe particular media at item level or at a level even more detailed than the item, such as sequence, shot, and so on. These rules do not govern such detailed levels of description because of the varying nature of institutional requirements in this area. Incorporating all possible rules for various types of media would result in a very large volume that would require regular monitoring of a number of specialized standards and frequent revisions of *DACS* as other standards changed. Where more detailed guidance is required, archivists are referred to Appendix B, which lists specialized standards for various types of material.

Data Elements Are Mutually Exclusive

The purpose and scope of each element has been defined so that the prescribed information can go in one place only. In some cases there are separate elements for closely related but distinct information, such as the several elements relating to conditions of access and use. The stated exclusions for each element indicate which other element can be used to provide the related information.

Order of Elements

Archival description is an iterative process that may suggest a certain sequence or order of elements in a given repository or output system. However, neither the arrangement of these rules nor their content mandate a given order. Archivists should be aware that some output systems may enforce a particular order of elements, and institutional or consortial guidelines may recommend or even require a given order.

Sources of Information

All the information to be included in archival descriptions must come from an appropriate source, the most common of which is the materials themselves. In contrast to library practice, archivists rarely transcribe descriptive information directly from archival materials; rather, they summarize or interpolate information that appears in the materials or supply information from appropriate external sources, which can include transfer documents and other acquisition records, file plans, and reference works. Each element has one or more prescribed sources of information.

Options and Alternatives

Some rules are designated as optional; others are designated as alternative rules.

- Where a rule represents an instruction that may or may not be used, it is introduced by the word "optionally." A repository may use it or not as a matter of institutional policy or on a case-by-case basis at the discretion of the archivist.

- Where a rule represents an alternative equal in status and value to another rule, it is introduced by the word "alternatively." A repository must use one or other as a matter of institutional policy or on a case-by-case basis.

These provisions arise from the recognition that different solutions to a problem and differing levels of detail and specificity are appropriate in different contexts. The use of some alternatives and options may be decided as a matter of description policy at the institutional level to be exercised either always or never. Other alternatives and options can be exercised on a case-by-case basis at the discretion of the archivist. Institutions are encouraged to distinguish between these two situations, and to keep a record of their policy decisions and of the circumstances in which a particular option may be applied.

Professional Judgment and Institutional Practice

The rules recognize the necessity for judgment and interpretation on the part of both the person who prepares the description and the institution responsible for it. Such judgment and interpretation may be based on the requirements of a particular description, on the use of the material being described, or on the descriptive system being used. The rules highlight selected, though certainly not all, points where the need for professional judgment is called for, using phrases such as "if appropriate," "if important," and "if necessary." While in no way contradicting the value of standardization, such words and phrases recognize that uniform rules for all types of descriptions are neither possible nor desirable, and they encourage institutions to develop and document a description policy based on specific local knowledge and consistent application of professional judgment. Furthermore, it is recognized that a particular data element may be formulated differently depending on the intended output system. For example, a scope and content note may be much more extensive in a multilevel finding aid than in a catalog record.

Descriptive Outputs

The application of these rules will result in descriptions of various kinds and the rules do not prescribe any particular output. It is up to the repository to determine what descriptive products will be produced and how they will be presented to the end user. Elements can be combined in a variety of ways, such as through use of punctuation, layout and typography, labels, etc. It is essential for the archivist to understand the particular output system being used. For example, a system may automatically display hierarchies and create links between different levels of description, or create links between a unit of description and other information such as appraisal or scheduling information, in such a way that a textual explanation of the relationship(s) is not necessary. Archivists should keep in mind, however, that standardization of the presentation or display of archival descriptive information greatly enhances recognition and understanding by end users.

Examples

The examples in Part I are illustrative, not prescriptive. They illustrate only the application of the rule to which they are appended. Furthermore, the presentation of the examples is intended only to assist in understanding how to use the rules and does not imply a prescribed layout, typography, or output. Some examples include citations for the body of archival materials from which they were drawn to help clarify the application of the rule to a particular level of description.

While the rules themselves are output neutral, examples are encoded in EAD and MARC 21, two widely used output mechanisms for archival descriptions, at the end of each chapter or section in Part I. The EAD examples frequently include attributes within elements. These are intended to illustrate aspects of the rules, and do not indicate that a specific attribute is required.[17] The MARC 21 examples include a blank space before and after each subfield for the sake of clarity. The fields that do not consist of standardized codes have a subfield a (‡a) at the beginning. Some systems require that ‡a be made explicit; others assume the ‡a is always the first subfield. Where MARC 21 two-position field indicators are not required or are not defined, a "b" (blank) is given in their place.

---

[17] See the *EAD Tag Library* for available attributes and their use.

CHAPTER 1

Levels of Description

DACS defines twenty-five elements that are useful in creating systems for describing archival materials. These systems can be of any type, ranging from simple paper-based files to complex digital information management systems. The output products of these systems—archival descriptions of all kinds and formats, printed on paper or encoded in EAD or MARC 21—must include at minimum a set of discrete descriptive elements that convey standardized information about the archival materials and creators being described. These *DACS* elements constitute a refinement of the twenty-six high-level elements of archival description defined in the *General International Standard Archival Description (ISAD(G))*.

Not all of the *DACS* elements are required in every archival description. Combinations of descriptive elements will vary depending on whether the archivist considers a specific description to be preliminary or complete, and whether it describes archival materials at a single level (e.g., collection level or item level) or at multiple levels that have a whole-part relationship.

Simple archival descriptive systems can be constructed using only the 25 elements articulated and defined by this standard; however, more detailed archival descriptive and management systems may require a number of additional elements, either defined by companion standards or standardized at the local level to meet the requirements of a specific repository.

The following requirements specify particular elements from Part I of *DACS* that should be used in output products—from basic collection-level accession records to fully encoded, multilevel finding aids—intended for the use of archivists or researchers in managing and using archival materials. They articulate a "minimum," "optimum," and "added value" usage of the elements defined by *DACS*, but are not intended to preclude use of other descriptive data that a repository deems necessary for its own descriptive systems or products. *DACS* does not specify the order or arrangement of elements in a particular descriptive output. Some systems or output formats, such as MARC 21 or EAD, provide specific guidance on the ordering of some or all elements. Others, such as a repository's preliminary accession record or a print finding aid, should include *DACS* elements in a logical and consistent manner determined by the repository's own procedures and standard practices. The requirements that follow are divided into two sections, one for single-level descriptions and one for multilevel descriptions.

Requirements for Single-level Descriptions

The following are examples of single-level descriptions:
- A preliminary accession record.
- A MARC 21 record not linked to other MARC 21 records.
- A database record in a repository's collections management database that describes archival materials only at a single level.
- A METS (Metadata Encoding and Transmission Standard)[18] record for a description of archival materials.

Single-level descriptions can describe archival materials at *any level*, from large accumulations commonly referred to by archivists as collections, record groups, fonds, or record series, to single items, and any level in between. They can, however, only describe that material at one level.

Single-level Minimum

A single-level description with the minimum number of *DACS* elements includes:
- Reference Code Element (2.1)
- Name and Location of Repository Element (2.2)
- Title Element (2.3)
- Date Element (2.4)
- Extent Element (2.5)
- Name of Creator(s) Element (2.6) *Note: At minimum, the person(s), family(ies) or organization(s) responsible for the creation or accumulation of the materials being described must be identified if known.*
- Scope and Content Element (3.1) *Note: In a minimum description, this element may simply provide a short abstract of the scope and content of the materials being described.*
- Conditions Governing Access Element (4.1)
- Language and Scripts of the Material Element (4.5)

---

[18] The METS standard is an XML schema for encoding descriptive, administrative, and structural metadata for objects within a digital library. It is an initiative of the Digital Library Federation and is maintained by the Library of Congress. Information is available at: <http://www.loc.gov/standards/mets/>

Single-level Optimum

A single-level description with the optimum number of *DACS* elements includes:
- All of the elements included in Single-level Minimum above, plus the following:
- Administrative/Biographical History Element (2.7)
- Scope and Content Element (3.1) *Note: In an optimum description, this element should include a full description of the scope and content of the material being described.*
- Access points (See Overview of Archival Description).

Single-level Added Value

A single-level description using *DACS* elements to provide added value for researchers includes:
- All of the elements included in Single-level Optimum above, plus any other relevant elements the repository wishes to include.

Requirements for Multilevel Descriptions

The following are examples of multilevel descriptions:
- A preliminary collection inventory or register (regardless of whether presented in print or encoded in EAD or another encoding scheme).
- A full collection inventory or register (regardless of whether presented in print or encoded in EAD or another encoding scheme).
- Multiple linked MARC 21 records.
- A database record in a repository's collections management database that describes archival materials at more than one level.

Multilevel descriptions can describe archival materials beginning at any level (e.g., collection level, series level) and must include at least one sublevel. Typical multilevel descriptions begin with large accumulations commonly referred to by archivists as collections, record groups, fonds, or record series. *ISAD(G)* envisions a descriptive framework that recognizes four levels: fonds, series, file, and item; however, *DACS* elements can be used to describe materials arranged according to this or any other scheme of articulating levels of arrangement of archival materials.

Multilevel Minimum

The *top* level of a multilevel description with the minimum number of *DACS* elements includes:
- Reference Code Element (2.1)
- Name and Location of Repository Element (2.2)
- Title Element (2.3)
- Date Element (2.4)
- Extent Element (2.5)
- Name of Creator(s) Element (2.6) *Note: At minimum, the person(s), family(ies), or organization(s) responsible for the creation or accumulation of the materials being described must be identified if known.*
- Scope and Content Element (3.1) *Note: In a minimum description, this element may simply provide a short abstract of the scope and content of the materials being described.*
- Conditions Governing Access Element (4.1)
- Language and Scripts of the Material Element (4.5)
- Identification of the whole-part relationship of the *top* level to at least the *next subsequent* level in the multilevel description. This may be done through internal tracking within a particular descriptive system; if so, the output must be able to explicitly identify this relationship.

Each *subsequent* level of a multilevel description should include:
- All of the elements used at higher levels, unless the information is the same as that of a higher level or if it is desirable to provide more specific information. *Notes:*
  - *Name of Creator(s) Element (2.6): At subsequent levels of a multilevel description, this element is required only if the person(s) or organization(s) responsible for the creation or accumulation of the material at the subsequent level differs from the higher level(s). This can also be accomplished by using the Name Segment of the Title Element (2.3).*
  - *Scope and Content Element (3.1): Scope and contents are typically necessary for large units of aggregation and are not required at the file or item level if the Title Element (2.3) is sufficient to describe the material.*
- Identification of the whole-part relationship of *each* level to at least the *next subsequent* level in the multilevel description. This may be done through internal tracking within a particular descriptive system, or through an explicit statement of the relationship.

Multilevel Optimum

The *top* level of a multilevel description with the optimum number of *DACS* elements includes:
- All of the elements included in Multilevel Minimum above, plus the following:
- Administrative/Biographical History Element (2.7)
- Scope and Content Element (3.1) *Note: In an optimum description, this element should include a full description of the scope and content of the materials being described.*
- Access points (See Overview of Archival Description).

Each *subsequent* level of that multilevel description should include:
- All of the elements included at the higher levels of the multilevel description, unless the information is the same as that of a higher level or if it is desirable to provide more specific information.
- Identification of the whole-part relationship of *each* level to at least the *next subsequent* level in the multilevel description. This may be done through internal tracking within a particular descriptive system, or through an explicit statement of the relationship.

Multilevel Added Value

A multilevel description using *DACS* elements to provide added value for researchers should include:
- All of the elements included in Multilevel Optimum above, plus any other elements the repository wishes to include.

Each *subsequent* level of that multilevel description should include:
- All of the elements included at the higher levels of the multilevel description, unless the information is the same as that of a higher level or if it is desirable to provide more specific information.
- Identification of the whole-part relationship of *each* level to at least the *next subsequent* level in the multilevel description. This may be done through internal tracking within a particular descriptive system, or through an explicit statement of the relationship.

CHAPTER 2

Identity Elements

2.1 Reference Code
2.2 Name and Location of Repository
2.3 Title
2.4 Date
2.5 Extent
2.6 Name of Creator(s)
2.7 Administrative/Biographical History

2.1 Reference Code Element

Purpose and Scope

This element provides a unique identifier for the unit being described. The identifier may consist of three subelements: a local identifier, a code for the repository, and a code for the country.

> Commentary: This typically alphanumeric identifier frequently serves as a succinct local means of referring to the materials. When delivering a descriptive record outside of the repository holding the materials, this element should also contain a nationally sanctioned code for the repository and an internationally standardized code for the country in which the repository is located. Taken together, these three subelements form a unique machine-readable identifier for the materials being described.

- The local identifier code is a means of gaining access to the description of the materials or to the documents themselves. Determining the structure and function(s) of a local identifier code are matters of institutional policy. Examples of local identifiers include accession numbers, record group numbers, and call numbers.
- The repository identifier code is required only for purposes of consortial, national, or international exchange. The full name of the institution is recorded in the Name and Location of Repository Element (2.2).
- The country identifier code is required only for purposes of consortial, national, or international exchange.

Sources of Information

2.1.1. The codes for country and repository are taken from national and international code lists. Repositories should develop a local system that uniquely identifies discrete materials.

General Rules

2.1.2. Record a reference code that consists of a local identifier, a repository identifier, and a country identifier in accordance with the following rules.

Local Identifier

2.1.3. At the highest level of a multilevel description or in a single level description, provide a unique identifier for the materials being described in accordance with the institution's administrative control system. Optionally, supply unique identifiers at lower levels of a multilevel description.

> 95-24
>> *Records collection identifier, Gay, Lesbian, Bisexual, Transgender Historical Society*
>
> MC22
>> *Personal papers collection identifier, Scripps Institute of Oceanography Archives*
>
> 632
>> *Manuscript group identifier, Manuscripts and Archives, Yale University Library*
>
> 79-GC-2-134
>> *Record group, series, album, and item identifier, National Archives and Records Administration*

Repository Identifier

2.1.4. Provide a repository code assigned by the national organization responsible for assigning and maintaining repository identifiers.[19]

> CUI
>> *Repository code for the University of California, Irvine Libraries*
>
> TxU-Hu
>> *Repository code for the Harry Ransom Humanities Research Center, The University of Texas at Austin*

---

[19] The Library of Congress is responsible for assigning repository codes and maintaining the list of assigned codes in the United States. National repository codes are constructed in accordance with the latest version of ISO 15511 (*International standard identifier for libraries and related organizations*).

Country Identifier

2.1.5. Provide a country code for the location of the repository as assigned by the International Standards Organization.[20]

> US
>> *Code for the United States*
>
> Ca
>> *Code for Canada*

EXAMPLES OF ENCODING FOR 2.1 REFERENCE CODE ELEMENT

Encoding at the highest level of description in EAD:

```
<unitid countrycode="us" repositorycode="cui">MS-SEA016</unitid>

<unitid countrycode="us" repositorycode="cus">MSS 0112</unitid>
```

Encoding at the highest level of description in MARC 21:

```
008  bb   031014i19781998cau      eng d
040  bb   ‡a CUI ‡e dacs ‡c CUI
099  b9   ‡a MS-SEA 016
852  bb   ‡a University of California, Irvine Libraries. ‡e 525
          Adjunct Lane, Irvine, CA 20033-1126. ‡n cau

008  bb   941228i19461998cau      eng d
040  bb   ‡a CUS ‡e dacs ‡c CUS
099  b9   ‡a MSS 0112
```

---

[20] The two-character country code is found in the latest version of ISO 3166-1 (*Codes for the representation of names of countries and their subdivisions*). While EAD requires the use of the ISO 3166-1 standard for names of countries, the MARC 21 standard has not yet adopted this code list. Use the code appropriate to the output system for a given description. The MARC Code List for Countries is used in archival cataloging (e.g., mixed materials) to indicate the country of the repository in the 008 field.

2.2 Name and Location of Repository Element

Purpose and Scope

This element identifies the name and location of the repository that holds the materials being described.

> Commentary: It may be possible for a system to generate the name of the repository from the repository identifier as specified in Rule 2.1.4.

Sources of Information

2.2.1. Take the information from institutional policies and procedures.

General Rules

2.2.2. Explicitly state the name of the repository, including any parent bodies.

    The University of Texas at Austin, Harry Ransom Humanities
    Research Center

    The Minnesota Historical Society

2.2.3. Provide the location of the repository. If desirable, include the mailing address and other contact information.

    Alabama Department of Archives and History. 624 Washington
    Avenue, Montgomery, AL 36130-0100. (334) 242-4435.

EXAMPLES OF ENCODING FOR 2.2 NAME AND LOCATION OF REPOSITORY ELEMENT

Encoding in EAD:

    <repository>
    <corpname>The University of Texas at Austin
    <subarea>Harry Ransom Humanities Research Center</subarea>
    </corpname>
    </repository>

Encoding in MARC 21:

    852 bb   ‡a Alabama Department of Archives and History. ‡e 624
               Washington Avenue, Montgomery, AL 36310-0100.

2.3 Title Element

Purpose and Scope

This element provides a word or phrase by which the material being described is known or can be identified. A title may be supplied or formal.

> Commentary: A *supplied title* is one provided by the archivist when there is no formal title for the materials being described, or where the formal title is misleading or inadequate. The rules for recording a supplied title differ from the rules for recording a formal title. Archivists usually supply titles for archival materials.
>
> Supplied titles generally have two parts:
> - the name of the creator(s) or collector(s)
> - the nature of the materials being described
>
> A *formal title* is one that appears prominently on or in the materials being described and is most commonly found in material that has been published or distributed, such as a title on a book, report, map, or film. Formal titles can also be found on unpublished material that bears a meaningful name consciously given by the creator of the material, (e.g., a caption on a photograph, label on a folder, or leader on a film).
>
> In the absence of a meaningful formal title, a title must be supplied. The archivist must use professional judgment to determine when it is appropriate to supply a title rather than transcribing a label on a container that may be misleading. When they occur at all in archival materials, formal titles are most commonly found on files or items.

Sources of Information

2.3.1. When supplying a title, take the information from any reliable source, including the internal evidence of the materials being described, an external source such as a records schedule or communication with a donor, or a title on another copy or version of the materials being described.

2.3.2. When recording a formal title, transcribe the information from the prescribed source as described in the appropriate chapters in *AACR2* (which specify that formal titles are recorded exactly as to wording, order, and spelling, but not necessarily as to punctuation or capitalization) or to specialized standards for various types of material cited in Appendix B. Rules for transcribing formal titles are not provided here.

General Rules

2.3.3. When supplying title information, compose a brief title[21] that uniquely identifies the material, normally consisting of a name segment, a term indicating the nature of the

---

[21] The supplied title should not be mistaken for a statement or abstract of the content of the unit being described; the supplied title simply names the unit as succinctly as possible. The contents of the unit, e.g., that of an individual letter, should be described in the Scope and Content Element.

unit being described,[22] and optionally a topical segment as instructed in the following rules. Do not enclose supplied titles in square brackets.

> Commentary:
> - In multilevel descriptions the name segment may be inherited from a higher level of description and may not need to be explicitly stated at lower levels.
> - When the repository is responsible for assembling a collection, do not provide, as part of the supplied title, the institution's name as the collector.
> - The topical segment should be used only when the identification of the material cannot be made clear from the name and nature elements.

Name segment

2.3.4. Record the name(s) of the person(s), family (families), or corporate body[23] predominantly responsible for the creation, assembly, accumulation, and/or maintenance of the materials.

```
Graciany Miranda Archilla papers

Bacot family papers

Bank of Cape Fear (Wilmington, N.C.) Hillsboro Branch records

Wisconsin Environmental Policy Act files

Cameron family account book

Caroline and Erwin Swann collection of caricature and cartoon
```

2.3.5. Record the name(s) in the form by which the creator or collector is generally known.[24] Record the name(s) in the natural language order of the language of the person's or corporate body's country of residence or activity or the official language of the corporate body. The name may be abbreviated if a fuller form of the name appears elsewhere in the descriptive record (e.g., in the administrative/biographical history) or as an access point.

```
Bessye B. Bearden papers
    not Bearden, Bessye B. papers

WAPOR records
    Name of Creator(s) Element is World Association for Public Opinion Research
```

---

[22] The order of these elements is not prescribed.

[23] The name of more than one person or family can appear in the title; however, the name of only one corporate body can appear in the title.

[24] Guidance for choosing between different names of persons (including name changes) or between variant forms of the same name can be found in Chapter 12 (rules 12.1–12.3). Guidance for choosing between different names of corporate bodies or between variant forms of the same name can be found in Chapter 14 (rules 14.1–14.3).

2.3.6. If the name of the creator, assembler, or collector is not known, or if the repository has assembled the materials, do not record a name. In such cases, supply the nature of the archival materials for the title as instructed in rules 2.3.18-2.3.20 and 2.3.22.

Name segment for more than one person

2.3.7. If three or fewer persons are credited with, or predominantly responsible for, the creation of the materials as a whole, record their names in direct order.

```
John and Leni Sinclair papers

Eugenia Rawls and Donald Seawell theater collection
```

2.3.8. If responsibility for the creation of the materials is dispersed among more than three persons, record the name of the individual whose material predominates. If this does not apply, choose the name considered most appropriate.

2.3.9. Optionally, include all the names of the persons who are credited with or predominantly responsible for the creation of the materials.

Name segment for families

2.3.10. If the materials were created, assembled, accumulated, and/or used in the context of familial relations by individuals who share a common surname, record that name followed by the word "family."

```
Harvey family papers
```

2.3.11. If the materials were created, assembled, accumulated, and/or used in the context of familial relations by individuals who do not share a common surname, record all their names followed by the word "family."

```
Paul Hibbet Clyde and Mary Kestler family papers
```

2.3.12. Optionally, if the materials were created, assembled, accumulated, and/or used in the context of familial relations but one person's material predominates, record that person's full name followed by the word "family."

```
Andrew Swanson family papers
```

2.3.13. If two or three families are credited with, or predominantly responsible for, the creation of the materials, record all the family names followed by the word "families."

```
Short, Harrison, and Symmes families papers
```

2.3.14. If responsibility for the creation of the materials is dispersed among more than three families, record only the name of the family whose material predominates. If no one family's material predominates, choose the name considered most appropriate.

2.3.15. Optionally, include all the names of the families who are credited with, or predominantly responsible for, the creation of the materials.

Name segment for corporate bodies

Single corporate body see Rule 2.3.4.

More than one corporate body

2.3.16. If the records of more than one corporate body are included in the materials, record only one name in the title. Establish a consistent policy for selecting the name of the corporate body to be used in the title. While the name of only one corporate body can be included in the title, names of other corporate bodies whose records are included in the materials may be recorded in the Name of Creator(s) Element as specified in rule 9.9.

> British American Tobacco Company records
>> *This body of corporate records includes records of* Cameron and Cameron, D.B. Tennant and Company, David Dunlop, Export Leaf Tobacco Company, and T.C. Williams Company, *all of which were tobacco exporting companies acquired by British American Tobacco Company.*

Corporate body whose name has changed

2.3.17. Where the name of the corporate body has changed, use the last (latest) name of the corporate body represented in the materials being described. Predecessor names of the corporate body may be recorded in the Name of Creator(s) Element as specified in rule 9.9.

> University of California, Irvine, Office of Research and Graduate Studies records
>> *These records include those from this same body under two previous names,* Graduate Division (1964-1981) *and* Division of Graduate Studies and Research (1981-1987).

> Allied Theatres of Michigan records
>> *These materials include records of this same body under its earlier name,* Motion Picture Theatre Owners of Michigan *(name changed in 1931).*

Nature of the archival unit

2.3.18. Where the materials being described consist of three or more forms of documents created, assembled, accumulated, and/or maintained and used by a government agency or private organization such as a business or club, supply the word "records" for the nature of the archival unit. Where the materials being described consist of three or more forms of documents created, assembled, accumulated, and/or maintained and used by a person or family, supply the word "papers" for the nature of the archival unit. When describing an intentionally assembled collection, supply the word "collection" to indicate the nature of the unit being described. This rule is generally only applied to the highest level of the archival unit being described.[25]

---

[25] "Papers," "records,"and "collection" include materials in all media.

```
Coalition to Stop Trident records

St. Paul African Methodist Episcopal Zion Church records

Mortimer Jerome Adler papers

Allyn Kellogg Ford collection of historical manuscripts

Semans family papers
```

2.3.19. Where the materials being described consist solely of one or two specific forms, supply those form(s) [26] for the nature of the archival unit. Express the forms in their order of predominance.

```
English Stage Company at the Royal Court Theatre correspondence

John E. Brennan outdoor advertising survey reports

William Gedney photographs and writings

Troy Kinney etchings and engravings

Sarah Dyer zine collection

Andrew Jackson letter

Speeches
```
    Supplied title for a series within the Bessye B. Bearden papers

```
Audio and video recordings
```
    Supplied title for a series within the Jacques Derrida papers

```
National Academy of Sciences correspondence
```
    Supplied title for a file within the Frederick Reines papers

```
Council for Refugee Rights correspondence and reports
```
    Supplied title for a file within the Project Ngoc records

2.3.20. Optionally, if one or two specific forms predominate but there are also other material types present, record the one or two most predominant forms followed by the phrase "and other material" in the supplied title and indicate the specific forms of material in the Scope and Content Element.

```
James M. Woodbury diary, letters, and other material

Sociedad Amigos de Arteaga, Inc. correspondence, flyers, and
other material
```
    Supplied title for a file within the Genoveva de Arteaga papers

---

[26] *Form* means the physical (e.g., watercolor, drawing) or intellectual (e.g., diary, journal, daybook, minute book) characteristics of a document. Repositories are strongly encouraged to use standardized vocabulary when supplying form(s) of material as part of the supplied title.

Topic of the archival unit

2.3.21. Optionally, supply a brief term or phrase that most precisely and concisely characterizes the unit being described. The term or phrase should incorporate the form(s) of material that typifies the unit and reflects the function, activity, transaction, subject, individuals, or organizations that were the basis of its creation or use.

```
Clarence McGehee collection on Ruth St. Denis

Catherine Clarke civil rights collection

Collection of California vacation albums
```
Supplied title for a collection of purchased vacation albums assembled by Special Collections and Archives, University of California, Irvine.

```
Russian referendum collection
```
Supplied title for a collection of materials on the 1993 Russian referendum in support of the policies of Boris Yeltsin that was assembled by Manuscripts and Archives, Yale University.

```
Land agreements between the University of California and the
Irvine Company

Edith Wharton correspondence with Morton Fullerton

Oneida Nation petition to Jasper Parrish

Frank and Frances Robinson files on Upper Newport Bay

Correspondence regarding graduate assistantships

James Joyce letter to Maurice Saillet

Richard Nixon letter to H.R. Haldemann regarding the Watergate
break-in
```

2.3.22. When the subject of the collection is a person, and if no name has been recorded because the repository is the collector, express the title of the collection in a way that clearly indicates that the subject of the collection is not the collector.

```
Collection on Isadora Duncan
```
Collection is about Isadora Duncan, she is not the collector.

```
Collection of Robert Browning materials
```
Collection is materials by Robert Browning, he is not the collector.

2.4 Date Element

Purpose and Scope

This element identifies and records the date(s) that pertain to the creation, assembly, accumulation, and/or maintenance and use of the materials being described. This section describes types of dates and forms of dates.

> Commentary: It may be useful or necessary for archivists to record different types of dates for the materials being described, including
>
> **Date(s) of creation** are the dates that the documents in the unit being described were originally created (e.g., date of writing a letter, drawing a map, or painting a portrait) or the date that an event or image was captured in some material form (e.g., date that a photograph was taken, sound was originally recorded, or a film was shot). Dates of creation refer only to the activity of creation of individual documents that make up each unit (as opposed to the "creation" of an aggregate such as a series or file). This is the type of date recorded most often by archivists and manuscript catalogers not describing government or organizational records.
>
> **Date(s) of record-keeping activity** are the dates during which the unit being described was created, assembled, accumulated, and/or maintained and used *as a unit* in the conduct of affairs by the organization or individual responsible for its provenance. They are distinct from the dates of creation of individual documents. Although the dates of record-keeping activity may often coincide with the dates of creation, the date types differ in two ways. First, the date(s) of record-keeping activity refer to the dates of a number of interrelated activities (including, but not limited to, creation and accumulation); and secondly, the activities pertain to the unit as a whole as opposed to individual documents. Records may be accumulated and used for a current purpose long after they were originally created, for example, where much earlier records are assembled to support an investigation or a legal action.
>
> When dates of creation and dates of record-keeping activity are the same, record only the former. Dates of record-keeping activity are most often recorded by archivists working with government records, organizational archives, or other materials where it is important to account for functions and activities.
>
> **Date(s) of publication** are recorded if the unit being described is a commercially issued or mass-produced item. Record this date information (including dates of publishing, distributing, releasing, and issuing of items) according to rules in various chapters of *AACR2* or other appropriate standards (see Appendix B). Dates of publication are most often recorded when describing items.
>
> **Date(s) of broadcast** are dates on which sound recordings or moving image materials were broadcast on radio or television. Record this date information according to rules in various chapters of *AACR2* or other appropriate standards (see Appendix B). Dates of broadcast are most often recorded when describing items.

Exclusions

2.4.1. If the material being described is a reproduction, record the details about the reproduction, including the date(s) of reproduction, if known, in the Scope and Content Element (3.1.7). If the material being described is the original and the repository wishes to provide details about the availability of copies, record that information in the Existence and Location of Copies Element (6.2).

Sources of Information

2.4.2. Take the information from any reliable source, including the internal evidence of the materials being described.

General Rules

2.4.3. Record dates of creation, record-keeping activity, publication, or broadcast as appropriate to the materials being described.

2.4.4. Alternatively, if relevant and deemed necessary by the repository and if the descriptive system permits it, record multiple types of dates, labeling each clearly.[27] When recording multiple date types, explain each in the Scope and Content Element (3.1).

2.4.5. Record the year(s) in Western-style Arabic numerals. If the date found in or on the unit being described is not of the Gregorian or Julian calendar,[28] record the date as found and follow it with the year(s) of the Gregorian or Julian calendar in parentheses. Specify the name of the calendar, such as Republican, Jewish, Chinese, in a note (see 7.1.2)

> 2628 (1968)
> *Note: Dated in accordance with the Chinese calendar.*
>
> an 14 (i.e., 1805)
> *Note: Dated in accordance with the French Republican calendar.*

2.4.6. Record the date(s) of the unit being described either as a range of dates or as a single date.

Date Ranges

Inclusive dates

2.4.7. If the materials comprising or the record-keeping activity relating to the unit being described span a period of time, always record the inclusive dates, that is, the earliest and latest dates of the materials or activity in question.

> 1849-1851

---

[27] Most MARC-based systems will allow only one date type and the repository's ability to label dates will be very limited. EAD and other systems are more flexible in this area.
[28] Direction for converting dates after 1582 from the Julian calendar to the Gregorian calendar is provided in *AACR2* rule 22.17A n. 16.

2.4.8. When further accruals are expected, record the inclusive dates pertaining to the holdings currently in the custody of the repository. Record information about expected accruals in the Accruals Element (5.4). When the accruals are received, revise the date information accordingly.

```
1979-1993
not 1979-
not 1979-(ongoing)
```

2.4.9. The date(s) of a unit being described must fall within the range of dates of the unit of which it forms a part. This rule applies to both dates of creation and dates of record-keeping activity.

```
1934-1985
```
Dates of record-keeping activity for a body of corporate records.

```
1945-1960
```
Dates of record-keeping activity for a series within the above.

```
1950-1955
```
Dates of record-keeping activity for a file within the above.

Predominant or bulk dates

2.4.10. Optionally, where the dates pertaining to the majority of the documents in the unit being described differ significantly from the inclusive dates, provide predominant or bulk dates. Specify them as such, preceded by the word "predominant" or "bulk." Never provide predominant or bulk dates without also providing inclusive dates.

```
1785-1960, bulk 1916-1958

1942-1998, predominant 1975-1991
```

2.4.11. Optionally, if there is a significant gap in the chronological sequence of the documents in the unit being described, where providing predominant/bulk dates would be misleading, record the anomalous date(s) separated by commas.[29] Explain significant chronological gaps in the materials in the Scope and Content Element (3.1).

```
1827, 1952-1978

1975, 2002
```

---

[29] Repositories are encouraged to establish consistent policies and procedures regarding the maximum number of anomalous dates to record.

Estimated date ranges

2.4.12. At all levels of description, where the earliest or latest dates pertaining to the unit being described are estimates, indicate the estimated dates in a clear and consistent fashion.[30]

```
approximately 1952-1978

circa 1870-1879
```

Single dates

2.4.13. If the materials fall within a single year, record that date or a more specific date therein.

```
1975

1975 March-August
```

Exact single dates

2.4.14. For descriptions of a single item, record exact dates in a consistent and unambiguous fashion, preferably expressed as year-month-day.[31]

```
1906 March 17
```

Estimated single dates

2.4.15. If no date can be found on or in the material itself or determined from any other source, estimate the nearest year, decade, century or other interval as precisely as possible. Record estimated dates in a consistent fashion.

```
probably 1867

approximately 1925

before 1867

after 1867 January 5

1892 or 1893

1890s

circa August 1975
```

---

[30] It is recommended, though not required, that terms reflecting estimation be spelled out rather than abbreviated, as abbreviations may not be understood by all users.
[31] Expression of dates as all numerals is discouraged due to the differing conventions in the order of information.

No dates

2.4.16. When recording date(s) for files and items, if the unit being described bears no date and the institution does not wish to or it may be misleading to record an estimated date, use "undated." Do not use the abbreviations "n.d." or "s.d."

EXAMPLES OF ENCODING FOR 2.4 DATE ELEMENT

Encoding at any level of description in EAD. Dates that a repository wishes to be computer searchable should be normalized according to ISO 8601 *Representation of Dates and Times.*

```
<unitdate normal="1975">1975</unitdate>

<unitdate type="inclusive" normal="1849/1851">1849-1851</unitdate>

<unitdate normal="19060317">1906 March 17</unitdate>

<unitdate type="inclusive" normal="1785/1960">1785-1960</unitdate>
<unitdate type="bulk" normal="1916/1958">bulk 1916-1958</unitdate>

<unitdate type="inclusive" normal="1870/1879">circa 1870-
1879</unitdate>

<unitdate normal="1892/1893">1892 or 1893</unitdate>

<unitdate type="inclusive" normal="1862/1969" label="Dates of
Creation">1862-1969</unitdate>
<unitdate type="inclusive" normal="1957-1969" label="Dates of
Record-keeping Activity">1957-1969</unitdate>
```

Encoding at the highest level of description in MARC 21:

```
245  00   ‡a Project Ngoc records, ‡f 1978-1998.

245  10  ·‡a Henry David Thoreau letter and engraving, ‡f 1847.

245  10   ‡a Willis H. Warner papers, ‡f 1884-1964, ‡g bulk 1920-
          1963.

245  10   ‡a United Farm Workers Information Fair collection, ‡f
          circa 1968-1972.

245  00   ‡a David Douglas Duncan photographs
260  bb   ‡c 1935-2004
```

2.5 Extent Element

Purpose and Scope

This element indicates the extent and the physical nature of the materials being described. This is handled in two parts, a number (quantity) and an expression of the extent or material type. The second part of the extent element may be either:

- the physical extent of the materials expressed either as the items, containers or carriers, or storage space occupied; or
- an enumeration of the material type(s), usually physical material type(s), to which the unit being described belongs. Material types may be general or specific.

Repositories should establish a consistent method of articulating statements of extent.

If the description of particular media or individual items requires more detail, such as other physical characteristics or dimensions, see the specific chapters in *AACR2* or the medium-specific rules indicated in the Introduction to Part I and Appendix B.

If the material type has been provided in the title statement, do not repeat it in the statement of extent.

> Commentary: It is important to include information about the quantity and physical nature of the materials for several reasons. It enables users to eliminate material that is irrelevant to their needs; for example, a user may want only the material containing photographs. It also enables users to plan their research: knowing the quantity is important because it takes longer to go through 30 boxes or 20 hours of sound recordings than it does to go through one box or five hours. The amount of detail provided at any level of description is a matter of institutional policy, depending on user needs and available resources. At lower levels in a multilevel description, extent may be expressed as an enumeration of boxes or folders rather than as a narrative extent statement.
>
> Further details about quantity and physical characteristics may also be provided in the Scope and Content Element (3.1).

Exclusions

2.5.1. Record information about physical characteristics that affect the use of the unit being described in the Physical Access Element (4.2).

Sources of Information

2.5.2. Derive the information from the materials themselves or take it from transfer documents.

General Rules

2.5.3. Record the numerical quantity associated with each expression of physical extent, containers or carriers, number of items, or material type, using the imperial system of measurement in Arabic numerals, unless the repository has made a decision to use the metric system.

2.5.4. Record the quantity of the material in terms of its physical extent as linear or cubic feet, number of items, or number of containers or carriers.[32]

```
45 linear feet

5,321 items

16 boxes

2 film reels

15 folders

Box 10    Folder 6
```

2.5.5. Optionally, record the quantity in terms of material type(s). Material types may be general, such as textual materials,[33] graphic materials, cartographic materials, architectural and technical drawings, moving images, and sound recordings, or more specific types such as those found in *AACR2* and various thesauri.[34]

```
10 boxes of textual materials

1,000 photographs

50 technical drawings

800 maps

12 audio cassettes
```

2.5.6. Optionally, qualify the statement of physical extent to highlight the existence of material types that are important.

```
45 linear feet, including 200 photographs and 16 maps

3 boxes, including photographs and audio cassettes
```

---

[32] It is recommended, though not required, that terms reflecting physical extent be spelled out rather than abbreviated, as abbreviations may not be understood by all users.

[33] It is usually assumed that archival materials are generally textual in nature, so it may not be necessary to supply the term "textual materials" unless it is desirable to distinguish from other material types.

[34] See especially *Art and Architecture Thesaurus, Thesaurus for Graphic Material,* and *Library of Congress Authorities* (full citations provided in Appendix B).

Multiple Statements of Extent

2.5.7. If a parallel expression of extent is required or desirable, add this information in parentheses.

```
2,400 photographs (12 linear feet)

89.3 linear feet (150 boxes and 109 oversize folders)

71 maps (3.5 cubic feet)

1 diary (352 pages)
```

2.5.8. Optionally, provide multiple statements of extent to highlight the existence of material types that are important.

```
12 linear feet of textual materials, 68 photographs, 16
architectural drawings
```

Approximate Statements of Extent

2.5.9. If parts of the material being described are numerous and the exact number cannot be readily ascertained, record an approximate number and indicate that it is an estimate.

```
approximately 35 linear feet

about 24,000 maps

circa 11,000 photographs
```

EXAMPLES OF ENCODING FOR 2.5 EXTENT ELEMENT

Encoding at any level of description in EAD:

```
<physdesc><extent>45 linear feet</extent></physdesc>

<physdesc><extent>50 technical drawings</extent></physdesc>

<physdesc><extent>3 boxes, including photographs and audio
    cassettes</extent></physdesc>

<physdesc><extent>89.3 linear feet (150 boxes and 109 oversize
    folders)</extent></physdesc>

<physdesc><extent>12 linear feet of textual materials</extent>,
    <extent>68 photographic prints</extent>, <extent>16 architectural
    drawings</extent></physdesc>

<container type="Box">10</container>
<container type="Folder">6</container>
```

Encoding at the highest level of description in MARC 21:

```
300  bb ‡a 45 ‡f linear feet

300  bb ‡a 3 ‡f boxes, ‡b including photographs and audio cassettes

300  bb ‡a 89.3 ‡f linear feet (150 boxes and 109 oversize folders)

300  bb ‡a 12 ‡f linear feet of textual materials

300  bb ‡a 68 ‡f photographs

300  bb ‡a 33,000 ‡f items (69.0 linear feet)
```

2.6 Name of Creator(s) Element

A description of the context in which the materials being described were created, assembled, accumulated, and/or maintained is as important as the description of the materials themselves. One of the most significant aspects of establishing the context of creation is to identify the individual, family, or organization responsible for that process. Depending on the materials being described, the archivist may express that relationship by various terms: creator, author, collector, artist, cartographer, or, more generically, as the provenance of the materials. Multiple individuals and organizations may serve multiple roles with respect to a given body of records. For example, a published document might be filed with a regulatory agency. The company that created a report would be its author, while the government body was responsible for assembling this report with others into a series of records. Both played a role in the creation of the materials that have come to the repository.

Detailed rules in Part II, Chapter 9, Identifying Creators, specify which name(s) should be provided in the Name of Creator(s) Element to document the processes by which the records were created, assembled, accumulated, and/or maintained. Specific systems may store information about creators either in the descriptions of records or separately in a linked authority file. In addition, names of creators serve as access points (see Overview of Archival Description).

2.7 Administrative/Biographical History Element

A description of the context in which the materials being described were created, assembled, accumulated, and/or maintained is as important as the description of the materials themselves. One of the most significant aspects of the description of the context of creation is the Administrative/Biographical History Element. Such descriptions may be a part of the description of the materials, but they may also be created and stored in an authority system separate from the description of the materials. To facilitate such systems, the rules for creating an administrative or biographical history are provided in Part II, Chapter 10. The rules apply to either situation—administrative history and biographical information as part of the description of the materials or as maintained in a separate authority system.

CHAPTER 3

Content and Structure Elements

3.1 Scope and Content
3.2 System of Arrangement

3.1 Scope and Content Element

Purpose and Scope

This element provides information about the nature of the materials and activities reflected in the unit being described to enable users to judge its potential relevance. The scope and content element may include information about any or all of the following, as appropriate:

- the function(s), activity(ies), transaction(s), and process(es) that generated the materials being described;
- the documentary form(s) or intellectual characteristics of the records being described (e.g., minutes, diaries, reports, watercolors, documentaries);
- the content dates, that is, the time period(s) covered by the intellectual content or subject of the unit being described;
- geographic area(s) and places to which the records pertain;
- subject matter to which the records pertain, such as topics, events, people, and organizations; and
- any other information that assists the user in evaluating the relevance of the materials, such as completeness, changes in location, ownership and custody while still in the possession of the creator, etc.

No attempt has been made to distinguish between what constitutes *scope* and what constitutes *content*; scope and content are treated as a single element, and the following rules simply enumerate the types of information that could be included in this element. Repositories should establish institutional policies and guidelines for consistent practice regarding the level of detail to be recorded in the scope and content statement. This element is a good source for the access points discussed in the Overview of Archival Description.

Commentary: A brief summary of the scope and content and biographical information may be combined in an abstract for presentation purposes to enhance resource discovery. Such an abstract does not serve as a substitute for the Scope and Content Element.

Exclusions

3.1.1. Record information about the context in which the unit being described was created, used, etc., in the Administrative/Biographical History Element (see Chapter 10).

3.1.2. Record information about gaps in the unit being described resulting from archival appraisal decisions in the Appraisal, Destruction, and Scheduling Information Element (5.3).

Sources of Information

3.1.3. Derive the information from the materials themselves and any relevant documentation.

General Rules

3.1.4. Record information of the types listed in the statement of purpose and scope above appropriate to the unit being described.

> Minutes, membership and dues records, journals, daybooks, forms, circulars, and correspondence from a carpenters' union local in St. Paul, Minnesota. Correspondence and minutes contain data on the union's formation, internal affairs, assessments and benefits, social functions, organizing activities, relations with other local and national unions, and political participation. There is also information on St. Paul labor issues, hiring practices, boycotts, strikes, and employers' attitudes toward unions. Present also are minutes (1914-1923) of Millmen's Local Number 1868, which affiliated with the carpenters in 1923.
>
> *Scope and content for the* Carpenters and Joiners Brotherhood of America. Local No. 87 (Saint Paul, Minn.) records.

> This collection documents the activities of Willis H. Warner, who was a member of the Orange County Board of Supervisors for 24 years, including the activities of the Board of Supervisors and numerous Orange County governmental units from the 1930s through the 1960s. It also contains personal materials, including the records of Warner's business, the Warner Hardware Store (Huntington Beach, California), and materials documenting his prolific career in the public sector working for the Westminster Drainage District, the Beach Protective Association of Huntington Beach, and other Orange County public institutions and political organizations. Some of the significant topics represented in these files are airport development; environmental issues such as air and water pollution, beach erosion, and shoreline development (including reports by consulting engineer R.L. Patterson); civil defense; county finances; employment; fire programs; land use and planning; freeway and highway development; county buildings; correctional facilities; parks and recreation; oil drilling; public health and hospitals, particularly the Orange County General Hospital; publicity and tourism; schools and school districts; and welfare and public works programs. The collection

also documents Warner's public service prior to joining the Board of Supervisors, particularly the financial and legal activities of the Westminster Drainage District, accumulated while he was working as its secretary; his active participation in the commercial development of Huntington Beach and nearby communities; his work on the board of trustees for Huntington Beach Union High School; and his involvement with the Beach Protective Association of Huntington Beach, which sought to prevent oil drilling in the area. Materials are largely textual, comprising correspondence, memoranda, minutes and agendas, financial and legal material, clippings, publications, blueprints, maps, and related printed matter. Among other formats scattered throughout the collection are photographs, a small number of negatives, artifacts such as plaques, ephemera, and campaign paraphernalia.

Scope and content for the Willis H. Warner papers.

Series comprises primarily letters to or from the secretary-treasurer of the North Carolina Folklore Society and the editor of *North Carolina Folklore*. Arthur Palmer Hudson and Daniel W. Patterson were secretary-treasurers until 1966; most of the early correspondence is to or from one of them and concerns subscriptions, dues, and annual meetings (especially the 1964 meeting). Most of the later correspondence is directed to Richard Walser as editor of *North Carolina Folklore*. Included as an attachment is a story dictated by North Carolina Governor Robert W. Scott in 1970, "The Governor Fowles Ghost Story."

Scope and content for a series in the North Carolina Folklore Society records.

File includes primarily correspondence, data and analysis, notes, and daily reports from East Rand Proprietary Mine (ERPM). Notebook II is primarily dictaphone transcriptions of daily reports.

Scope and content for a file in the Frederick Reines papers.

Plat map depicting town plaza and perimeter, including mission church and courtyard, adobe walls, some roads, orchards, vineyards, and cemetery. Scale is listed as 3 chains to 1 inch.

Scope and content for an item in the Richard Egan Manuscript Maps of Orange County.

Letter presented by 21 Oneida Indians, signed with their marks, requesting that Jasper Parrish pay them the amount they are owed for serving in the War of 1812. They state that they are aware that he received the money three months previously and they are anxious to settle the account.

Scope and content for the Oneida Nation petition to Jasper Parrish.

3.1.5. When the unit being described is known to be incomplete due to reasons other than archival appraisal decisions, record information about the gaps.

File contains telex printouts of almost daily discussions between various members of the collaboration team spread out between Ohio, California, and South Africa. Significant gaps for which no telex printouts exist include August 1967-February 1968.

Scope and content for a file in the Frederick Reines papers.

Files are incomplete, since many items of significant commercial value were sold piecemeal in the 1980s and some files from later years are held by Weidenfeld and Nicholson, which took over the Dent firm in 1986.

Scope and content for a series in J. M. Dent & Sons records.

3.1.6. Where the material includes a uniform set of documents (e.g., marriage certificates), indicate the kinds of information recorded in the documents.

Investigative files include correspondence, witness interviews, autopsy reports, and lab test reports; official court records include deposition transcripts, pleading books, transcripts of trial testimony, and "discovery" material; court exhibit files contain "scene evidence" collected by the police at the murder scene and copies of investigation reports from the FBI, the BATF, and the Greensboro Police Department.

Collection-level scope and content from the Greensboro Civil Rights Fund records.

Court exhibit files contain copies of reports, maps, photographs, and investigation notes from the FBI, the BATF, and the Greensboro Police Department. Physical evidence includes "scene evidence" picked up by police at the murder scene on 3 November, including CWP banners, blood-stained clothing removed from the bodies of victims, shotgun pellets removed from the victims, and a Klan effigy utilized by the demonstrators. Some additional physical evidence (e.g., a guitar shattered by shotgun pellets) was returned to the plaintiffs.

Series-level scope and content from the Greensboro Civil Rights Fund records.

3.1.7. If the material being described is a reproduction, indicate that fact, and if considered important, also indicate the date of reproduction.

File contains reproductions of original plats made circa 1960–circa 1980. These plat maps depict the following ranchos and communities: San Jose de Buenos Ayres, La Cienegas, La Brea, Cahuenga Tract, San Antonio (or Rodeo de Las Aquas), San Vicente y Santa Monica, Los Felis, and Cuati.

Scope and content for a file in the Collection of Orange County and California maps.

Pictures are of William Gaston (reproduction of engraving from painting and photograph of painting), Zebulon Baird Vance (reproduction of engraving), William A. Graham (reproduction of engraving), Willie Person Mangum (reproduction of engraving), John Motley Morehead (reproduction of engraving), and John Louis Taylor (carte-de-visite).

Scope and content for a series in William Gaston papers.

EXAMPLES OF ENCODING FOR 3.1 SCOPE AND CONTENT ELEMENT

Encoding at any level of description in EAD:

```
<scopecontent>
<p>File contains telex printouts of almost daily discussions between
various members of the collaboration team spread out between Ohio,
California, and South Africa. Significant gaps for which no telex
printouts exist include August 1967-February 1968.</p>
</scopecontent>
```

Encoding at the highest level of description in MARC 21:

```
520  2b   ‡a Minutes, membership and dues records, journals,
          daybooks, forms, circulars, and correspondence from a
          carpenters' union local in St. Paul, Minnesota. ‡b
          Correspondence and minutes contain data on the union's
          formation, internal affairs, assessments and benefits,
          social functions, organizing activities, relations with
          other local and national unions, and political
          participation. There is also information on St. Paul labor
          issues, hiring practices, boycotts, strikes, and employers'
          attitudes toward unions. Present also are minutes (1914-
          1923) of Millmen's Local Number 1868, which affiliated with
          the carpenters in 1923.
```

3.2 System of Arrangement Element

Purpose and Scope

This element identifies the various aggregations of archival materials, their relationships, or the sequence of documents within them.

Sources of Information

3.2.1. Derive the information from the materials themselves.

General Rules

3.2.2. Describe the current arrangement of the material in terms of the various aggregations within it and their relationships.

```
Arranged in 5 series: 1. Subject files concerning refugee issues,
1978-1997. 2. Project Ngoc organizational files, 1987-1997. 3.
Visual and audiovisual materials, 1985-1997. 4. Artwork, 1987-
1997. 5. Newspaper clippings, 1980-1998.
                    ------------------------
The records are arranged in five series, three of which have been
further arranged in subseries. The contents of each series or
subseries are arranged alphabetically with the exception of
Series 1, Subseries 1, which is arranged hierarchically to
reflect the organizational structure of the AAIA. The series and
subseries arrangement of the records is as follows:
  Series 1, Organizational Files,1922-1995
      Subseries 1, Administration, 1923-1994
      Subseries 2, Affiliates and Offices, 1922-1964
      Subseries 3, Correspondence, 1929-1995
      Subseries 4, Finances, 1933-1995
  Series 2, Subject Files, 1851-1995
      Subseries 1, General, 1868-1995
      Subseries 2, Tribal, 1852-1994
      Subseries 3, Legislation, 1851-1994
      Subseries 4, Legal Cases, 1934-1991
      Subseries 5, Programs, 1927-1994
      Subseries 6, Publications and Circulars, 1924-1994
  Series 3, Personal Files, 1927-1991
      Subseries 1, Henry S. Forbes, 1954-1981
      Subseries 2, Hildegarde B. Forbes, 1927-1991
      Subseries 3, Oliver La Farge, 1939-1963
      Subseries 4, Corinna Lindon Smith, 1932-1965
      Subseries 5, Alden Stevens, 1941-1971
  Series 4, Photographs, 1928-1992
  Series 5, Audiovisual Materials, 1961-1987
                    ------------------------
Arranged in two series: 1. Correspondence (chronological); 2.
Professional organization files (alphabetical by organization
name).
```

3.2.3. Optionally, give information about the system of ordering the component files or items.

```
Resources arranged alphabetically by subject, personal name, or
corporate name.
```
   Arrangement for a series in the William Noffke papers

```
Arrangement: chronological.
```
   Arrangement for a series in the Caffery Family papers

```
This subseries is arranged alphabetically by the geographic
location of the photograph and then by the item number assigned
by the photographer.
```
   Arrangement for a subseries in the Edward W. Cochems photographs

3.2.4. Provide significant information about other aspects of the arrangement of the materials, such as maintenance/reconstitution of original order, arrangement by the archivist, or previous arrangements or reorganization(s) by the creator if known and important to the understanding of the materials.

```
Unless otherwise noted in the series and subseries descriptions,
the arrangement scheme for the collection was imposed during
processing in the absence of a usable original order.
```
   Arrangement of the Frederick Reines papers

```
The original chronological arrangement of the series was
maintained during processing.  The sole exception to this
arrangement is several files of correspondence with physicists
that Reines maintained separately from the chronological files,
which are arranged alphabetically by the physicists' surnames at
the end of the series.
```
   Arrangement of a series in the Frederick Reines papers

EXAMPLES OF ENCODING FOR 3.2 SYSTEM OF ARRANGEMENT ELEMENT

Encoding at any level of description in EAD:

```
<arrangement>
<p>This subseries is arranged alphabetically by the geographic
location of the photograph and then by the item number assigned
by the photographer.</p>
</arrangement>


<arrangement>
<p>The papers are arranged in 11 series:</p>
<list type="simple">
<item>Series 1. Early career, circa 1932-1995. 0.5 linear ft.
</item>
<item>Series 2. Case Institute of Technology files, 1958-
1976.</item>
<item>Series 3. University of California committee files, 1970-
1992.</item>
<item>Series 4. University of California, Irvine files, circa
1931-1996.</item>
<item>Series 5. Professional activities, 1934-1997.</item>
<item>Series 6. Correspondence files, 1952-1995.</item>
<item>Series 7. Publications and writings, 1945-1999.</item>
<item>Series 8. Data books, 1946-1991.</item>
<item>Series 9. Experiments, 1943-1997.</item>
<item>Series 10. Collaborations, 1952-1995.</item>
<item>Series 11. Funding agency files, 1959-1994.</item>
</list>
<p>Unless otherwise noted in the series and subseries
descriptions, the arrangement scheme for the collection was
imposed during processing in the absence of a usable original
order.</p>
</arrangement>
```

Encoding at the highest level of description in MARC 21:

```
351  bb   ‡a Arranged in 5 series: 1. Subject files concerning
          refugee issues, 1978-1997. 2. Project Ngoc
          organizational files, 1987-1997. 3. Visual and
          audiovisual materials, 1985-1997. 4. Artwork, 1987-
          1997. 5. Newspaper clippings, 1980-1998.
```

CHAPTER 4

Conditions of Access and Use Elements

4.1 Conditions Governing Access
4.2 Physical Access
4.3 Technical Access
4.4 Conditions Governing Reproduction and Use
4.5 Languages and Scripts of the Material
4.6 Finding Aids

4.1 Conditions Governing Access Element

Purpose and Scope

This element provides information about access restrictions due to the nature of the information in the materials being described, such as those imposed by the donor, by the repository, or by statutory/regulatory requirements.

> Commentary: In many cases it will be necessary or desirable to provide a very succinct statement regarding access restrictions rather than a lengthy explanation. This would particularly be the case for a MARC 21 record when restrictions are complex or likely to change over time.

Exclusions

4.1.1. Record any physical conditions affecting the use of the materials being described in the Physical Access Element (4.2).

4.1.2. Record any technical requirements affecting the use of the materials being described in the Technical Access Element (4.3).

4.1.3. Record any restrictions governing reproduction, publication, or other uses after access is given in the Conditions Governing Reproduction and Use Element (4.4).

Sources of Information

4.1.4. Derive the information from a reliable source, such as donor agreements, statutes, and regulations and repository policies.

General Rules

4.1.5. Give information about any restrictions on access to the unit being described (or parts thereof) as a result of the nature of the information therein or statutory/contractual requirements. As appropriate, specify the details of the restriction, including the length of the period of closure or the date when it will be lifted; the authority that imposed and enforces the conditions governing access; contact information for the person or office to whom the restriction may be appealed; authorized users; etc. If there are no restrictions, state that fact.

```
The collection is open for research use.
------------------------
Records are closed, per agreement with the creating office, for
fifteen years after the date of their creation unless otherwise
stated.
------------------------
Researchers must receive prior written permission to use the
collection from the Trustees of the Kenneth Winslow Charitable
Remainder Unitrust. The collection is partially processed. Please
contact Special Collections for more information.
------------------------
The records of the president contain personnel and student
academic records that are restricted in accordance with
university policy and applicable law. Restrictions, where
applicable, are noted at the series, subseries, or file levels.
In addition, this record group has the following unique
restrictions:
    • Files of a president, while still in office, are
      restricted.
    • Once a president has left office, files over ten years old
      are open to researchers; those under ten years old are
      restricted.
For records of the president added to the record group after 1
January 2001, the restriction is twenty years from the date of
accession in accordance with the university's policy on the
records of Executive Officers, Deans, Directors, and their
support offices.  Records in this category are identified with an
"ER restricted" note.
------------------------
Only electronic records more than five years old may be used by
researchers.
------------------------
All student records in this series are subject to Family
Educational Rights and Privacy Act (FERPA) restrictions of 75
years from the date of creation of the record.
------------------------
Access to files containing information on University personnel
matters is restricted for 50 years from the latest date of the
materials in those files. Access to student records is restricted
for 75 years from the latest date of the records in those files.
Restrictions are noted at the file level.
------------------------
Access to correspondence in this file is restricted until 2020.
```

4.1.6. Alternatively, simply indicate the fact of restriction.

```
Access is restricted; consult repository for details.
```

```
EXAMPLES OF ENCODING FOR 4.1 CONDITIONS GOVERNING ACCESS ELEMENT
```

Encoding at any level of description in EAD:

```
<accessrestrict>
<p>Researchers must receive prior written permission to use the
collection from the Trustees of the Kenneth Winslow Charitable
Remainder Unitrust. The collection is partially processed. Please
contact Special Collections for more information.</p>
</accessrestrict>
```

Encoding at the highest level of description in MARC 21:

506 bb   ‡a **Dream diaries are closed to research use until the
death of the donor.**

506 bb   ‡a **Correspondence between Smith and his first wife is not
available for research use until 2010.**

4.2 Physical Access Element

Purpose and Scope

This element provides information about access restrictions due to any physical characteristics or storage locations that limit, restrict, delay, or otherwise affect access to the materials being described. Such restrictions may include:

- location (e.g., offsite, cold storage);
- physical condition of the material that limits use; and
- requirement to use copies instead of originals for preservation reasons.

Exclusions

4.2.1. Record any access restrictions due to the nature of the information in the Conditions Governing Access Element (4.1).

4.2.2. Record any technical requirements affecting the use of the materials being described in the Technical Access Element (4.3).

4.2.3. Record any restrictions governing reproduction, publication, or other uses after access is given in the Conditions Governing Reproduction and Use Element (4.4).

Sources of Information

4.2.4. Derive the information from the materials themselves and repository policy.

General Rules

4.2.5. Provide information about the physical characteristics or condition of the unit being described that limit access to it or restrict its use.

```
Records are heavily foxed.

Some of the letters in this series are illegible due to water
damage.

The majority of the materials in this file are torn along edges
and folds.

Emulsion flaking.

Recorded with a constant audible hum.
```

4.2.6. Provide information about the location of the unit being described, if that location affects access to it.

The audio cassettes are located in cold vault storage and must be acclimated before delivery to the research room.

Forty-eight hours advance notice is required for access because materials are stored offsite.

4.2.7. If the original materials may not be used at all for preservation reasons, provide information about the reasons and the availability of reproductions.

As a preservation measure, researchers must view the reference set of color slide reproductions of the posters in this collection rather than the originals.

Originals not available due to fragility. Use microfilm copy.

This film reel has shrunk and may not be viewed.

EXAMPLES OF ENCODING FOR 4.2 PHYSICAL ACCESS ELEMENT

Encoding at any level of description in EAD:

```
<accessrestrict>
<p>Use of audio cassettes may require production of listening copies.</p>
</accessrestrict>

<phystech>
<p>Some of the letters in this series are illegible due to water damage.</p>
</phystech>

<physloc>
<p>Forty-eight hours advance notice is required for access because materials are stored offsite.</p>
</physloc>
```

Encoding at the highest level of description in MARC 21:

506 bb   ‡a **Researchers must use microfilm copies.**

506 bb   ‡a **Some of the letters in this series are illegible due to water damage.**

4.3 Technical Access Element

Purpose and Scope

This element provides information about access restrictions due to any technical requirements that restrict or otherwise affect access to the materials being described, such as equipment or specific hardware/software required for use.

Exclusions

4.3.1. Record any access restrictions due to the nature of the information in the Conditions Governing Access Element (4.1).

4.3.2. Record any physical conditions affecting the use of the materials being described in the Physical Access Element (4.2).

4.3.3. Record any restrictions governing reproduction, publication, or other uses after access is given in the Conditions Governing Reproduction and Use Element (4.4).

Sources of Information

4.3.4. Derive the information from the materials themselves and repository policy.

General Rules

Commentary: Special equipment may be required to view or access some material, particularly audiovisual materials and records in electronic form. In some cases the equipment required may be obvious from the Extent Element, as in "42 slides" or "30 audio cassettes." In other cases, however, the type of equipment required should be indicated in the Physical Access Element; for example, the playing speed of audio discs (e.g., 45 or 78 rpm), a video's recording mode (e.g., Betamax, D2, VHS, Video 8, etc.), or broadcast format (e.g., NTSC, PAL, SECAM, HDTV, etc.), the gauge (width) of the film (e.g., 16 or 35 mm), and so on.

4.3.5. Provide information about any special equipment required to view or access the unit being described, if it is not clear from the Extent Element (2.5).

```
Parade recorded on Super8 film.

Membership files are in an Access database.
```

4.3.6. Record information about the technical requirements for access to records in electronic form. Give the following characteristics in any appropriate order: make and model of the computer(s) on which the records are designed to run, amount of memory required, name of the operating system, software requirements, and kind and characteristics of any required or recommended peripherals.

The Personnel Master File contains 14 rectangular flat files stored in standard label EBCDIC. The files contain numeric and character data. The files are stored on 14 reels of tape at 6250 bpi. The data can be manipulated using a common statistical package. Tape copies are in standard label EBCDIC format. Floppy disk copies are in ASCII format.

System requirements: 48K RAM; Apple Disk II with controller; color monitor required to view this file.

EXAMPLES OF ENCODING FOR 4.3 TECHNICAL ACCESS ELEMENT

Encoding at any level of description in EAD:

```
<phystech>
<p>Umstead for governor radio advertisement, 1952 July 7, recorded
on radio transcription disc.</p>
</phystech>

<phystech>
<p>Membership files are in an Access database.</p>
</phystech>
```

Encoding at the highest level of description in MARC 21:

```
538  bb   ‡a Disk characteristics:  Floppy disk, single sided,
          double density, soft sectored.
```

4.4 Conditions Governing Reproduction and Use Element

Purpose and Scope

This element identifies any restrictions on reproduction due to copyright or other reasons, as well as restrictions on further use of the materials being described, such as publication, after access has been provided.

> Commentary: In many cases it will be necessary or desirable to provide a very succinct statement regarding reproduction and use (see 4.4.8 and the first example under 4.4.12), particularly when restrictions are complex or likely to change over time.

Exclusions

4.4.1. Record any access restrictions due to the nature of the information in the materials being described in the Conditions Governing Access Element (4.1).

4.4.2. Record any physical conditions affecting the use of the materials being described in the Physical Access Element (4.2).

4.4.3. Record any technical requirements affecting the use of the materials being described in the Technical Access Element (4.3).

Sources of Information

4.4.5. Derive the information from a reliable source, such as a donor agreement, statutes and regulations, or repository policies.

General Rules

4.4.6. Give information about copyright status and any other conditions governing the reproduction, publication, and further use (e.g., display, public screening, broadcast, etc.) of the unit being described after access has been provided.

4.4.7. Where possible and appropriate, combine the statements pertaining to copyright status, reproduction, publication, or use in the most efficient way.

```
Unpublished manuscripts are protected by copyright.
Permission to publish, quote, or reproduce must be secured
from the repository and the copyright holder.
```

Copyright Status

> Commentary: The statement of copyright status of a work indicates whether or not it is protected by copyright, and if it is protected, the duration and owner of the copyright. The copyright status is determined by the copyright legislation of the country in which the

archives preserving the work is located. Where the term of copyright protection has expired, it is useful to indicate that the work may be used freely for any purpose without the permission of the copyright owner or the payment of royalties. Where the work is still subject to copyright protection, it is useful to indicate the duration of copyright protection and the copyright owner, should the user require permission to use the work for purposes other than private study, scholarship, or research. Copyright laws provide the copyright owner with other rights in addition to copying, including the right to control publication, distribution, broadcast, public performance, etc. Copyright laws may also permit archives and libraries to copy items in their holdings for limited purposes, such as research or preservation, without the permission of the copyright owner, provided that certain conditions are met.

4.4.8. If the details of the copyright status of the materials being described are unknown, unclear, or complex, make a general statement about possible copyright restrictions.

```
Copyright restrictions may apply.
```

4.4.9. If the materials being described are protected by copyright, indicate the copyright owner, when the copyright restrictions will expire, and contact information for the copyright owner or the owner's agent, if known.

```
Copyright held by KOCE-TV.

Copyright in the unpublished writings of Clark M. Clifford in
these papers and in other collections of papers in the custody of
the Library of Congress has been dedicated to the public.

Copyright retained by the donor during her lifetime, at which
point it will revert to the Regents of the University of
California.

To the extent that she owns copyright, the donor has assigned the
copyright in her works to the Archives; however copyright in some
items in this collection may be held by their respective
creators. Consult the reference archivist for details.
```

4.4.10. If the term of copyright has expired, indicate that the material being described is no longer subject to copyright restrictions.

```
Material in this collection is in the public domain.
```

Conditions Governing Reproduction

Commentary: Reproduction is defined as the making of copies of all or part of an item in the unit being described. It does not involve other uses such as publication, public viewing, broadcast, etc. While copyright legislation may place statutory restrictions on reproduction (as well as other uses), reproduction may be restricted for other reasons, for example, the wishes of the donor, physical condition, etc.

4.4.11. If the conditions governing reproduction are fully expressed in the copyright status statement, do not repeat them in a separate statement.

4.4.12. Give information about any conditions that may restrict the making of copies of all or part of the materials being described. As appropriate, specify the details of the restriction, including the length of the period of closure or the date when it will be lifted; the authority that imposed the restriction(s); and the contact information for the person or office from whom permission to copy may be sought.

```
All requests for copying of materials must be submitted to the
Director of Archives in writing for approval by the donor.  Please
consult the Reference Archivists for further information.

Cartographic material in this series cannot be reproduced without
the written permission of the donor. This restriction is in
effect until 30 June 2010. Contact the repository for further
information.
```

Conditions Governing Publication and Other Uses

Commentary: Publication means the issuing or distribution of copies of a work to the public. A variety of uses other than reproduction or publication may be subject to certain conditions, including display, public viewing, broadcast, presentation on the World Wide Web, etc.

4.4.13. If the conditions governing publication and other uses are fully expressed in the copyright status statement, do not repeat them in a separate statement.

4.4.14. Give information about any conditions that may restrict publication or other uses of all or part of the unit being described. As appropriate, specify the details of the condition(s), including the duration of the restriction or the date when it will be lifted; the authority that imposed the condition(s); and the contact information for the person or office from whom permission to publish may be sought.

```
Authorization to publish, quote, or reproduce must be obtained
from Watkinson Library, Trinity College, Hartford, Connecticut
06106.

Donor permission is required for public screening of films in
this collection.

Drawings not to be used for construction as they have not been
coordinated with engineer's drawings, which were unavailable.
```

EXAMPLES OF ENCODING FOR 4.4 CONDITIONS GOVERNING REPRODUCTION AND USE ELEMENT

Encoding at any level of description in EAD:

```
<userestrict>
<p>Transcripts and cassette recordings of interviews conducted in
1996-1997 may be read or heard for information only.  Copying,
citation, quotation, or publication of any material from them is
prohibited without the written permission of the interviewer and
interviewee.</p>
</userestrict
```

Encoding at the highest level of description in MARC 21:

```
540  bb   ‡a All requests for copying of materials must be submitted
          to the Director of Archives in writing for approval by the
          donor.  Please consult the Reference Archivist for further
          information.

540  bb   ‡3 Series 5 ‡a No photocopying of materials is permitted
          without permission from a trust officer of the Wachovia
          Bank and Trust Company.
```

4.5 Languages and Scripts of the Material Element

Purpose and Scope

This element identifies the language(s), script(s), and symbol systems employed in the materials being described, particularly as they may affect its use.

> Commentary: While most repositories in the U.S. will provide descriptions in English, it is frequently the case that some or all of a body of archival material is in other languages.
>
> Language and script information may also be represented as codes for machine processing using the appropriate ISO codes for languages (ISO 639-1 and ISO 639-2: *Codes for the representation of names of languages*) or scripts (ISO 15924: *Codes for the representation of names of scripts*).

Sources of Information

4.5.1. Derive the information from the materials themselves.

General Rules

4.5.2. Record the language(s) of the materials being described.

```
Materials entirely in English.

Collection is predominantly in Vietnamese; materials in English
are indicated at the file level.

Most of the material in this series is in Finnish. Some
correspondence in English, French, and Swedish.

All records are in Latvian unless otherwise noted.

In Dakota, with partial English translation.

Captions on photographs are in English, French and Spanish.

Japanese film subtitled in English and dubbed in French.
```

4.5.3. Record information about any distinctive alphabets, scripts, symbol systems, or abbreviations employed.

```
Later additions are in a seventeenth century hand.

Several pamphlets in this series are in German Fraktur.
```

EXAMPLES OF ENCODING FOR 4.5 LANGUAGES AND SCRIPTS OF THE MATERIAL ELEMENT

Encoding at any level of description in EAD:

```
<langmaterial>Collection is predominantly in <language
langcode="vie">Vietnamese</language>; materials in <language
langcode="eng">English</language> are indicated at the file
level.</langmaterial>

<langmaterial>Audio recordings in <language>Arabic</language>
</langmaterial>
```

Encoding at the highest level of description in MARC 21:

```
546  bb   ‡3 Diaries in ‡a Spanish.

546  bb   ‡3 Pamphlets in ‡a German; ‡b Fraktur.

546  bb   ‡a In Korean.
```

4.6 Finding Aids Element

Purpose and Scope

This element identifies any other finding aids to the materials being described, particularly if they are available to the user, and provides information about the form and content of those finding aids.

> Commentary: Finding aid is a broad term that covers any type of description or means of reference made or received by an archival repository in the course of establishing administrative or intellectual control over archival materials. The term "finding aid" can include a variety of descriptive tools prepared by an archives (e.g., guides, calendars, inventories, box lists, indexes, etc.) or prepared by the creator of the records (e.g., registers, indexes, transfer lists, classification schemes, etc.). Such tools provide a representation of, or a means of access to, the materials being described that enables users to identify material relating to the subject of their inquiries. An archival repository's descriptive system will likely consist of various types of finding aids, each serving a particular purpose.

Sources of Information

4.6.1. Derive the information from the other finding aids.

General Rules

4.6.2. Record information about any existing finding aids that provide information relating to the context and contents of the unit being described. As appropriate and available, include information about the type (e.g., list, index, guide, calendar, etc.), medium (e.g., cards, electronic, etc.), and content (e.g., names of correspondents, subjects, etc.) of the finding aid, the number or other identifier of the finding aid (if any), any relevant information about its location or availability, and any other information necessary to assist the user in evaluating its usefulness. Include finding aids prepared by the creator (e.g., registers, indexes, etc.) that are part of the unit being described.

```
Box list available.

Electronic finding aid available via the Internet in the Online
Archive of California; folder level control:
http://www.oac.cdlib.org/findaid/ark:/13030/kt8z09p8pd.

An item list, a file of calendar sheets, and indexes by subject,
type of author, and (selectively) place written from are
available in the repository; filed under M316.

A Marriage Index database of information from these records is
maintained by the Ulster County Clerk's Office Archives.

Register of outgoing correspondence in this series found in the
first folder.
```

An index to the content of the written briefs and presentations
is included at the beginning of series 2.

4.6.3. Optionally, provide information on where to obtain a copy of the finding aid(s).

Finding aid available on the Online Archive of California.

4.6.4. Optionally, if the materials have not yet been completely arranged and described by the repository, indicate the existence of any relevant descriptive tools for administrative or intellectual control over the materials that existed at the time the repository acquired the unit being described and that are available for consultation, such as records disposition schedules, transfer lists, and so on.

Contact the archivist for access to transfer lists of box
contents for this series.

Unpublished accession inventory for this unprocessed but usable
collection is available; please contact the repository.

Published Descriptions

4.6.5. Optionally, where descriptions of the materials or other finding aids (e.g., abstracts, calendars, indexes, etc.) have been published in standard lists or reference works, provide this information in a standard and concise form.

Described in: Library of Congress Acquisitions: Manuscript
Division, 1979. Washington, D.C.: Library of Congress, 1981.

Listed in: Ricci. Census, vol.1, p. 857, no. 4.

The entire calendar has been published in 12 volumes from the set
of cards held by the University of Illinois. *The Mereness
Calendar: Federal Documents of the Upper Mississippi Valley
1780-1890* (Boston: G.K. Hall and Co., 1971).

EXAMPLES OF ENCODING FOR 4.6 FINDING AIDS ELEMENT

Encoding at any level of description in EAD:

```
<otherfindaid>
<p>A Marriage Index database of information from these records is
maintained by the Ulster County Clerk's Office Archives.</p>
</otherfindaid>

<otherfindaid>
<p>Card file for correspondents in Series 1 also available.</p>
</otherfindaid>
```

Encoding at the highest level of description in MARC 21:*

```
555  bb    ‡a Electronic finding aid available via the Internet in
           the Online Archive of California; folder level control:
           ‡u http://www.oac.cdlib.org/findaid/ark:/13030/kt8z09p8pd

856  42    ‡a Finding aid ‡u
           http://www.lib.unc.edu/mss/uars/ead/40002.html
```

Some MARC systems may not yet have implemented ‡u in the 555 field, in which case this information can be placed in the 856 field.

CHAPTER 5

Acquisition and Appraisal Elements

5.1 Custodial History
5.2 Immediate Source of Acquisition
5.3 Appraisal, Destruction, and Scheduling Information
5.4 Accruals

5.1 Custodial History Element

Purpose and Scope

This element provides information on changes of ownership or custody of the material being described, from the time it left the possession of the creator until it was acquired by the repository, that is significant for its authenticity, integrity, and interpretation.

> Commentary: The archivist should determine when it is desirable to create an access point for a custodian. It is probably not necessary to do so for custodians who merely stored the materials.

Exclusions

5.1.1. Record information about the donor or source from which the archives directly acquired the unit being described in the Immediate Source of Acquisition Element (5.2).

Sources of Information

5.1.2. Derive the information from transfer documents such as donor agreements.

General Rules

5.1.3. Record the successive transfers of ownership, responsibility, or custody or control of the unit being described from the time it left the possession of the creator until its acquisition by the repository, along with the dates thereof, insofar as this information can be ascertained and is significant to the user's understanding of the authenticity.

```
Franklin Delano Roosevelt's gubernatorial records were initially
deposited at the Roosevelt Presidential Library following his
death. In 1982 they were returned by the Roosevelt Library to the
New York State Archives.

Many of the records in this series were created or compiled by
the U.S. Army prior to the Japanese invasion of the Philippines.
Just before the surrender of U.S. forces, the records were buried
```

to prevent capture and were retrieved after the U.S. forces
reoccupied the Philippines in 1945.

EXAMPLES OF ENCODING FOR 5.1 CUSTODIAL HISTORY ELEMENT

Encoding at any level of description in EAD:

```
<custodhist>
<p>The Annuity Payments to Native-Americans were left on a loading
dock by the Comptroller's Office where they were inadvertently
picked up by a scrap paper dealer and taken to a paper mill. A
local history buff recognized the value of the records and
convinced the paper mill to cease destruction of the records.
This series represents the records that were saved, returned to
state custody and then transferred to the State Archives.</p>
</custodhist>
```

Encoding at the highest level of description in MARC 21:

561 bb   ‡a **The brothers Albert and Gaston Tissandier, French
balloonists and aeronautical pioneers and historians,
assembled this collection from many sources over many
years as part of their effort to document their own
balloon flights with original photographs and drawings
and to compile published illustrated histories of early
aeronautics throughout Europe and the U.S.**

5.2 Immediate Source of Acquisition Element

Purpose and Scope

This element identifies the source from which the repository directly acquired the materials being described, as well as the date of acquisition, the method of acquisition, and other relevant information.

> Commentary: The immediate source of acquisition is the person or organization from which the materials being described were acquired through donation, purchase, or transfer. Because some information relating to acquisitions may be considered confidential, each institution must establish a consistent policy to determine the information to be included in publicly available descriptive records.

Exclusions

5.2.1. Record information about changes of ownership or custody of the materials being described that do not involve direct acquisition by the repository and that are significant for its authenticity, integrity, and interpretation in the Custodial History Element (5.1).

Sources of information

5.2.2. Take the information from transfer documents such as deeds of gift.

General Rules

5.2.3. Record the source(s) from which the materials being described were acquired, the date(s) of acquisition, and the method of acquisition, if this information if not confidential.

```
Received from Charles Edward Eaton, Chapel Hill, N.C., in a
number of installments beginning in 1977.

Gifts, 1962-1963.
```

5.2.4. Optionally, record the source/donor's relationship to the materials, and any other information considered relevant (e.g., address of the source/donor, agent, price, source of funding), if this information is not confidential.

```
The Yale University Library acquired the Whitney Papers through
gifts in 1941 and 1953 from Eli Whitney's great-granddaughters,
Susan Brewster Whitney, Elizabeth Fay Whitney, Henrietta Edwards
Whitney Sanford, Anne Farnam Whitney Debevoise, and Frances
Pierrepont Whitney Knight.
```

Identifying Numbers

5.2.5. Optionally, record identifying number(s) of the acquisitions, such as an accession number or reference code.

> This collection was donated by the Michigan Organization for Human Rights in May 1983; material was added in February and September 1994. The Robert Lundy files were added in 1998. Donor no.6933.
>
> Gift and purchase, 1996 (G10669, R13821).

EXAMPLES OF ENCODING FOR 5.2 IMMEDIATE SOURCE OF ACQUISITION ELEMENT

Encoding at any level of description in EAD:

```
<acqinfo>
<p> This collection was donated by the Michigan Organization for
Human Rights in May 1983; material was added in February and
September 1994. The Robert Lundy files were added in 1998. Donor
no.6933.</p>
</acqinfo>
```

Encoding at the highest level of description in MARC 21:

```
541  bb   ‡c Gift and purchase, ‡d 1996 ‡e (G10669, R13821).

541  bb   ‡c Purchase, ‡d 1978.

541  bb   ‡c Gifts, ‡d 1996-2000.
```

5.3 Appraisal, Destruction, and Scheduling Information Element

Purpose and Scope

This element provides information about the rationale for appraisal decisions, destruction actions, and disposition schedules that are relevant to the understanding and use of the materials being described.

> Commentary: Not all materials offered to, or acquired by, a repository merits permanent retention. The process of determining the archival value of records (and thus the attendant disposition of unwanted records) is known as appraisal. A number of considerations go into appraisal decisions, including the current administrative, legal, and fiscal use of the records; their evidential, intrinsic, and informational value; their arrangement and condition; and their relationship to other records. In many cases, material is not selected for permanent retention or only a sample is retained. In other cases, material not normally selected may be retained for particular reasons. Documenting appraisal decisions and the rationale for retention or destruction of selected archival materials provides significant information relevant to the interpretation of the materials being described.
>
> Organizations with a records management program transfer materials to archives in accordance with records schedules. A records schedule is a document that describes the records of an organization, establishes the length of time the records are required to carry out the organization's business, and provides authorization for their disposition. Disposition can include destruction or retention in a repository. Thus, appraisal decisions and the justification for them are an inherent part of records schedules. Archives that receive regular transfers of records from their parent bodies may wish to include in their descriptions (or by means of links to the records management system) the rationale for the appraisal decisions documented in records schedules.

Exclusions

5.3.1. Record information about expected accruals in the Accruals Element (5.4).

5.3.2. Record information about gaps in the unit being described due to reasons other than appraisal/destruction actions in the Scope and Content Element (3.1).

Sources of Information

5.3.3. Take the information from repository documentation such as retention schedules.

General Rules

5.3.4. Where the destruction or retention of archival materials has a bearing on the interpretation and use of the unit being described, provide information about the materials destroyed or retained and provide the reason(s) for the appraisal decision(s), where known.

```
Appraisal criteria for file retention included the presence of
attorney's handwritten notes, substantiating correspondence,
depositions, and transcripts, which are seldom or never present
in the Supreme Court's files.
                        ---------------------------
The State Archives will retain all pre-1920 patient case files in
their entirety. The State Archives will retain a representative
sample of post-1920 patient case files from the following
facilities: Binghamton, Pilgrim, .... The sample captures
specific patient populations and treatments as defined in the
detailed appraisal report, as well as providing geographic
coverage. The sample is necessary because over 110,000 cubic feet
of patient case files currently exist, and cannot be microfilmed
or retained in paper form. Admission and discharge ledgers for
all patients will be retained by the State Archives to ensure
that core information survives on all patients for all
facilities.
                        ------------------------
After they were microfilmed, the original letterpress copies were
destroyed due to their illegibility.
```

5.3.5. Where appropriate, record the authority for the action.

```
All files in this series are appraised as 'retain permanently'
under disposal authorities RDS440/10.1, RDA458/8.1 and
RDA1176/8.1.
```

5.3.6. Optionally, record the date(s) of the appraisal/destruction action(s).

```
Originals were destroyed by the National Archives in 1982 in
accordance with the Department's approved Appraisal and
Disposition Schedule.
```

```
Originals destroyed after microfilming, 1981.
```

Encoding at any level of description in EAD:

```
<appraisal>
<p>Appraisal criteria for file retention included the presence of
attorney's handwritten notes, substantiating correspondence,
depositions, and transcripts, which are seldom or never present in
the Supreme Court's files.</p>
</appraisal>

<appraisal>
<p>The State Archives will retain all pre-1920 patient case files
in their entirety. The State Archives will retain a representative
sample of post-1920 patient case files from the following
facilities: Binghamton, Pilgrim, .... The sample captures specific
patient populations and treatments as defined in the detailed
appraisal report, as well as providing geographic coverage. The
sample is necessary because over 110,000 cubic feet of patient case
files currently exist, and cannot be microfilmed or retained in
paper form. Admission and discharge ledgers for all patients will
be retained by the State Archives to ensure that core information
survives on all patients for all facilities.</p>
</appraisal>
```

Encoding at the highest level of description in MARC 21:

```
583  bb   ‡a Appraisal criteria for file retention included the
          presence of attorney's handwritten notes, substantiating
          correspondence, depositions, and transcripts, which are
          seldom or never present in the Supreme Court's files.
```

5.4 Accruals Element

Purpose and Scope

This element informs the user of anticipated additions to the unit being described. An accrual is an acquisition of archival materials additional to that already in the custody of the repository.

Sources of Information

5.4.1. Take the information from donor agreements, records schedules, and institutional policy.

General Rules

5.4.2. If known, indicate whether or not further accruals are expected. When appropriate, indicate frequency and volume.

```
Further accruals are expected.

No further accruals are expected.

The repository continues to add materials to this collection on a
regular basis.

Records from the Office of the Protocol and Ceremonials are
transferred to the archives five years following the academic
year to which the records relate. On average, 1 linear foot of
records is transferred to the archives annually on August 1.

Since 1964, approximately 50 maps have been transferred to the
archives on an annual basis.

Files older than ten years are transferred in accordance with the
records retention schedule for the Department of Housing.
```

```
EXAMPLES OF ENCODING FOR 5.4 ACCRUALS ELEMENT
```

Encoding of at any level of description in EAD:

```
<accruals>
<p>Records from the Office of the Protocol and Ceremonials are
transferred to the archives five years following the academic year
to which the records relate. On average, 1 linear foot of records
is transferred to the archives annually on August 1.</p>
</accruals>
```

Encoding at the highest level of description in MARC 21:

```
584  bb   ‡a Records from the Office of the Protocol and
          Ceremonials are transferred to the archives five years
          following the academic year to which the records relate.
          On average, 1 linear foot of records is transferred to
          the archives annually on August 1.
```

CHAPTER 6

Related Materials Elements

6.1 Existence and Location of Originals
6.2 Existence and Location of Copies
6.3 Related Archival Materials
6.4 Publication Note

6.1 Existence and Location of Originals Element

Purpose and Scope

This element indicates the existence, location, and availability of originals when the materials being described consist of copies, and the originals are not held by the repository.

Exclusions

6.1.1. If the repository owns both the original(s) and a copy or copies, record information about the copy or copies in the Existence and Location of Copies Element (6.2).

6.1.2. If the originals have been destroyed, record information about the destruction of materials in the Appraisal, Destruction, and Scheduling Information Element (5.3).

Sources of Information

6.1.3. Take the information from a reliable source, such as the materials themselves, transfer documents, records from other repositories, etc.

General Rules

6.1.4. If the materials being described are reproductions and the originals are located elsewhere, give the location of the originals.

```
Originals are in the Minnesota Historical Society.

Original letters in the collection of the Watkinson Library,
Trinity College, Hartford, CT.
```

6.1.5. Optionally, record the address and other contact information for the individual or institution holding the originals, if it is not confidential.

6.1.6. Record any identifying numbers that may help in locating the originals in the cited location.

```
Original diaries in the James Francis Thaddeus O'Connor Diaries
and Correspondence (BANC MSS C-B 549), The Bancroft Library,
University of California, Berkeley, CA 94720-6000.
```

6.1.7. Optionally, if the location of the originals is unknown, record that information.

```
Location of the original is unknown.
```

EXAMPLES OF ENCODING FOR 6.1 EXISTENCE AND LOCATION OF ORIGINALS ELEMENT

Encoding at any level of description in EAD:

```
<originalsloc>
<p>Original letters in the collection of the Watkinson Library,
Trinity College, Hartford, CT.</p>
</originalsloc>
```

Encoding at the highest level of description in MARC 21:

```
535  1b    ‡3 Original letters ‡a Watkinson Library, Trinity
           College, Hartford, CT.
```

6.2 Existence and Location of Copies Element

Purpose and Scope

This element indicates the existence, location, and availability of copies or other reproductions of the materials being described when they are available for use in an institution, or for loan or purchase, or available electronically. Do not mention copies in private hands or copies made for personal use.

Exclusions

6.2.1. If copies must be used instead of originals for preservation reasons, record this information in Physical Access Element (4.2).

Sources of Information

6.2.2. Take the information from repository records or the materials themselves.

General Rules

Copies and Originals Available in the Same Institution[35]

6.2.3. If a copy of all or part of the material being described is available, in addition to the originals, record information about the medium and location of the copy, any identifying numbers, and any conditions on the use or availability of the copy. If a copy of only a part of the unit being described is available, indicate which part. If the materials being described are available via remote access (electronically or otherwise), provide the relevant information needed to access them.

```
Also available on videocassette.

Microfilm copies available for interlibrary loan.

Diaries available on microfilm for use in repository only.

Digital reproductions of the Christie family Civil War
correspondence are available electronically at
http://www.mnhs.org/collections/christie.html.

The diary has been published in Dunlap, Kate. The Montana Gold
Rush Diary of Kate Dunlap, edited and annotated by J. Lyman
Tyler. (Denver:  F.A. Rosenstock Old West Publishing Co., 1969).
```

---

[35] If the institution holds both the originals and a copy (or copies), the institution should establish a consistent policy regarding whether it will prepare a separate descriptive record for the copy, or whether it will indicate the availability of the copy within the description of the original(s) as instructed in this element.

6.2.4. If appropriate, record information to distinguish between multiple generations of the material.

> Prints in this series made from copy negatives, produced in 1974, of the original photographs.

> Reference videocassette recorded from the internegative and optical sound track.

> Modern silver gelatin print from original negative made 1915.

Copies Available in Another Institution

6.2.5. If a copy of all or part of the materials being described is available in another institution, and information about the copy(ies) is deemed important by the repository holding the original, record that information, including contact information for the repository holding the copy(ies).

> A microfilm of the Alexander W. Chase Overland Journal is available at the Bancroft Library, University of California, Berkeley.

EXAMPLES OF ENCODING FOR 6.2 EXISTENCE AND LOCATION OF COPIES ELEMENT

Encoding at any level of description in EAD:

```
<altformavail>
<p>Diaries available on microfilm for use in repository only.</p>
</altformavail>
```

Encoding at the highest level of description in MARC 21:

    530 bb   ‡a Diaries available on microfilm for use in repository
               only.

    530 bb   ‡3 Postcards ‡a available as digital images at ‡u
               http://www.mnhs.org/postcards

6.3 Related Archival Materials Element

Purpose and Scope

This element indicates the existence and location of archival materials that are closely related to the materials being described by provenance, sphere of activity, or subject matter, either in the same repository, in other repositories, or elsewhere.

Exclusions

6.3.1. Record information about records control tools that are part of the materials they describe, such as an index, and that also serve as finding aids, in the Finding Aids Element (4.6).

6.3.2. Record information about originals of the unit being described (if the unit being described is a copy) in the Existence and Location of Originals Element (6.1).

6.3.3. Record information about copies of the unit being described in the Existence and Location of Copies Element (6.2).

Sources of Information

6.3.4. Take the information from other descriptions of archival materials.

General Rules

6.3.5. If there are materials that have a direct and significant connection to those being described by reason of closely shared responsibility or sphere of activity, provide the title, location, and, optionally, the reference number(s) of the related materials and their relationship with the materials being described.

```
Related materials providing visual documentation of racially
segregated facilities may be found in the following collections
in this repository: Birmingfind Project Photographs and Common
Bonds Project Photographs.

James Gulick was the half brother of Alice Gulick Gooch, the
photographer of a small collection of Orange County photographs
also held by Special Collections.  The Gulick collection also
adds family context to materials in the Huntley Family Papers.
The Edna Phelps Collection contains photographs, family history,
and correspondence on the Gulicks.
```

The following sources provide additional information on
Gordon Gray's personal and professional life and on the
development of the Consolidated University during his tenure as
President.
   Southern Historical Collection:
     GORDON GRAY PAPERS #3824
   University Archives:
     RECORDS OF THE BOARD OF TRUSTEES
     RECORDS OF THE VICE PRESIDENT FOR FINANCE
     RECORDS OF THE VICE PRESIDENT FOR ACADEMIC AFFAIRS
     RECORDS OF THE OFFICE OF CHANCELLOR: R.B. HOUSE SERIES

Motion picture films and sound and video recordings transferred
to Library of Congress Motion Picture, Broadcasting and Recorded
Sound Division.

EXAMPLES OF ENCODING FOR 6.3 RELATED ARCHIVAL MATERIALS ELEMENT

Encoding at any level of description in EAD:

```
<relatedmaterial>
<p>Related materials providing visual documentation of racially
segregated facilities may be found in the following collections in
this repository: Birmingfind Project Photographs and Common Bonds
Project Photographs.</p>
</relatedmaterial>
```

Encoding at the highest level of description in MARC 21:

544 1b   ‡a **Related materials providing visual documentation of
          racially segregated facilities may be found in the
          following collections in this repository: Birmingfind
          Project Photographs and Common Bonds Project Photographs.**

544 bb   ‡3 **Motion picture films and sound and video recordings
          transferred to** ‡a **Library of Congress Motion Picture,
          Broadcasting and Recorded Sound Division.**

6.4 Publication Note Element

Purpose and Scope

This element identifies any publications that are about or are based on the use, study, or analysis of the materials being described.

Exclusions

6.4.1. Record information about published descriptions or other finding aids in the Finding Aids Element (4.6).

6.4.2. Record information about published transcriptions or facsimiles in the Existence and Location of Copies Element (6.2)

Sources of information

6.4.3. Take the information from any reliable source.

General Rules

6.4.4. Record a citation to, or information about, a publication that is about or is based on the use, study, or analysis of the materials being described. Provide sufficient information to indicate the relationship between the publication and the unit being described. This includes annotated editions.

```
Arctic field notebooks cited in:  Day, Harold. "Statistical
Methods for Population Transport estimation." Journal of
Ecological Studies 7 (1974): 187.

An annotated edition of the letters in this collection was
published in Montana: the Magazine of Western History 37:1
(Winter 1987), 14-33.
```

EXAMPLES OF ENCODING FOR 6.4 PUBLICATION NOTE ELEMENT

Encoding at any level of description in EAD:

```
<bibliography>
<p>An annotated edition of the letters in this collection was
published in <title render="italic">Montana: the Magazine of
Western History</title> 37:1 (Winter 1987), 14-33.</p>
</bibliography>

<bibliography>
<bibref>An annotated edition of the letters in this collection
was published in
<title render="italic">Montana: the Magazine of Western
History</title>
<imprint>
<geogname>Helena, MT</geogname>
<publisher>Montana Historical Society</publisher> 37:1
<date>(Winter 1987)</date>, 14-33.
</imprint>
</bibref>
</bibliography>
```

Encoding at the highest level of description in MARC 21:

```
581  bb    ‡a An annotated edition of the letters in this
           collection was published in Montana: the Magazine of
           Western History 37:1 (Winter 1987), 14-33.
```

CHAPTER 7

Notes Element

7.1 Notes Element

Purpose and Scope

This element provides information that cannot be accommodated in any of the defined elements of description.

> Commentary: The use of all notes is optional. They may be used on a case-by-case basis, or an institution may wish to establish a policy regarding what notes to use and how detailed to make them. If it is desirable to provide information on sources of descriptive information, title variations, statements of responsibility, signatures and inscriptions, attributions and conjectures, editions, dates, and publishers' series, see the appropriate chapter(s) in *AACR2* or other descriptive standards as described in the Overview of Archival Description.

Sources of Information

7.1.1. Take the information from any reliable source.

General Rule

7.1.2. Record, as needed, information not accommodated by any of the defined elements of description.

```
See also the 1970 Strasbourg conference "La Mythologie blanche:
La Métaphore dans le texte philosophique" in Series 3.

Interviewed by Helen Hungerford under the auspices of the Canyon
County Historical Society on 10 July 1973.

Part of the Cooperative HBCU Archival Survey Project (CHASP) to
survey the archival collections housed in the Historically Black
Colleges and Universities (HBCUs).
```

Specialized Notes

Conservation

7.1.3. Describe any specific conservation treatment.

```
Re-bound in 1987 as two volumes for conservation purposes.
```

```
Album pages were detached from their original bindings,
encapsulated in Mylar, and re-bound, 1988.

Cleaned ultrasonically.

Perforations have been repaired.
```

7.1.4. If the materials being described are in electronic form, give details of any migration or logical reformatting since its transfer to archival custody. Indicate the location of any relevant documentation. Information regarding digitization is provided in the Existence and Location of Copies Element (6.2).

```
Computer files migrated by the National Archives of Canada from
original word-processing software (MICOM) to WordPerfect version
4.2 to maintain readability of data. Technical specifications of
the migration are filed with the printed documentation.
```

Citation

7.1.5. Indicate the preferred style for the citation of the unit being described.

```
Percival Farquhar Papers. Manuscripts and Archives, Yale
University Library.
```

Alpha-Numeric Designations

7.1.6. If appropriate at the file or item level of description, make a note of any important numbers borne by the unit being described.

```
ISBN 0-919223-5.

ISR study no. 56.

Original negative no. 64260.

Plans numbered 4073-52-1 to 4073-52-3.
```

EXAMPLES OF ENCODING FOR 7.1 NOTES ELEMENT

Encoding at any level of description in EAD:

```
<note>
<p>See also the 1970 Strasbourg conference "La Mythologie blanche:
La Métaphore dans le texte philosophique" in Series 3.</p>
</note>

<prefercite encodinganalog="524">
<head>Preferred Citation</head>
<p>[Identification of item], in the Foust Family Papers #3860,
Southern Historical Collection, Wilson Library, University of North
Carolina at Chapel Hill.</p>
</prefercite>

<unitid countrycode="us" repositorycode="TxU">ISR study no.
56</unitid>
```

Encoding at the highest level of description in MARC 21:

```
500  bb    ‡a Album pages were detached from their original bindings,
           encapsulated in Mylar, and re-bound, 1988.

524  bb    ‡a Percival Farquhar Papers. Manuscripts and Archives, Yale
           University Library.
```

CHAPTER 8

Description Control Element

8.1 Description Control Element

Purpose and Scope

The purpose of this element is to document the creation and revision of archival descriptive records. There are four aspects to this: sources used, the rules or conventions on which it is based, the name(s) of the person(s) who prepared or revised it, and the date(s) it was created or revised. Establish a consistent policy regarding the content, form, and placement of citation of sources.

Exclusions

8.1.1. Rules for documenting the creation and maintenance of an authority record are found in Chapter 11.

Sources of Information

8.1.2. Take the information from institutional policies and procedures.

General Rules

Sources Used

8.1.3. Record relevant information about sources consulted in establishing or revising the description.

> *Dictionary of North Carolina Biography* (vol. 4, 1991) consulted during
> preparation of biographical note.

Rules or Conventions

8.1.4. Record the international, national, or local rules or conventions followed in preparing the description.

> Description based on *DACS*
>
> Collection description based on *DACS*, with the exception of
> descriptions of oral histories, which use the Oral History Cataloging
> Manual (Chicago, SAA, 1995)
>
> Series controlled and described under the rules of the National
> Archives of Australia's Commonwealth Records Series (CRS) System

Archivist and Date

8.1.5. Record the name(s) of the person(s) who created or revised the description, as well as the creation or revision date.

```
Created 6 May 1985

Finding aid written by Dan Smith, 1998. Revised by Violet Jones on 18
December 2002.
```

EXAMPLES OF ENCODING FOR 8.1 DESCRIPTION CONTROL ELEMENT

Encoding at the highest level of description in EAD:

```
<profiledesc>
<descrules>Finding aid prepared using DACS</descrules>
<profiledesc>

<processinfo>
<p>Finding aid written by Mary Hanson, <date>2002</date></p>
</processinfo>
```

Encoding at any level of description in MARC 21:

```
040  bb ‡a TxU-Hu ‡c TxU-Hu ‡e dacs*

583  bb ‡a Collection processed in 1993.
```

Note: DACS has not yet been defined as a value in the MARC Code List for Relators, Sources, Description Conventions.

PART II

Describing Creators

Introduction to Describing Creators

The structure and content of archival materials cannot be completely understood without some knowledge of the context in which they were created. It is insufficient for the archivist simply to include the name of the creator in the title of the description of the materials. Additional information is required regarding the persons, families, and corporate bodies responsible for the creation, assembly, accumulation, and/or maintenance and use of the archival materials being described. Part II describes the information that is required to establish this context. It is the logical outcome of Principle 8 in the Statement of Principles: that the creators of archival materials, as well as the materials themselves, must be described.

There are three steps in the process of creating the documentation that establishes archival context.

- The archivist must first identify the individuals, families, and corporate bodies that played a significant role in the creation of the materials.

  Chapter 9, Identifying Creators, provides specific guidance as to which of these entities need to be associated with the description of the materials, based on their role in the creation, assembly, accumulation, and/or maintenance and use of the records.

- The archivist must assemble biographical information about these individuals and families or data about the history, structure, functions, and relationships of the relevant organization.

  Chapter 10 provides guidance on recording biographical data or administrative histories.

- Finally, the names of these entities must be rendered in a standardized form to facilitate the retrieval of information across descriptions, systems, and institutions.

  Three chapters in Part III cover the construction of the proper form of names, based on *AACR2*. Chapter 12 covers personal and family names, Chapter 14 addresses corporate names, and Chapter 13 provides rules for geographic entities that serve as the names of corporate bodies.

Once formulated, this information may be presented to the user in either of two ways. Traditionally, archivists have incorporated the names of creators and contextual information about them directly into archival descriptions, both in catalog records and in finding aids. Such information, created according to the rules in *DACS*, may certainly continue to be employed in this manner.

However, *DACS* also provides an alternative: information about creators of archival materials can be captured and maintained in a separate system of archival authority records that are linked to the archival descriptions rather than being embedded within them. This approach reflects the model created by the International Council on Archives where the *General International Standard for Archival Description (ISAD(G))* provides rules on description and the *International Standard Archival Authority Record for Corporate Bodies, Persons and Families (ISAAR(CPF))* governs the creation of information about creators. Chapter 11 provides guidance on the construction of archival authority records based on the structure of *ISAAR(CPF)*.

Separating the capture and maintenance of contextual information has a number of advantages. The ability to link a description of a creating entity to several descriptions of records from the same creator held within the same repository eliminates the need to duplicate the administrative/biographical history in each description. Furthermore, the practice enables the linking of descriptions of creating entities to descriptions of records from the same creator(s) held by more than one repository, as well as to descriptions of related library and museum materials, Web sites, etc. Relationships between creating entities also can be documented in authority records. Finally, certain functions can be efficiently performed in authority records, such as maintaining a record of variant and related terms, which cannot be done well (or at all) within descriptions.

Where several repositories hold records of the same provenance, they can share or exchange contextual information about the creator more easily if it has been maintained in a standardized manner. Archival authority records do not merely *record* contextual information, they also provide a means of *standardizing* access points and the contextual information. They are similar to library authority records in that both support the creation of standardized access points in descriptions. Such standardization has two aspects: consistency and uniqueness. *Consistency* requires that the name of a creator be identical each time it is used as an access point in the descriptive system. This is achieved by implementing rules that establish an authorized form of the name where different forms exist. *Uniqueness* requires that each person, family, or corporate body have a heading that applies to it alone. This is achieved by making additions to otherwise identical names in order to distinguish between them. Rules for achieving this consistency are provided in Part III. Whenever possible, repositories should use the form of personal and corporate names found in the *Library of Congress Authorities* (formerly Library of Congress Name Authority File (LCNAF)).[36]

While archival authority records and the bibliographic authority records used in library systems are similar, they differ in significant ways. A bibliographic authority record consists of an authorized heading that standardizes the form of the name, as well as other information elements that describe the named entity or point to other authority records. Archival authority records contain the following elements similar to bibliographic authority records:

---

[36] The *Library of Congress Authorities* (LCNAF) is available online at <http://authorities.loc.gov/>. It is also possible to search for subject headings at this site.

- the authority entry (i.e., a standardized access point established by an archival agency uniquely identifying the corporate body, person, or family associated with the creation of the archival materials);
- references to related names and variant names; and
- documentation of how the authority record was established and maintained.

Beyond this, archival authority records support a much wider set of requirements than library authority records. These additional requirements derive from the importance of documenting the context of records creation in archival description and control systems. As such, archival authority records usually contain much more information than library authority records.

While archival authority records generally are distinguished from library authority records in that they focus on identifying and providing information about those associated in some way with the creation of archival materials, they do not include topical subjects, forms or genres, functions, or uniform titles. Archivists may also maintain authority files to control the terms used to provide access in these ways, however, such applications are beyond the scope of this standard.[37]

The two methods of presenting archival context information, i.e., within the description or in a separate authority file, are not mutually exclusive. Indeed, archives may quite reasonably maintain separate files of authority data for internal control purposes even when the names reflected in those records are embedded in descriptions.

Purpose and Scope

Part II provides rules for documenting the context in which archival materials were created, and, in Chapter 11, guidance on the creation of authority records based on the data elements found in *ISAAR(CPF)*.

Exclusions

Instructions for describing the archival materials themselves are found in Part I.

Instructions for formatting names of persons, families, or corporate bodies identified as creators using the rules in Chapter 9 are found in Part III.

---

[37] *DACS* does not provide rules for the construction and maintenance of subject authorities. However, a corporate body, person, or family can also be the subject of a unit of description, and an archival authority record that conforms to *DACS* may also serve to control the form of name and identity of a corporate body, person, or family named in a subject access point. See Appendix B. Companion Standards.

Structure and Numbering

Part II consists of three chapters. Two of the chapters provide content rules for elements defined in Part I: Chapter 9 contains the rules for the Name of Creator(s) Element (2.6), and Chapter 10 contains rules for the Administrative/Biographical History Element (2.7). Chapter 11 provides rules for creating authority records for repositories that wish to maintain separate authority systems.

Descriptive Outputs

The rules provide for data input, but do not prescribe particular outputs or display. Presentation of this information to the user, including the way that the authority information is linked with the descriptions of the materials, will be determined by institutional policy within each repository's descriptive system.

Examples

The examples in Part II are illustrative, not prescriptive. They illustrate only the application of the rule to which they are appended. Furthermore, the presentation of the examples is intended only to assist in understanding how to use the rules and does not imply a prescribed layout, typography, or output. Some examples include citations for the body of archival materials from which they were drawn to help clarify the application of the rule to a particular level of description.

While the rules themselves are output neutral, examples are encoded in EAD and MARC 21, two widely used output mechanisms for archival descriptions, at the end of Chapters 9 and 10. The EAD examples may include attributes within elements. These are intended to illustrate aspects of the rules, and do not indicate that a specific attribute is required.[38] The MARC 21 examples include a blank space before and after each subfield for the sake of clarity. The fields that do not consist of standardized codes have a subfield a (‡a) at the beginning. Some systems require that ‡a be made explicit; others assume the ‡a is always the first subfield. Where MARC two-position field indicators are not required or are not defined, a "b" (blank) is given in their place.

---

[38] See the *EAD Tag Library* for available attributes and their use.

CHAPTER 9

Identifying Creators

Purpose and Scope

The purpose of this chapter is to identify the corporate bodies, persons, and families associated with the creation, assembly, accumulation, and/or maintenance and use of the materials being described so that they might be appropriately documented and used to create access points by which users can search for and retrieve descriptive records. For archival materials, the creator is typically the corporate body, family, or person responsible for an entire body of materials. However, a creator can also be responsible for the intellectual or artistic content of a single item, as in the writer of a letter or the painter of a portrait. A collector of materials, for example, Vietnam War memorabilia, letters of presidents of the United States, or materials relating to suffragettes, is considered the creator of the collection.

> Commentary: Various relationships exist between records and the organizations or individuals associated with them. The primary one is responsibility for the creation, assembly, accumulation, and/or maintenance and use of the materials being described. Depending on the nature of those materials, one may express that relationship by various terms: author, collector, artist, cartographer, photographer, etc., or, more generically, as the provenance of the materials. The archivist may also wish to identify entities who had custody of the records at some time (see 5.1).
>
> This chapter provides rules for determining which entities need to be documented as creators. The names selected in this process will also serve as access points—index terms by which users can search for and locate relevant archival materials.
>
> The use of the names of creators as access points enables researchers to gain access to an institution's holdings, and provides a means of linking all records created by a particular person, family, or corporate body. The selection of access points is discussed in the Overview of Archival Description. The formation of nominal access points is discussed in Part III.

Exclusions

9.1. The rules for the consistent formation of names of persons, families, and corporate bodies identified as creators and chosen as access points are found in Chapters 12–14.

9.2. The rules for documenting relationships between creating entities are found in Chapter 11.

Sources of Information

9.3. Take the information from the archival descriptions of the material as created according to the rules in Part I and Chapter 10,[39] as instructed in the following rules.

General Rules

9.4. Record the name(s) of creators at all levels of description as specified in the following rules, except as restricted by 9.10 or in accordance with institutional policy.

9.5. Record as access points only names that appear in the archival description to which they relate.

9.6. If it is appropriate in the context of a particular descriptive system to record a name other than those prescribed in this chapter, do so.

9.7. Where the institution maintains a separate system of authority files, create authority records for the authorized forms of the names of the persons, families, and corporate bodies that are identified as creators using the rules in Chapter 11.

Identifying Creators

Commentary: The source for the name of the creator is usually the name element in the supplied title (2.3.4-2.3.17). In many cases there will be only one creator; however, when there is more than one, the archivist must sometimes look in other parts of the description to ensure that all creators are identified. When describing the records of a person or family for which there are several creators, the supplied title *may* contain all the creators' names; however, the repository may also choose to include only one name in the title. When supplying a title for the records of a corporate body, only one creator can be named in the title. Other creators will be mentioned in the Administrative/Biographical History Element (Chapter 10), and recorded as access points.

9.8. Record the name(s) of the creator(s) identified in the name element in the supplied title of the materials in the authorized form specified in Chapters 12-14.

> Hamilton, Alexander, 1757-1804
> *Title:* Alexander Hamilton papers
>
> Lyon, Phyllis
> Martin, Del
> *Title:* Phyllis Lyon and Del Martin papers
>
> Richardson, James Burchell
> *Title:* James Burchell Richardson family papers
>
> Schramm family
> *Title:* Schramm family papers

---

[39] The administrative/biographical history can be part of a description of the archival materials or it can be maintained in a separate authority file that is linked to the description and displays with it.

```
Wharton, Edith, 1862-1937
Fullerton, William Morton, b. 1865
```
    Title: Edith Wharton correspondence with Morton Fullerton

```
Bollingen Foundation
```
    Title: Bollingen Foundation records

```
United States.  Bureau of Insular Affairs
```
    Title: United States Bureau of Insular Affairs records

```
Irvine Company
University of California (System). Regents.
```
    Title: Land agreements between the University of California and the Irvine Company

9.9. Where the names of all creators are not included in the supplied title, in addition to those named in the title, record in the authorized form specified in Chapters 12-14 the names of other persons, families, or corporate bodies identified in the Administrative/Biographical History Element as creators of the materials being described.

```
Pettigrew family papers
```
    (*Record* Pettigrew family; Pettigrew, Charles, 1744-1807; Pettigrew, Charles Lockhart, 1816-1873; Pettigrew, Ebenezer, 1783-1848; Pettigrew, James Johnston, 1828-1863; *and* Pettigrew, William S., 1818-1900)

9.10. Optionally, if the name(s) of the creator(s) of series, files, or items is included in the supplied title for that level or in an Administrative/Biographical History Element, do not record it at lower levels of description.

```
Collection title: Eugene Loring papers
Series title:  H.N. Clugston and Mary Ann Maudlin dance
scrapbooks
```
    (*Record at the collection level*: Loring, Eugene, 1914-1982)
    (*Optionally, do not record at the series level*: Clugston, H. N. *and* Maudlin, Mary Ann)

```
Collection title: Collection on Refugee Forums
File title:  Santa Ana College fliers on courses and services for
continuing education students
```
    (*Record the collector at the collection level*: Frank, Anne, 1937-)
    (*Optionally, do not record at the file level*: Santa Ana College)

```
Collection title: Alexander Graham Bell family papers, 1834-1970
Item title:  Biography of Gardiner Greene Hubbard
```
    (*Record at the collection level*: Bell family)
    (*Optionally, do not record at the item level*: Hubbard, Gardiner Greene)

```
EXAMPLES OF ENCODING FOR 2.6 (CHAPTER 9) NAME OF CREATOR(S) ELEMENT

Encoding at any level in EAD:

    <origination>
    <corpname source="lcnaf">University of Michigan.
    <subarea>President.</subarea>
    </corpname>
    </origination>

    <controlaccess>
    <persname source="lcnaf">Bollinger, Lee C. 1946-  </persname>
    </controlaccess>

Encoding at the highest level in MARC 21:

    110  2b    ‡a University of Michigan. ‡b President.
    700  1b    ‡a Bollinger, Lee C., ‡d 1946-

    100  30    ‡ a Smythe family
    245  10    ‡ a John A. Smythe family papers
    600  30    ‡ a Smith family
```

CHAPTER 10

Administrative/Biographical History

Purpose and Scope

The purpose of this element is to provide information about the organization(s) or individual(s) associated in some way with the creation, assembly, accumulation, and/or maintenance and use of the unit being described in order to place the material in context and make it better understood. The administrative/biographical history provides relevant information about corporate bodies, families, or persons who are identified using the Name of Creator(s) Element and who therefore function as nominal access points.

> Commentary: Information about the corporate body, person, or family that created, assembled, accumulated, and/or maintained and used the materials being described may be incorporated into the description or it may be held in a separate system of authority files that are linked to the archival descriptions and displayed together. In the latter situation, the administrative/biographical history is part of the authority record for that person, family, or corporate body. *DACS* provides rules to cover both practices.
>
> Archivists may wish to supply more or less detail depending on the system being used and other local variables. For example, the administrative/biographical history information in a MARC 21 record describing the materials should be brief, while an authority record or creator sketch in a multilevel finding aid may be much more extensive, consisting of a narrative description, chronology, or both.
>
> There may be instances in describing collections where providing information about the collector is not necessary; for example, when the repository is the collector.

Exclusions

10.1. Record information about the scope and content of the materials in the Scope and Content Element (3.1).

10.2. Record information about the structure or arrangement of the materials in the System of Arrangement Element (3.2).

10.3. Record information about the custodial history in the Custodial History Element (5.1).

Sources of Information

10.4. Assemble the information from reliable sources, such as the materials themselves and reference works. Establish a consistent policy regarding the content, form, and placement of citation of sources and quotations.

General Rules

Separate Authority File

10.5. If the institution maintains a separate authority file, provide administrative/ biographical history information, as instructed in rules 10.6-10.7 and 10.13-10.36.

10.6. For each entity recorded as a creator access point, provide administrative/ biographical history information about the functions, activities, etc., of that corporate body, family, or person as instructed in rules 10.13-10.36.

10.7. Optionally, for each entity recorded as a non-creator nominal access point, provide relevant administrative/biographical information about that corporate body, family, or person.

Within the Description

10.8. Where the administrative/biographical history is provided within the description, provide administrative/biographical history at the highest levels of description as instructed in rules 10.9-10.36.

10.9. At the highest level of description, give information about the history of the corporate body(ies), person(s), or family(ies) that created, assembled, accumulated, and/or maintained and used the material as a whole.

10.10. Optionally, at subsequent levels of description, if the creator of the subordinate unit is different from the creator of the material as a whole, give information about the history of the corporate body(ies), person(s), or family(ies) that created, assembled, accumulated, and/or maintained and used that subordinate unit.

10.11. When primary responsibility for the creation, assembly, accumulation, and/or maintenance and use of the materials is shared between two or more corporate bodies, or two or more persons, or two or more families, create separate administrative/biographical histories for each corporate body, person, or family.

10.12. When primary responsibility for the creation, assembly, accumulation, and/or maintenance and use of the materials is shared between two or more members of a family, create separate biographical histories for the family and for each person.

Selection of the Sub-Elements

10.13. Include in the Administrative/Biographical History all of the following sub-elements[40] that are relevant to the corporate body, family, or person being described and

---

[40] The way in which the sub-elements are presented to users is a matter of institutional policy. Repositories may choose the order in which to present the sub-elements, or whether to present them in a narrative format or in a structured format with each element introduced by an introductory word or phrase.

that provide the information necessary to explain the context in which the materials were created, assembled, accumulated, and/or maintained and used.

Biographical History of Individuals or Families

10.14. Record information relevant to the understanding of the life, activities, and relationships of the person or family, applying rules 10.15-10.24 as necessary.

> Bessye J. Bearden was born in Atlantic City, New Jersey in 1891, the youngest child of George and Carrie Banks. She attended local schools in North Carolina, Hartshorn Memorial College in Richmond, and Virginia Normal and Industrial Institute from which she graduated. In later years Mrs. Bearden did graduate work at the University of Western Pennsylvania and Columbia University.
>
> At the age 20, Bessye Banks married R. Howard Bearden. They had one son, Romare, who became an internationally renowned artist.
>
> Mrs. Bearden managed the New York office of the E. C. Brown Real Estate Company of Philadelphia for many years. She was also the New York representative for the Chicago "Defender," starting in 1927, and did free lance writing for other publications. On June 11, 1935 Mrs. Bearden was appointed Deputy Collector of Internal Revenue, serving first in the Processing Division, and later, as an auditor. In 1922 she was the first black woman to be elected to local School Board No. 15 in New York City where she served until 1939.
>
> Mrs. Bearden was involved in numerous civic activities and belonged to several organizations, among them the New York Urban League, where she served as secretary of the executive board, the Council of Negro Women where she served as treasurer, and the executive boards of the Harlem Community Council and the Colored Women's Democratic League, of which she was the first president.
>
> Mrs. Bearden died in September 1943 at Harlem Hospital in New York City.
>   *Biographical sketch for the* Bessye B. Bearden papers

> Chang and Eng Bunker (1811-1874), the original Siamese twins, were born in Meklong, Siam, and were brought from Bangkok to Boston in 1829. After extensive tours in North America and Europe, they settled in Wilkes County (later Surry County), N.C., were naturalized, and received the surname Bunker by act of the legislature. In 1843, Chang and Eng Bunker married Sarah and Adelaide Yates, daughters of David Yates of Wilkes County, N.C. Chang had ten children; Eng had nine children. They continued to make exhibition tours until about 1870.
>   *Biographical sketch for the* Chang and Eng Bunker papers

```
1886          Born 14 October, Fayetteville, N.C., son of Katherine
              Sloan and Alexander Graham
1909          Received A.B. from University of North Carolina
1910          Licensed to practice law in North Carolina
1911-1913     English teacher at Raleigh High School
1914-1916     Instructor of history, UNC
1916          Received M.A. from Columbia University
1917-1919     U.S. Marine Corps private (mustered out as first
              lieutenant)
1920-1921     Assistant professor, UNC
1921-1927     Associate professor, UNC; member of the President's
              Committee on Education; twice president of the North
              Carolina Conference of Social Service (sponsored and
              prepared first worker's compensation act in North
              Carolina); founded Citizens' Library Movement of
              North Carolina
1927-1930     Professor of history, UNC
1930-1932     President of UNC (Chapel Hill)
```
Chronology for the Frank Porter Graham papers

10.15. Optionally, at the beginning of the biographical history, provide a brief summary of the most relevant aspects of a person's or family's life, typically including name, dates, profession, and geographic location.

```
Frederick Reines (1918-1998) was a particle physicist, Nobel
laureate, and educator internationally recognized for his
verification of the existence of the neutrino and investigation
of its properties.
```
Biographical sketch for the Frederick Reines papers

```
Political activist Allard Kenneth Lowenstein (1929-1980) served
as a lawyer, teacher, speaker, author, U.S. congressman from New
York, U.S. ambassador to the United Nations, and founder and
leader of several organizations.
```
Biographical sketch for the Allard K. Lowenstein papers

```
Guion Griffis Johnson (1900- ) of Chapel Hill, N.C., was a
professor, author, scholar, journalist, women's advocate, and
general civic leader.
```
Biographical sketch for the Guion Griffis Johnson papers

Name(s)
10.16. Record the full name, title(s), married name(s), alias(es), pseudonym(s), and common or popular name(s) of persons.

```
Edgar Allardyce Wood wrote under the name of Kerry Wood.  He was
also known as Nobby.
```

```
Michael Rigsby Revere, formerly Michael Darrell Rigsby, was born
in 1951.
```

10.17. For families, record information about the origin of the family and the names of persons forming it, including the facts of marriages; and the names of children.

The Gordon family of Savannah, Ga., included William Washington (W. W.) Gordon (1834-1912), lawyer, Confederate Army officer, cotton merchant, state legislator, and brigadier general during the Spanish-American War of 1898; his wife, Eleanor (Nelly) Lytle Kinzie Gordon (1835-1917); her mother, Juliette Magill (Mrs. John) Kinzie of Chicago, author; and the children of W. W. and Nelly, especially G. Arthur (Arthur) Gordon (1872-1941), cotton merchant and civic leader of Savannah; Juliette (Daisy) Gordon Low (1860-1927), founder of the Girl Scouts; and Mabel Gordon Leigh, who lived in England and was honored for her relief work during World War I.

Biographical sketch for the Gordon family papers

The Ker family was related to the Baker and other families of Mississippi and Louisiana. Prominent family members included John Ker (1789-1850) of Natchez, Miss., and Concordia Parish, La., who was a surgeon, planter, 1830s Louisiana state senator, and vice president of the American Colonization Society; his wife Mary Baker Ker (d. 1862); their daughter schoolteacher Mary Susan Ker (1838-1923), who taught at the Natchez Institute; and two grandnieces whom Mary Susan raised: Matilda Ralston (Tillie) Dunbar (fl. 1890s-1960s), who clerked in a Fayette, Miss., bank, and Catharine Dunbar Brown (d. 1959), who first taught at the Natchez Institute and later owned a rare book and antiques store.

Biographical sketch for the Ker family papers

Dates

10.18. For persons, record the dates or approximate dates of birth and death.[41]

Charles Bishop Kuralt, 1934-1997, was a newspaper, radio, and television journalist and author.

Biographical sketch for the Charles Kuralt papers

George Moses Horton (1798?-ca.1880) was a Chatham County, N.C., slave who taught himself to read and compose poetry.

Biographical sketch for the George Moses Horton poem

Place(s) of residence

10.19. Indicate the geographical place(s) of residence of the person or family and the length of residence in each place, as well as any other place with which the person or family has a connection.

Edward Hammond Boatner was born November 13, 1898 in New Orleans, Louisiana. His father, Dr. Daniel Webster Boatner, was an itinerant minister who took his family with him on his travels from church to church. Impressed by the singing he heard in those churches, Boatner began to collect spirituals at an early age. He was educated in the public schools of St. Louis, Missouri, where his family lived during his childhood. He also attended the public schools of Kansas City, Kansas, where his family later moved. Upon graduation in 1916, Boatner took

---

[41] While *DACS* generally discourages the use of abbreviations, the use of "ca." and other abbreviations in birth and death dates follows the authority form as established in the *Library of Congress Authorities*.

lessons in voice and piano at Western University in Quindaro, Kansas, for a short time. Later that year Boatner sang for the famous tenor Roland Hayes, who encouraged the young baritone to continue his vocal studies in Boston. Boatner followed Hayes' advice, and moved to Boston in 1917. In 1925, Boatner moved to Chicago, in order to complete his formal education. He earned his Bachelor's degree in music from the Chicago College of Music in 1932. During his student years in Chicago, Boatner directed the choirs at Olivet Baptist Church, and concertized widely as a singer. His reputation grew during the years 1925-1933, when he was director of music for the National Baptist Convention. In 1933, Boatner was appointed director of music at Samuel Huston College in Austin, Texas. He later taught at the Wiley College in Marshall, Texas, where he was appointed Dean of Music. During the late 1930s, he settled permanently in New York City, where he opened the Edward Boatner Studio.

Biographical sketch for the Edward Boatner papers

Born in eastern Ukraine, Vsevolod Holubnychy fled with his family to Bavaria in 1943 to escape the Red Army. In 1951, he moved to New York City where he attended Columbia University. He was professor at the City University of New York from 1962 until his death.

Biographical sketch for the Vsevolod Holubnychy fonds

The Cameron family of Orange and Durham counties and Raleigh, N.C., was among antebellum North Carolina's largest landholders and slave holders; the Camerons also owned substantial plantations in Alabama and Mississippi.

Biographical sketch for the Cameron family papers

Antonina Hansell Looker (1898-1987) was an author, teacher, and psychiatric worker of Atlanta and Lakemont, Rabun County, Ga., and New York City.

Biographical sketch for the Antonina Hansell Looker papers

Education

10.20. Record information about the formal education of persons, including members of families whose education is important to an understanding of their life.

With the outbreak of World War II, the Yasutake family, together with all other ethnic Japanese residing in Washington, Oregon, and California, was removed to an internment camp. The family was sent to the Minidoka Relocation Center in Hunt, Idaho. This internment made a deep impression on Yamada that informed much of her later literary and political career. After the war, she completed a B.A. at New York University (1947) and an M.A. at the University of Chicago (1953), both in English literature.

Biographical sketch for the Mitsuye Yamada papers

Floyd B. McKissick (1922-1991), the son of Ernest Boyce and Magnolia Thompson McKissick, was born in Asheville, N.C., on 9 March 1922. He earned his undergraduate and law degrees from North Carolina Central University. During the course of his educational pursuits, he became the first African American man to

attend the Law School at the University of North Carolina at
Chapel Hill.
> *Biographical sketch for the* Floyd B. McKissck papers

Occupation, Life, and Activities

10.21. Record information about the principal occupation(s) and career or lifework of persons or about the activities of families. Also indicate any other activities important to an understanding of the life of the person or family. Give information about significant accomplishments or achievements, including honors, decorations, and noteworthy public recognition.

> Blyden Jackson, African American professor of English at the
> University of North Carolina at Chapel Hill, wrote novels and
> works on African-American and southern literature. He also
> served from 1973 to 1981 as the Assistant Dean/Special Assistant
> to the Dean of the Graduate School at UNC-CH charged with
> promoting the recruitment and retention of minority graduate
> students and working with the University's Student Aid Office to
> secure scholarships and fellowships for graduate students.
> > *Biographical sketch for the* Blyden Jackson papers

> Paul Green's contributions were widely recognized. In addition to
> the early Pulitzer Prize and the Guggenheim Fellowship, he
> received the Belasco Little Theatre Tournament trophy in 1925.
> Other honors included the National Theatre Conference plaque, the
> American Theater Association citation for distinguished service
> to the theater, the North Carolina Civil Liberties Union's Frank
> P. Graham Award, the Morrison Award, the North Caroliniana
> Society Award, the North Carolina Writers Conference Award, and
> the Sir Walter Raleigh cup. In 1979 the General Assembly named
> him North Carolina's dramatist laureate. He received honorary
> doctorates from the University of North Carolina, Davidson
> College, Campbell College, the North Carolina School of the Arts,
> and four out-of-state colleges and universities.
> > *Biographical sketch for the* Paul Green papers

10.22. Identify important relationships with other persons or organizations and indicate any office(s) held.

> Susan M. Arkeketa, Otoe-Missouri and Muscogee (Creek), has worked
> for nonprofit Indian organizations such as the Oklahoma City
> Native American Center, the Native American Rights Fund, and the
> Native American Journalists Association (NAJA). She served the
> latter as executive director when it was known as the Native
> American Press Association (NAPA), and later as a member of its
> board of directors. She has taught writing and speech at Haskell
> Indian Nations University, Tulsa Community College, and the
> University of Phoenix. She continues to work as a freelance
> writer and consultant to tribes and organizations.
> > *Biographical sketch for the* Susan Arkeketa papers

> Jessie Daniel Ames (1883-1972) was a civil rights worker of
> Atlanta, Ga.; Georgetown, Tex.; and Tryon, N.C. Beginning in
> 1922, Ames served separate roles as secretary and vice-president

of the Texas Commission on Interracial Cooperation. By 1929, she had moved to Atlanta, where she was director of women's work for the Commission on Interracial Cooperation. During this time, Ames established the Association of Southern Women for the Prevention of Lynching, which functioned as a volunteer component within the Commission.

Biographical sketch for the Jessie Daniel Ames papers

10.23. For families, describe family relationships that have a bearing on the understanding of the unit being described.

Lenoir family members include William Lenoir, Revolutionary War general and N.C. politician of Fort Defiance, Caldwell County, N.C.; Lenoir's friend and father-in-law of two of Lenoir's sons Waightstill Avery, lawyer, legislator, and signer of the Mecklenburg Declaration; and his son-in-law Israel Pickens, N.C. congressman, 1811-1817, governor of Alabama, 1821-1825, and U.S. senator from Alabama, 1826.

Biographical sketch for the Lenoir family papers

Thomas Gale (fl. 1815-1881), a physician who served with Indian-fighting soldiers in Alabama Territory in 1815 and afterwards became a planter in Jefferson and Yazoo counties, Miss., and later in Davidson, Tenn., married Ann M. Greene (fl. 1820-1845). William Dudley Gale (fl. 1844-1881), their son, married Katherine ("Kate") Polk (fl. 1858-1895) in 1858, after his first wife died.

Biographical sketch for the Gale and Polk family papers

Other Significant Information

10.24. Record any other important information not recorded elsewhere in the biographical history.

Administrative History of Corporate Bodies

10.25. Give information relevant to the understanding of the creator's functions, activities, and relations with other corporate bodies, applying rules 10.26-10.36 as necessary.

The American Missionary Association was established in 1846 as an interdenominational missionary society devoted to abolitionist principles. From its beginning the major support for the Association came from Congregationalists, but it also received support from Wesleyan Methodists, Free Presbyterians, and Free Will Baptists. In 1865 it became the official agency of the Congregational churches for conducting educational work among the freedmen. Support from other denominations gradually declined until the Association became exclusively a Congregational organization.

Administrative history for the American Missionary Association records

10.26. Optionally, at the beginning of the administrative history, provide a brief summary of the most relevant aspects of the corporate body's existence, typically including name, dates of existence, main functions or activities, and geographic location.

The Goldband Recording Corporation of Lake Charles, La., has played a key role in documenting and shaping musical traditions, tastes, and trends, both regionally and on an international level since 1944.

Administrative history for the Goldband Recording Corporation records

A. P. Watt and Company of London, England, was the world's first literary agency and, for thirty years after its founding in the early 1880s, was the largest in the world.

Administrative history for the A.P. Watt and Company records

The Anne C. Stouffer Foundation was established in 1967 by Anne Forsyth of Winston-Salem, N.C., to promote the integration of preparatory schools in the South.

Administrative history for the Anne C. Stouffer Foundation records

Dates of Founding and/or Dissolution

10.27. Give the date and place of the founding of the corporate body, and if applicable, the date and place of its dissolution.

Glencoe Mills, established in 1880 by James Henry Holt (1833-1897) and William Erwin Holt (1839-1917), operated until 1954, producing cotton fabric.

Administrative history for the Glencoe Mills records

The White Rock Baptist Church was founded in 1866 in Durham, N.C., by two clergymen, the Reverend Zuck Horton and the Reverend Samuel "Daddy" Hunt, who organized the church in the home of Margaret "Maggie" Faucette.

Administrative history for the White Rock Baptist Church records

Geographical Areas

10.28. Give the location of the head office and of any branch or regional offices, as well as the geographic region in which the organization operated.

The Research Triangle Foundation (RTF) is the owner and developer of Research Triangle Park, N.C., a research park housing research institutes and other businesses in Piedmont North Carolina.

Administrative history for the Research Triangle Foundation records

The Carolina Panel Company of Lexington, N.C., began manufacturing high quality hardwood plywood in 1927 to supply the local furniture industry's demand for plywood.

Administrative history for the Carolina Panel Company records

Mandate

10.29. Record the enabling legislation or other legal or policy instrument(s) that act as the source of authority for the corporate body in terms of its powers, responsibilities, or sphere of activities, including any significant changes in its authority and functions.

In 1959 the North Carolina General Assembly appropriated funds to the Consolidated University of North Carolina to establish a

```
long-range planning effort for capital improvements. In September
of that year the Chapel Hill campus used $15,000 from the
appropriation to create the University Planning Office, with
Arthur Norman Tuttle, Jr., as director.
```
Administrative history for the Facilities Planning and Design Office of the University of North
Carolina records

Functions

10.30. Record information about the functions and activities performed by the corporate
body being described.

```
Throughout the antebellum period, the faculty was responsible for
enforcing social as well as academic regulations and for handling
cases of student misconduct. After 1875 the faculty assumed an
increasing role in establishing policies governing educational
activities and the awarding of degrees by the University.
```
Administrative history for the General Faculty and Faculty Council of the University of North
Carolina at Chapel Hill records

Administrative Structure

10.31. Describe the internal structure of the corporate body and the dates of any changes
to the structure that are significant to the understanding of the way the corporate body
conducted its affairs. Name any higher body(ies) having authority or control over the
corporate body, or any corporate body(ies) over which it exercised authority or control,
and describe the nature and any change of the authority or controlling relationship.

```
The Office of the Associate Vice Chancellor for Business was
created 1 January 1970 as part of a major reorganization of the
University's Division of Business and Finance. Among the units
initially supervised by the Associate Vice Chancellor for
Business were the campus auxiliary enterprises, which included
the Horace Williams Airport, the Carolina Inn, the Laundry,
Student Stores, and the campus utilities. The Associate Vice
Chancellor also supervised the Campus Police (later named
Security Services, then Public Safety Department), the Health and
Safety Office, Traffic and Parking, and Purchases and Stores. The
position later assumed responsibility for additional units,
including the Food Service, other University conference centers
(Quail Roost and the William Rand Kenan, Jr. Center), the
Internal Audit Department, and Trademark Licensing.
```
Administrative history for the Office of the Associate Vice Chancellor for Business of the
University of North Carolina at Chapel Hill records

Predecessor and Successor Bodies

10.32. Give the facts of the relationship of the body with predecessor or successor bodies
to its mandate, functions, or activities.

```
The University's Physical Plant Department is responsible for the
operation and maintenance of campus facilities and grounds and
for the provision of utilities. It was created in the mid-1930s
to coordinate and oversee the functions performed by the
```

previously separate Buildings Department and Groups Superintendent.
> *Administrative history for the* Physical Plant of the University of North Carolina records

10.33. In cases of corporate or administrative amalgamations or mergers, name the administrative or corporate entities involved and summarize the nature of the amalgamation.

```
In 1984, the Southern Furniture Manufacturers Association (SFMA)
and the National Association of Furniture Manufacturers (NFMA)
merged to form the American Furniture Manufacturers Association
(AFMA). Headquartered in High Point, N.C., AFMA provides
educational services to its member companies, a comprehensive
public relations program to represent the industry to consumers,
government relations to relay member interests to national
agencies and officials, and statistical information about home
furnishings manufacturing.
```
> *Administrative history for the* American Furniture Manufacturers Association records

Names of the Corporate Bodies
10.34. Record any changes in the official name of the body not recorded in one of the other elements, any popular or common names by which it has been known, and its name(s) in other languages.

```
The Office of the Vice President for Academic Affairs was created
in 1951 and was then called simply Vice President; subsequently
it was called Provost, Vice President and Provost, Vice President
for Graduate Studies and Research, Vice President for Academic
Affairs (in 1964), Vice President for Academic Affairs and Senior
Vice President, and Senior Vice President and Vice President for
Academic Affairs (beginning in 1995).
```
> *Administrative history for the* Office of the Senior Vice President and Vice President for Academic Affairs of the University of North Carolina (System) records

```
In 1900, Sidney Halstead Tomlinson founded Tomlinson Chair
Manufacturing Company in High Point, N.C. The company became
Tomlinson of High Point, Inc., in 1934.
```
> *Administrative history for the* Tomlinson of High Point, Inc., records

Name(s) of Chief Officers
10.35. Record the personal name(s) of persons holding the position as chief officer of the organization or corporate body if appropriate.

```
Frank Porter Graham (1886-1972) was the first president, 1932-
1949, of the Consolidated University of North Carolina, which
included the University of North Carolina in Chapel Hill, North
Carolina State College in Raleigh, and Woman's College in
Greensboro.
```
> *Administrative history for the* Office of President of the University of North Carolina (System): Frank Porter Graham records

Other Significant Information

10.36. Record any other important information not recorded elsewhere in the administrative history.

EXAMPLES OF ENCODING FOR 2.7 (CHAPTER 10) ADMINISTRATIVE/BIOGRAPHICAL HISTORY ELEMENTS

Encoding at any level in EAD:

```
<bioghist>
<p>Journalist Betty Ann Arnold Hodges (1926- ) was born in
Waynesboro, Va., where she apprenticed as a linotype operator
during World War II when shortages forced employers to hire women
for jobs traditionally held by men. She received an A.B. degree in
English from the University of North Carolina in 1950. Moving to
Durham, N.C., in 1954, Hodges worked at the Durham Morning Herald,
where she served in several capacities, including style editor
and, for 43 years, book columnist. Hodges married newspaperman Ed
Hodges in 1954. They had two children.</p>
</bioghist>

<bioghist>
<chronlist>
<chronitem>
<date>1886</date>
<event>Born 14 October, Fayetteville, N.C., son of Katherine Sloan
and Alexander Graham</event>
</chronitem>
<chronitem>
<date>1909</date>
<event>Received A.B. from University of North Carolina</event>
</chronitem>    etc.
</chronlist>
</bioghist>
```

Encoding at the highest level in MARC 21:

```
545  bb  ‡a Algonquin Books of Chapel Hill is a publishing house
         incorporated in 1982 by University of North Carolina
         English Professor Louis Rubin, Jr., and Shannon Ravenel,
         a St. Louis fiction editor who had been one of Rubin's
         creative writing students, with the aim of publishing
         non-fiction and literary fiction of unpublished young
         writers. By 1993, Algonquin had published 178 books. In
         1989, Algonquin was acquired by Workman Publishing
         Company of New York City. Algonquin retains editorial
         control over works of fiction while Workman must approve
         non-fiction books. In 1990, Rubin turned over control of
         Algonquin to his son Robert and to Ravenel.
```

CHAPTER 11

Authority Records

Purpose and Scope

The purpose of this chapter is to describe the elements of a fully documented archival authority record. Because of the variety of ways in which this data might be stored and used, *DACS* prescribes only the elements of information that need to be recorded and not the precise formats in which they are stored or presented to users.

Commentary: An authority record is a description of a personal, family, or corporate entity associated with a body of archival materials, typically where that name is used as an access point to a description of those records. The *International Standard Archival Authority Record for Corporate Bodies, Persons, and Families (ISAAR(CPF))* identifies the four types of information found in an archival authority record:

- the authoritative form of the name of the entity as established by cataloging rules such as those found in Chapters 12-14, along with references to any variant forms of that name by which researchers might know that entity,
- a description of the history and activities of the entity that are pertinent to the records with which it is associated, written in accordance with the rules in Chapter 10,
- references to related persons, families, and corporate bodies, and
- management information regarding the creation and status of the record which is of use to the archivist.

This chapter also describes the ways in which authority records may be linked to other resources such as descriptions of archival materials, or to other data about the entity such as biographical directories.

Authority information may be recorded and used in a variety of ways. It may be available electronically as part of a publicly accessible information system linked to descriptions of archival materials (see the introduction to Part II). This data may be presented to the user in a paper-based system of finding aids in the manner of traditional *see* and *see also* references in a card catalog, or it might be kept in a "shelf list" or official file strictly for internal staff control of the information, especially the form of headings.

While these rules address the formation of descriptions for persons, families, and corporate bodies associated with the creation and custody of archival materials (frequently referred to in the rules as "entities"), authority records may also be created to document entities that are the subject of materials in such records. The same type of data is appropriate in either situation.

Exclusions

11.1. Record information about the relationships between descriptions of archival materials in the Related Materials Element (6.3).

11.2. Record information about the relationships between levels of arrangement within a description in the System of Arrangement Element (3.2).

Sources of Information

11.3. Take the information from any reliable source.

General Rule

11.4. Create an authority record for each person, family, or corporate body associated with the creation of archival materials as specified in the rules in Chapter 9.

Form of the Name

Authorized Form

11.5. Record the name of the entity being described in the authority record in the standardized form prescribed by Chapters 12-14.

    Haworth, Kent MacLean, 1946- [42]

    Stibbe, Hugo L. P.

11.6. Indicate by codes or text whether the entity named in the heading is a corporate body, a person, or a family.

    100 3b ‡a William Smith family
      MARC 21 encoding indicating that the entry is a family name.

    <corpname>Hal Leonard Publishing Corporation</corpname>
      EAD encoding indicating that the entry is a corporate body.

Parallel Forms of the Name

Commentary: A *parallel name* is an alternative form of the authorized name for the same person, family, or corporate body, formulated in alternative languages (as when there are two or more official languages). An institution may, as a matter of policy, choose to create separate authority records for each authorized form of the name, in which case the parallel form of the name would be treated as a related or variant name. If, however, the institution or agency maintains records in only one language, the name in another language would be recorded as a parallel form of the authorized form of the name in a single authority record for that entity.

11.7. If an institution maintains records in two or more official languages, record as a related name the form of the authorized name as it occurs in the other language(s).

    National Library of Canada *(authorized name)*
      Parallel name(s): Bibliothèque nationale du Canada

---

[42] This is the *Library of Congress Authorities* form of the name. Archivists may choose to add the death date, 2003.

11.8. If the institution maintains records in only one language, record as a variant in the same authority record the parallel form of the authorized name as it occurs in the other language(s), as instructed in rule 11.10.

> United Church of Canada *(authorized name)*
> *Variant name(s):* L'église unie du Canada

Standardized form of the name according to other rules

11.9. Record the name of the entity as it would be constructed according to the rules of other, for example earlier, cataloging conventions when the entity is represented as such in an existing catalog.

> Minnesota. Section on Wildlife
> *Pre-AACR2 form:* Minnesota. Division of Fish and Wildlife. Section on Wildlife

> Washington National Cathedral
> *Pre-AACR2 form:* Washington, D.C. Cathedral of Saint Peter and Saint Paul

Other forms of names

11.10. Record all other names or forms of name(s) that might reasonably be sought by a user, but were not chosen as the authorized form of name.

> Clark, Joe *(authorized name)*
> *Variant name(s)*: Clark, Charles Joseph
>   Clark, C. J.

> Prichard, Robert *(authorized name)*
> *Variant name(s):* Prichard, John Robert Stobo
>   Prichard, J. Robert S.
>   Prichard, Rob

> World Health Organization *(authorized name)*
> *Variant name(s):* W.H.O.
>   Organisation de la Santé Mondiale

> Massachusetts *(authorized name)*
> *Variant name(s):* Commonwealth of Massachusetts

> Montgomery, L. M. *(authorized name)*
> *Variant name(s):* Montgomery, Lucy Maud
>   MacDonald, Lucy Maud Montgomery

> Society of American Archivists. National Information Systems
> Task Force *(authorized name)*
> *Variant name(s):* National Information Systems Task Force
>   NISTF

Identifiers for Corporate Bodies

11.11. Record where possible an official or other identifier for the corporate body and the jurisdiction that assigned it.

> Registered company 01003142 (Companies House, England)
> *For the corporate body* Rolls Royce PLC

Description of the Person, Family, or Corporate Body

11.12. Describe the entity that is the subject of the authority record as prescribed in Chapter 10.

> Hubert H. Humphrey was born in Wallace, South Dakota, on May 27, 1911. He left South Dakota to attend the University of Minnesota but returned to South Dakota to help manage his father's drug store early in the depression. He attended the Capitol College of Pharmacy in Denver, Colorado, and became a register pharmacist in 1933. On September 3, 1936, Humphrey married Muriel Fay Buck. He returned to the University of Minnesota and earned a B.A. degree in 1939. In 1940 he earned an M.A. in political science from Louisiana State University and returned to Minneapolis to teach and pursue further graduate study, he began working for the W.P.A. (Works Progress Administration). He moved on from there to a series of positions with wartime agencies. In 1943, he ran unsuccessfully for Mayor of Minneapolis and returned to teaching as a visiting professor at Macalester College in St. Paul. Between 1943 and 1945 Humphrey worked at a variety of jobs. In 1945, he was elected Mayor of Minneapolis and served until 1948. In 1948, at the Democratic National Convention, he gained national attention when he delivered a stirring speech in favor of a strong civil rights plank in the party's platform. In November of 1948, Humphrey was elected to the United States Senate. He served as the Senate Democratic Whip from 1961 to 1964.
>
> In 1964, at the Democratic National Convention, President Lyndon B. Johnson asked the convention to select Humphrey as the Vice Presidential nominee. The ticket was elected in November in a Democratic landslide. In 1968, Humphrey was the Democratic Party's candidate for President, but he was defeated narrowly by Richard M. Nixon. After the defeat, Humphrey returned to Minnesota to teach at the University of Minnesota and Macalester College. He returned to the U.S. Senate in 1971, and he won re-election in 1976. He died January 13, 1978 of cancer.

Related Persons, Families, and Corporate Bodies

Commentary: In describing the parties that created, assembled, accumulated, and/or maintained and used archival records, it will be useful to identify related persons, families, and organizations. They may be connected in a variety of ways, such as members of families, hierarchical relationships between parts of organizations, chronological (i.e., predecessor/successor) relationships between organizations or parts of organizations, or offices held by a person within an organization. Related names might also be used within a descriptive system as alternative access points to descriptions of archival records, or as links to other authority records.

11.13. Record the authorized names and any relevant unique identifiers, including the authority record identifier, of corporate bodies, persons, or families that have a significant relationship with the entity named in the authority record.

> Brown, Muriel Buck Humphrey
>   n 83312367 *(Library of Congress authority record control number)*

11.14. Briefly describe the nature of the relationship unless it is clearly indicated in the Administrative/Biographical History.

> Minnesota. Dept. of Game and Fish *(authorized name)*
>   *Related name:* Division of Game and Fish
>
> The Department became the Division of Game and Fish in the newly organized Conservation Department in 1931.
>
> Humphrey, Hubert H. (Hubert Horatio), 1911-1978 *(authorized name)*
>   *Related name:* Brown, Muriel Buck Humphrey
>
> Wife of Hubert Humphrey. Muriel Humphrey was appointed by the Governor of Minnesota to the United States Senate, January 25, 1978, to fill the vacancy caused by the death of her husband. She served from January 15, 1978 to November 7, 1978. She married Max Brown in 1979.

11.15. Alternatively, provide a brief indication of the nature of the relationship, such as predecessor, father, younger brother, subordinate body, etc. Relationships may be hierarchical, temporal, familial, or associative.

> Minnesota. Dept. of Game and Fish *(authorized name)*
>   *Related name:* Division of Game and Fish. *(successor agency)*
>
> Humphrey, Hubert H. (Hubert Horatio),1911-1978 *(authorized name)*
>   *Related Name:* Humphrey, Hubert H., 1942- *(son)*

11.16. Record the dates of the existence of the relationship, if known.

11.17. If required, also record an explanation of the relationship between the two names, such as "earlier name."

> MacDonald, Lucy Maud Montgomery *(married name)*
>   *See* Montgomery, L. M.
>
> Ontario. Office of Arbitration
>   *(Replaced Ontario Labour-Management Arbitration Commission on 1 Sept. 1979)*
>   *See also earlier name*
>   Ontario Labour-Management Arbitration Commission

Authority Record Management

Repository Code

11.18. Record the code for the institution creating the authority record, as assigned by the Library of Congress in the *MARC Code List for Organizations*.

    MnHi

Authority Record Identifier

11.19. Record a number that uniquely identifies the authority record. The number may be assigned locally or taken from a regional or national database such as the *Library of Congress Authorities*.

> Commentary: The combination of this number and the Repository Code described above creates a globally unique identification for the authority record.

    02-87152480

Rules or Conventions

11.20. Record the international, national, or local rules or conventions followed in creating the authority record. Establish an institutional policy on how to cite published standards, that is, detail provided, use of abbreviations, and so on.

    DACS

    Anglo-American Cataloguing Rules, 2nd edition (AACR2)

11.21. Optionally, record the number or other identifier of the particular rule followed.

    DACS Rule 12.2A1

Status

11.22. Indicate whether the record is a draft, finalized, revised, or obsolete. This data may be recorded as text or codes.

    Heading is obsolete.

    00731cz
    (The character "c" in the fifth position of the leader of this MARC authority record indicates
    that it is a "corrected" record.)

Level of detail

11.23. Indicate whether the record contains partial or full information. This data may be recorded as text or codes.

    006521nz_2200067n
    (The character "n" in the seventeenth position of the leader of this MARC authority record
    indicates that it meets "national level record requirements.")

Date(s) of Authority Record Creation

11.24. Record the action taken and the date(s) on which the authority record was prepared or revised.

```
Created 12 August 1998.  Revised 18 December 2002.
```

Language or scripts

11.25. Record the language or scripts of the archival authority record if it is to be exchanged internationally.

Sources

11.26. Record relevant information about sources consulted in establishing or revising the authority record. Establish a consistent policy regarding the content, form, and placement of citation of sources.

```
Caro, Robert A.  The years of Lyndon Johnson.  New York, Knopf,
1982-2002.
```

Maintenance information

11.27. Record the name(s) of the person(s) who prepared or revised the authority record and any other information pertinent to its creation or maintenance.

```
Biographical data assembled by Lael Ramaley.
```

Related Archival Materials and Other Resources

Commentary: While authority records are created to document the context in which archival materials were created, it is also desirable to associate them with descriptions of the materials themselves and with other, external data that provides additional information about the entity described in the record. These connections may be electronic links within an archival information system between the authority record and associated descriptions or links to external files such as online biographical databases. They may also be recorded as citations in a print-based authority file.

Identifiers and titles of related resources

11.28. Provide the unique identifiers/reference codes or titles for the related resources necessary to establish a connection between the entity and the related resource.

```
Hubert H. Humphrey papers:  a summary guide, including the papers
of Muriel Buck Humphrey Brown.  St. Paul, Minnesota. Minnesota
Historical Society, 1983.

A biography of Vice-President Humphrey is available at
http://gi.grolier.com/presidents/ea/vp/vphumph.html
```

Types of related resources

11.29. Identify the type of related resources, such as archival materials, finding aid or other archival description, monograph, journal article, web site, photograph, museum collection, documentary film, or oral history recording.

```
Franklin Roosevelt is the subject of this reminiscence.
```

Nature of relationships

11.30 Describe the nature of the relationships between the corporate body, person or family and the related resource, for example, creator, author, subject, custodian, copyright owner, controller, owner.

Dates of related resources or relationships

11.31 Provide any relevant dates for the related resources or the relationship between the corporate body, person, or family and the related resource, and describe the significance of those dates.

EXAMPLES OF ENCODING FOR AN AUTHORITY RECORD IN MARC 21 FORMAT

```
010          ‡ a no 97063617
040          ‡ a NcU ‡ c NcU
100  1b      ‡ a Ballard, Rice C. ‡ q (Rice Carter), ‡ d d. 1860
400  1b      ‡ a Ballard, Rice Carter, ‡ d d. 1860
670  bb      ‡ a Rice C. Ballard papers, 1822-1888 ‡ b (Rice C.
             Ballard; slave trader of Richmond, Va., owner of several
             Mississippi Valley plantations; d. 1860)
```

The next two pages contain an archival authority record. Each data field cites the relevant DACS rule in parentheses.

Archival Authority Record

Authorized Form (11.4): Humphrey, Hubert H. (Hubert Horatio), 1911-1978

Type of Heading (11.6): Person

Form according to other rules (11.9): Humphrey, Hubert Horatio, 1911-1978 (pre-AACR form)

Dates (10.18): 1911-05-27/1978-01-13

Description (11.12):
Hubert H. Humphrey was born in Wallace, South Dakota, on May 27, 1911. He left South Dakota to attend the University of Minnesota but returned to South Dakota to help manage his father's drug store early in the depression. He attended the Capitol College of Pharmacy in Denver, Colorado, and became a register pharmacist in 1933. On September 3, 1936, Humphrey married Muriel Fay Buck. He returned to the University of Minnesota and earned a B.A. degree in 1939. In 1940 he earned an M.A. in political science from Louisiana State University and returned to Minneapolis to teach and pursue further graduate study, he began working for the W.P.A. (Works Progress Administration). He moved on from there to a series of positions with wartime agencies. In 1943, he ran unsuccessfully for Mayor of Minneapolis and returned to teaching as a visiting professor at Macalester College in St. Paul. Between 1943 and 1945 Humphrey worked at a variety of jobs. In 1945, he was elected Mayor of Minneapolis and served until 1948. In 1948, at the Democratic National Convention, he gained national attention when he delivered a stirring speech in favour of a strong civil rights plank in the party's platform. In November of 1948, Humphrey was elected to the United States Senate. He served as the Senate Democratic Whip from 1961 to 1964.

In 1964, at the Democratic National Convention, President Lyndon B. Johnson asked the convention to select Humphrey as the Vice Presidential nominee. The ticket was elected in November in a Democratic landslide. In 1968, Humphrey was the Democratic Party's candidate for President, but he was defeated narrowly by Richard M. Nixon. After the defeat, Humphrey returned to Minnesota to teach at the University of Minnesota and Macalester College. He returned to the U.S. Senate in 1971, and he won re-election in 1976. He died January 13, 1978 of cancer.

Places (10.19):
Born: Wallace, South Dakota
Lived: Minneapolis and St. Paul, Minnesota; Washington, DC

Occupation, life, activities (10.21):
Registered pharmacist
University professor
Mayor of Minneapolis, Minnesota
U.S. Senator
Vice President of the United States

Related entry (11.13):
Brown, Muriel Buck Humphrey
US LC 02-83312367

Description of the relationship (11.14):
Wife of Hubert Humphrey. Muriel Humphrey was appointed by the Governor of Minnesota to the United States Senate, January 25, 1978, to fill the vacancy caused by the death of her husband. She served from January 15, 1978 to November 7, 1978

Dates (11.16): 1936/1978-01-13

Related entry (11.13):
Humphrey, Hubert H., 1942-
US LC 02-86828402

Description of the relationship (11.14):
Son of Vice President Hubert H. Humphrey

Dates (11.16): 1942/1978-01-1

Authority record identifier (11.19): US DLC 02-79026910

Record creator code (11.18): US DLC

Rules (11.20): Anglo-American Cataloguing Rules, second edition, revised

Status (11.22): Final

Level of detail (11.23): Full

Date of creation (11.24): 2000-04-13

Language (11.25): English

Source (11.26): Centennial of the Territory of Minn., 1949

PART III

Forms of Names

Introduction to Forms of Names

Purpose and Scope

Part III provides information about creating standardized forms for the names of persons, families, or corporate bodies associated with archival materials as the creators, custodians, or subjects of the records. Such names, in the regularized format prescribed in Chapters 12-14, are used in any or all of the following contexts: when they are recorded in the Name of Creator(s) Element (2.6 and Chapter 9) of an archival description, when they are included in an archival authority record (Chapter 11), or when they are used as index terms in the form of nominal access points to a description of records or to a description of a creator of archival materials (see Overview of Archival Description).

Exclusions

Instructions for describing the archival materials themselves are found in Part I.

Instructions for identifying the persons, families, and corporate bodies who created, assembled, accumulated, and/or maintained and used the materials being described, as well as for providing contextual information about them, are found in Part II.

Structure and Numbering

Part III has three chapters. Chapter 12 provides rules for formulating the names of persons and families, Chapter 13 provides rules for formulating the names of geographic entities that are used as part of the names of corporate bodies, and Chapter 14 provides rules for formulating the names of corporate bodies.

These chapters are unlike Chapters 2-10 in that they do not provide rules for elements that form part of a description. Instead they provide rules for the consistent formation of names of persons, families, and corporate bodies. For that reason, they are not structured in the same way as the other chapters. *DACS* has moved considerably away from the bibliographic model of *AACR2*, which stresses authorship, to supporting the archival emphasis on creatorship, and that shift is reflected in these rules.

The syntax of these rules is also slightly different from those of other chapters in this standard because of their origins in *AACR2* which is principally concerned with the creation of only one form of descriptive format, the catalog record. When the rules in this section direct the cataloger to "create a heading" or employ a similar phrase, they can be understood to mean, "create a name in the following standard form for use in a Name of Creator(s) Element, for inclusion in an archival authority record, or for the creation of an index term or access point in an electronic database or as the heading in a card index."

However, the rules for formation of names in Chapters 12–14 have remained as close as possible to the most recent edition of *AACR2* to ensure that a search for a particular name in an integrated catalog containing descriptions of both archival and library holdings will yield all records regardless of their nature. The rules for formation of names differ from *AACR2* only where divergence is justified by archival practice. Minor changes to the rules have been made to make them less oriented toward published works, and some examples have been omitted or changed to make them more relevant to archival materials. However, the numbering system utilized by *AACR2* has been retained here to enable users to reference the same rules in both standards.

CHAPTER 12

Form of Names
for Persons and Families

Commentary: Once a personal or family name has been chosen for recording in a Name of Creator(s) Element, for inclusion in an archival authority record, or as a nominal access point, the form of that name must be standardized. The purpose of this chapter is to provide rules for the standardized form of the names of persons and families. Regularization of names is critical to the formulation of consistent citations to archival materials and, particularly in online environments, to the retrieval of all relevant records. Therefore it is important for archivists to use the authority form of a name, if one exists, from the *Library of Congress Authorities*.[43] If there is no authorized form in the Name Authority File, the rules in this chapter should be applied. Other sources of information to be used in particular circumstances are indicated at various places within the rules themselves. When a rule in this chapter contains an instruction to make a reference, do so in accordance with the rules in section 11.1.

In the examples in this chapter, variant names (i.e., names that are not authorized names or forms of the name) are indicated by the letter *x* in front of them. This means that the variant name would be included in an authority record as instructed in Chapter 11.

For the most part, the numbering system in Chapter 12 follows that of Chapter 22 of *AACR2*, except that the *DACS* chapter number is substituted for *AACR2* chapter number. Rule 22.16A3 in *AACR2*, for example, is 12.16A3 in *DACS*. The most significant difference between Chapter 22 of *AACR2* and Chapter 12 of *DACS* is the addition of rules for forming the names of families. These rules have been numbered 12.29, picking up where *AACR2* stops.

Choice of Name

12.1. GENERAL RULES

12.1A. In general, choose, as the basis of the heading for a person, the name by which he or she is commonly known. This may be the person's real name, pseudonym, title of nobility, nickname, initials, or other appellation. Treat a roman numeral associated with a given name (as, for example, in the case of some popes, royalty, and ecclesiastics) as part of the name. For the treatment of the names of persons using one or more pseudonyms or a real name and one or more pseudonyms, see 12.2B. For the form of names used in headings, see 12.4–12.16.

> William Shakespeare
>
> D. W. Griffith
> *not* David Wark Griffith

---

[43] The authorized form of a personal name in a LCNAF record is given in the 100 field in a MARC 21 record.

```
                Jimmy Carter
        not     James Earl Carter

                Capability Brown
        not     Lancelot Brown

                Anatole France
        not     Jacques-Anatole Thibault

                H. D.
        not     Hilda Doolittle

                Duke of Wellington
        not     Arthur Wellesley

                Sister Mary Hilary

                Queen Elizabeth II

                Pope John Paul II
```

12.1B. Determine the name by which a person is commonly known from the following sources and in the order of preference given:

  a) the name that appears most frequently in the person's published works (if any);
  b) the name that appears most frequently in the archival materials being described;
  c) the name that appears in reference sources;[44]
  d) the latest name.

If the name does not appear on a prescribed source of information (e.g., a photographer's papers that consists only of unsigned photographs) determine the name by which he or she is known from reference sources issued in his or her language or country of residence or activity.

12.1C. Include any titles of nobility or terms of honor (see also 12.12) or words or phrases (see also 12.8 and 12.16) that commonly appear either wholly or in part in association with names that do not include a surname. Omit such titles, terms, words, or phrases from any name that does include a surname (see also 12.5 and 12.15) unless the name consists only of a surname (see 12.15A) or the name is of a married woman identified only by her husband's name and a term of address (see 12.15B1). Include all terms of rank in headings for nobles when the term commonly appears with the name in works by the person or in reference sources (see 12.6 and 12.12). If an apparent addition to a name including a surname is in fact an intrinsic part of the name, as determined from reference sources or from works by or about that person, include the title. For the treatment of other terms appearing in association with the name, see 12.19B.

---

[44] The term *reference sources,* as used in this chapter, includes books and articles written about a person.

```
        Viscountess Astor

        Richard, Duke of York

        Otto Fürst von Bismarck

        Olga Maitland
 not    Lady Olga Maitland

        Miss Read

        Mrs. Humphry Ward
```

12.1D. Diacritical Marks and Hyphens

12.1D1. Accents, etc. Include accents and other diacritical marks appearing in a name. Supply them if it is certain that they are integral to a name but have been omitted in the source(s) from which the name is taken.

```
        Jasques Lefèvre d'Étaples

        Éliphas Lévi
            (Sometimes appears without diacritical marks)
```

12.1D2. Hyphens. Retain hyphens between given names if they are used by the bearer of the name.

```
        Gian-Carlo Menotti

        Jean-Léon Jaurès
```

Include hyphens in romanized names if they are prescribed by the romanization system adopted by the institution.

```
        Ch`oe Sin-dŏk
        Jung-lu
        Li Fei-kan
```

Omit a hyphen that joins one of a person's forenames to the surname.

```
        Lucien Graux
            (Name appears as: Lucien-Graux)
```

12.2. CHOICE AMONG DIFFERENT NAMES
12.2A Predominant Name

12.2A1. If a person (other than one using a pseudonym or pseudonyms, see 12.2B) is known by more than one name, choose the name by which the person is clearly most commonly known, if there is one. Otherwise, choose one name or form of name according to the following order of preference:

a) the name that appears most frequently in the person's published works (if any);

b) the name that appears most frequently in the archival materials being described;

c) the name that appears in reference sources;[45]

d) the latest name.

If a person's name shows a nickname in quotation marks or within parentheses as a part of other forename(s), omit the nickname in formulating the heading.

```
Name used:    Martin (Bud) Schulman
   Heading:    Schulman, Martin
```

If a married woman's name shows her own forenames in parentheses as part of her married name, omit the parenthesized elements in formulating the heading.

```
Name used:    Mrs. John A. (Edna I.) Spies
   Heading:    Spies, John A., Mrs.
```

12.2B. Pseudonyms

A pseudonym is defined as "a name assumed by a personal author[46] to conceal or obscure his or her identity." Apply these rules only if a person has published or distributed works under a pseudonym. Otherwise choose the person's real name.

12.2B1. One Pseudonym. If all the works or records of one person are identified only by a pseudonym, choose the pseudonym. If the real name is known, make a reference from the real name to the pseudonym. For the treatment of a pseudonym used jointly by two or more persons, see rule 21.6D in *AACR2*.

```
        George Orwell
   not  Eric Arthur Blair

        Martin Ross
   not  Violet Frances Martin

        Nevil Shute
   not  Nevil Shute Norway

        Woody Allen
   not  Allen Stewart Konigsberg
```

12.2B2. Separate Identities. If a person has established two or more identities, as indicated by the fact that works or records of one type appear under one pseudonym, and works or records of other types appear under the person's real name or other pseudonyms, choose, as the basis for the heading for each group of works or records, the name by which those works or records are identified. Make references to connect the

---

[45] The term *reference sources,* as used in this chapter, includes books and articles written about a person.

[46] *Personal author* is defined here as the person chiefly responsible for the creation of the intellectual or artistic content of a work.

names. In case of doubt, do not consider a person to have separate identities. For contemporary authors, see also 12.2B3.

> C. Day-Lewis
>   (*Real name used in poetic and critical works*)
> Nicholas Blake
>   (*Pseudonym used in detective novels*)
>
> Charles L. Dodgson
>   (*Real name used in works on mathematic and logic*)
> Lewis Carroll
>   (*Pseudonym used in literary works*)
>
> Frederic Dannay
>   (*Real name used in his papers*)
> Ellery Queen
>   (*Shared pseudonym used in detective novels with Manfred Lee; see also AACR2 rule 21.6D*)

12.2B3. Contemporary Authors. If a contemporary author uses more than one pseudonym, or his or her real name and one or more pseudonyms, use, as the basis for the heading for each unit being described, the name appearing in it. Make references to connect the names.

> Ed McBain
> Evan Hunter
>   (*Pseudonyms used by the same person*)
>
> Philippa Carr
> Victoria Holt
> Kathleen Kellow
> Jean Plaidy
> Ellalice Tate
>   (*Pseudonyms used by the same person*)
>
> Kingsley Amis
>   (*Real name used in most works*)
> Robert Markham
>   (*Pseudonym used in one work*)

If, in the works of contemporary authors, different names appear in different editions or versions of the same work or two or more names appear in one edition or version, choose, for all editions or versions, the name most frequently used in editions or versions of the work. If that cannot be determined readily, choose the name appearing in the latest available edition or version of the work. Make name-title references from the other name or names.

12.2B4. If a person using more than one pseudonym, or his or her real name and one or more pseudonyms, but the use of the pseudonym(s) is not consistent enough for the creator to be clearly known by any of them (i.e., the person has neither established separate identities (see 12.2B2), nor is a contemporary author (see 12.2B3)), choose, as the basis for the heading, the person's real name. Make references from other names.

12.2C. Change of Name

12.2C1. If a person (other than one using a pseudonym or pseudonyms) has changed his or her name, choose the latest name or form of name unless there is reason to believe that an earlier name will persist as the name by which the person is better known. Follow the same rule for a person who has acquired and become known by a title of nobility (see also 12.6). As required, make references from the other form(s).

	Dorothy Belle Hughes
not	Dorothy Belle Flanagan
	(*Name used in published works before author's marriage*)

	Jacqueline Onassis
not	Jacqueline Bouvier
not	Jacqueline Kennedy
	(*Names used before marriage and during first marriage*)

	Ford Madox Ford
not	Ford Madox Hueffer
	(*Name changed from Hueffer to Ford*)

	Muhammed Ali
not	Cassius Clay
	(*Name changed from Cassius Clay to Muhammed Ali*)

	Judy Garland
not	Frances Gumm
	(*Stage name adopted, by which she is commonly known*)

	Benjamin Disraeli
not	Earl of Beaconsfield
	(*Title acquired late in life; better known by another name*)

12.3. CHOICE AMONG DIFFERENT FORMS OF THE SAME NAME
12.3A. Fullness

12.3A1. If the forms of a name vary in fullness, choose the form of the name according to the following order of preference:

a) the name that appears most frequently in the person's published works (if any);
b) the name that appears most frequently in the archival materials being described;
c) the name that appears in reference sources;[47]
d) the latest name.

As required, make references from the other form(s).

---

[47] The term *reference sources,* as used in this chapter, includes books and articles written about a person.

```
Morris West
    (Most common form: Morris West)
    (Occasional form: Morris L. West)

P.X. Smith
    (Most common form: P.X. Smith)
    (Occasional forms: Peter Xavier Smith, Peter X. Smith, Xavier Smith)
```

If no one form predominates, choose the latest form. In case of doubt about which is the latest form, choose the fuller or fullest form.

12.3B. Language

12.3B1. People Using More than One Language. If the name of a person who has used more than one language appears in different language forms in his or her works, in reference sources, in his or her papers, in administrative acquisition records, or in other archival records, choose the form according to the following order of preference:

a) the form corresponding to the language of most of that person's published work (if any);
b) the form corresponding to the language of most of that person's papers;
c) the form that appears most frequently in reference sources.

```
        George Mikes
not     György Mikes

        Philippe Garigue
not     Philip Garigue
```

If, however, one of the languages is Latin or Greek, apply 12.3B2.

If no one form predominates, choose the form most commonly found in reference sources of the person's country of residence or activity.

For persons identified by a well-established English form of name, see 12.3B3. If the name chosen is written in a nonroman script, see 12.3C.

12.3B2. Names in Vernacular and Greek or Latin Forms. If a name occurs in reference sources or in the person's works, in his or her papers, in administrative acquisition records, or in other archival records, in a Greek or Latin form as well as in a form in the person's vernacular, choose the form most commonly found in reference sources.

```
        Sixt Birck
not     Xystus Betulius

        Hugo Grotius
not     Hugo de Groot
```

In case of doubt, choose the Latin or Greek form for persons who were active before, or mostly before, A.D. 1400. For persons active after that date, choose the vernacular form.

```
        Giovanni da Imola
not     Joannes de Imola
        (Died 1436)
```

12.3B3. Names Written in the Roman Alphabet and Established in an English Form. Choose the English form of name for a person entered under given name, etc., (see 12.8) or for a Roman of classical times (see 12.9A) whose name has become well-established in an English form in English-language reference sources.

```
        Saint Francis of Assisi
not     San Francesco d'Assisi

        Pope John XXIII
not     Joannes Papa XXIII

        Horace
not     Quintus Horatius Flaccus

        Charles V
not     Karl V
not     Carlos I
```

In case of doubt, use the vernacular or Latin form.

```
        Sainte Thérèse de Lisieux
not     Saint Theresa of Lisieux
```

12.3B4. Other Names. In all cases of names found in different language forms and not covered by 12.3B1–12.3B3, choose the form most frequently found in reference sources of the person's country of residence or activity.

```
        Hildegard Knef
not     Hildegarde Neff
```

12.3C. Names Written in a Nonroman Script[48]
12.3C1. People Entered under Given Name, etc. Choose the form of name that has become well-established in English-language reference sources for a person entered under given name, etc. (see 12.8) whose name is in a language written in a nonroman script. If variant English-language forms are found, choose the form that occurs most frequently. As required, make references from other forms.

```
        Alexander the Great
not     Alexandros ho Megas
```

---

[48] Systematic romanizations used in the examples in this chapter follow the tables (published by the Library of Congress in *Cataloging Service*, bulletin 118) adopted jointly by the American Library Association, the Canadian Library Association, and the Library of Congress.

```
        Confucius
not     K`ung-tzu

        Homer
not     Homeros
not     Homerus

        Isaiah the Prophet
not     Yesha`yahu
```

If no English romanization is found, or if no one romanization predominates, romanize the name according to the table for the language adopted by the institution.

12.3C2. People Entered under a Surname.[49] If the name of a person entered under surname (see 12.5) is written in a nonroman script, romanize the name according to the table for the language adopted by the institution. Add vowels to names that are not vocalized. As required, make references from other romanized forms.

```
        Lin Yü-t`ang
not     Lin Yutang

        P.S. Irāmaccantiran
not     P.S. Ramachandran

        Mosheh Dayan
not     Moshe Dayan

        Shelomit Kohen
not     Shlomit Cohen
```

If the name of a person is found only in a romanized form, use it as found.

```
        Ghaoutsi Bouali
not     Ghawthī `Abū `Alī
```

If such a person's name is found in more than one romanized form, choose the form that occurs most frequently.

---

[49] *Alternative rule.* This alternative rule may be applied selectively language by language.

Persons entered under a surname. Choose the romanized form of name that has become well-established in English-language reference sources for a person entered under a surname (see 12.5) whose name is in a language written in a nonroman script. For a person who uses Hebrew or Yiddish and whose name is not found to be well-established in English-language reference sources, choose the romanized form appearing in his or her works, or in the materials being described.

If variant romanized forms are found in English-language reference sources, choose the form that occurs most frequently.

As required, make references from other romanized forms.

```
        Lin Yutang
not     Lin Yü-t`ang
```

If a name is written in more than one nonroman script, romanize it according to the table for the original language of most of the works or of most of the archival records being described (in that order of preference). As required, make references from other romanized forms.

> Raghunātha Sūri
> *not* Irakunātasūri
> *(Wrote primarily in Sanskrit but also in Tamil)*

In case of doubt as to which of two or more languages written in the Arabic script should be used for the romanization, base the choice on the nationality of the person or the language of the area of residence or activity. If these criteria do not apply, choose (in this order of preference): Urdu, Arabic, Persian, any other language.

12.3D. Spelling

12.3D1. If variant spellings of a person's name are found and these variations are not the result of different romanizations, choose the form resulting from an official change in orthography, or, if this does not apply, choose the predominant spelling. In case of doubt, choose the spelling that seems most appropriate. For spelling differences resulting from different romanizations, see 11.3C.

Entry Element

12.4. GENERAL RULES

12.4A. If a person's name (chosen according to 12.1–12.3) consists of several parts, select as the entry element that part of the name under which the person would normally be listed in authoritative alphabetic lists[50] in his or her language or country of residence or activity. In applying this general rule, follow the instructions in 12.5–12.9. If, however, a person's preference is known to be different from the normal usage, follow that preference in selecting the entry element.

12.4B. Order of Elements

12.4B1. If the entry element is the first element of the name, enter the name in direct order.

> Ram Gopal
>
> Gray Lock

12.4B2. If the first element is a surname,[51] follow it by a comma.

---

[50] *Authoritative alphabetic lists* means publications of the "who's who" type or biographical dictionaries, encyclopedias, but not telephone directories or similar compilations.
[51] *Surname*, as used in this chapter, includes any name used as a family name (other than those used as family names by Romans of classical times, see 12.9A).

```
Chiang, Kai-shek
   (Name: Chiang Kai-shek)
   (Surname: Chiang)

Molnár, Ferenc
   (Name: Molnár Ferenc)
   (Surname: Molnár)

Trịnh, Vân Thanh
   (Name: Trịnh Vân Thanh)
   (Surname: Trịnh)
```

12.4B3. If the entry element is not the first element of the name, transpose the elements of the name preceding the entry element. Follow the entry element by a comma.

```
Cassatt, Mary
   (Name: Mary Cassatt)
```

12.4B4. If the entry element is the proper name in a title of nobility (see 12.6), follow it by the personal name in direct order and then by the part of the title denoting rank. Precede the personal name and the part of the title denoting rank by commas.

```
Leighton, Frederick Leighton, Baron

Caradon, Hugh Foot, Baron
```

12.5. ENTRY UNDER SURNAME
12.5A. General Rule
12.5A1. Enter a name containing a surname (or consisting only of a surname, see 12.15A) under that surname unless subsequent rules (e.g., 12.6, 12.10) provide for entry under a different element.

```
Anka, Paul

Fitzgerald, Ella

Byatt, A. S.

Ching, Frances K. W.

Mantovani
```

If the surname is represented by an initial, but at least one element of the name is given in full, enter under the initial that represents the surname.

```
G., Michael
```

12.5B. Element other than the First Treated as a Surname[52]

12.5B1. If the name does not contain a surname but contains an element that identifies the individual and functions as a surname, enter under this element followed by a comma and the rest of the name.

```
Hus, Jan

Ali, Muhammad
   (The American boxer)

X, Malcolm
```

12.5C. Compound Surnames

12.5C1. Preliminary Rule. The following rules deal with the entry of surnames consisting of two or more proper names (referred to as "compound surnames") and names that may or may not contain compound surnames. Apply the rules in the order given. Refer from elements of compound surnames not chosen as the entry element.

12.5C2. Preferred or Established Form Known. Enter a name containing a compound surname under the element by which the person bearing the name prefers to be entered.[53] If this is unknown, enter the name under the element under which it is listed in reference sources[54] in the person's language or country of residence or activity.

```
Fénelon, Francois de Salignac de la Mothe-

Lloyd George, David
   (Paternal surname:  George)

Machado de Assis, Joaquim Maria
   (Paternal surname:  de Assis)
```

12.5C3. Hyphenated Surnames. If the elements of a compound surname are regularly or occasionally hyphenated, enter under the first element (see also 12.5E1).

```
Day-Lewis, C.

Henry-Bordeaux, Paule

Chaput-Roland, Solange
```

---

[52] For Islamic names, see rules 22.22, 22.26C1a, and 22.27 in *AACR2*, 2002 revision.

[53] Take regular or occasional initializing of an element preceding a surname as an indication that that element is not used as part of the surname.

```
Chavarri, Eduardo López
   (Name sometimes appears as: Eduardo L. Chavarri)

Campbell, Julia Morrila de
   (Name sometimes appears as: Julia M. de Campbell)
```

[54] Disregard reference sources that list compound surnames in a uniform style regardless of preference or customary usage.

```
Lykke-Seest, Hans

Sainte-Marie, Buffy
```

12.5C4. Other Compound Surnames, Except those of Married Women whose Surname Consists of Surname before Marriage and Husband's Surname. Enter under the first element of the compound surname unless the person's language is Portuguese. If the person's language is Portuguese, enter under the last element.

```
Johnson Smith, Geoffrey

Hungry Wolf, Adolf

Cotarelo y Mori, Emilio

Straus und Torney, Lulu von

Halasy Nagy, József

Martel Richard, Micheline
```

but   `Silva, Ovidio Saraiva de Carvalho e`

12.5C5. Married Women whose Surname Consists of Surname before Marriage and Husband's Surname. Enter under the first element of the compound surname (regardless of its nature) if the person's language is Czech, French, Hungarian, Italian, or Spanish. In all other cases, enter under the husband's surname. For hyphenated names, see 12.5C3.

```
Bonacci Brunamonti, Alinda
   (Language of person: Italian)

Molina y Vedia de Bastianini, Delfina
   (Language of person: Spanish)
```

but   `Stowe, Harriet Beecher`
`   (Language of person: English)`

```
Wang Ma, His-ch'un
   (Language of person: Chinese)
```

12.5C6. Nature of Surname Uncertain. If a name has the appearance of a compound surname but its nature is not certain, treat it as a compound surname unless the language of the person is English, Danish, Faroese, Norwegian, or Swedish.

If the person's language is English, enter under the last part of the name and do not refer from the preceding part unless the name has been treated as a compound surname in reference sources.

```
Adams, John Crawford
```

```
Robertson, E. Arnot
```

If the person's language is Danish, Faroese, Norwegian, or Swedish, enter under the last part of the name and refer from the preceding part.

```
Mahrt, Haakon Bugge
  x Bugge Mahrt, Haakon

Olsen, Ib Spang
  x Spang Olsen, Ib
```

12.5C7. Place Names Added to Surnames. Treat a place name added to a person's surname and connected to it by a hyphen as part of the surname (see 12.5C3).

```
Müller-Breslau, Heinrich
```

12.5C8. Words Indicating Relationship Following Surname. Treat *Filho, Junior, Neto, Netto,* or *Sobrinho* following a Portuguese surname as part of the surname.

```
Castro Sobrinho, Antonio Ribeiro de

Marques Junior, Henrique
```

Omit similar terms (e.g., *Jr., Sr., fils, père*) occurring in languages other than Portuguese. If such a term is required to distinguish between two or more identical names, add it as instructed in 12.19B.

12.5D. Surnames with Separately Written Prefixes
12.5D1. Articles and Prepositions. If a surname includes an article or preposition or combination of the two, enter under the element most commonly used as entry element in alphabetically arranged directories or other resources in the person's language or country of residence or activity. The rules listed under languages and language groups below summarize entry element practice.

If such a name is listed in a nonstandard fashion in reference sources in the person's language or country of residence, enter under the entry element used in those sources.

If a person has used two or more languages, enter the name according to the language used in most of that person's published works, in the materials being described, or in reference sources (in that order of preference). In case of doubt, follow the rules for English if English is one of the languages. Otherwise, if the person is known to have changed his or her country of residence, follow the rules for the language of the adopted country. As a last resort, follow the rules for the language of the name.

Afrikaans: Enter under the prefix.

```
De Villiers, Anna Johanna Dorothea

Du Toit, Stephanus Johannes

Van der Post, Christiaan Willem Hendrik

Von Wielligh, Gideon Retief
```

Czech and Slovak: If the surname consists of a place name in the genitive case preceded by *z*, enter under the part following the prefix. Refer from the place name in the nominative case. Omit the *z* from the reference.

```
Žerotína, Karel z
    x Žerotín, Karel
```

Danish: See Scandinavian languages.

Dutch: If the surname is Dutch, enter under the part following the prefix unless the prefix is *ver*. In that case, enter under the prefix.

```
Aa, Pieter van der

Beeck, Leo op de

Braak, Menno ter

Brink, Jan ten

Driessche, Albert van

Hertog, Ary den

Hoff, Jacobus Henricus van 't

Wijngaert, Frank van den

Winter, Karel de

Ver Boven, Daisy
```

If the surname is not Dutch, enter the name of a Netherlander under the part following the prefix and the name of a Belgian according to the rules for the language of the name.

```
Faille, Jacob Baart de la
    (Netherlander)
```

```
Long, Isaäc le
   (Netherlander)

Du Jardin, Thomas
   (Belgian; French name)
```

English: Enter under the prefix.

```
À Beckett, Gilbert Abbott

D'Anvers, Knightley

De Morgan, Augustus

De la Mare, Walter

Du Maurier, Daphne

Le Gallienne, Richard

Le Page, John

Van Buren, Martin

Von Braun, Wernher
```

Flemish: See Dutch.

French: If the prefix consists of an article or of a contraction of an article and a preposition, enter under the prefix.

```
Le Rouge, Gustave

La Bruyère, René

Du Méril, Édélestand Pontas

Des Granges, Charles-Marc
```

Otherwise, enter under the part of the name following the preposition.

```
Aubigné, Théodore Agrippa d'

Musset, Alfred de

La Fontaine, Jean de
```

German: If the name is German and the prefix consists of an article or of a contraction of an article and a preposition, enter under the prefix.

```
Am Thym, August

Aus'm Weerth, Ernst
```

```
Vom Ende, Erich

Zur Linde, Otto
```

Follow the same rule for Dutch names with a prefix consisting of an article or of a contraction of an article and a preposition.

```
De Boor, Hans Otto
    (Name of Dutch origin)

Ten Bruggencate, Paul
    (Name of Dutch origin)
```

Enter other German and Dutch names under the part of the name following the prefix.

```
Goethe, Johann Wolfgang von

Mühll, Peter von der

Urff, Georg Ludwig von und zu
```

Enter names that are neither German nor Dutch according to the rules for the language of the name.

```
Du Bois-Reymond, Emil

Le Fort, Gertrud
```

Italian: Enter modern names under the prefix.

```
A Prato, Giovanni

D'Arienzo, Nicola

Da Ponte, Lorenzo

De Amicis, Pietro Maria

Del Lungo, Isidoro

Della Volpaia, Eufrosino

Li Greci, Gioacchino

Lo Savio, Niccolò
```

For medieval and early modern names, consult reference sources about whether a prefix is part of a name. If a preposition is sometimes omitted from the name, enter under the part following the preposition. *De, de', degli, dei,* and *de li* occurring in names of the period are rarely part of the surname.

```
Alberti, Antonio degli

Anghiera, Pietro Martire d'

Medici, Lorenzo de'
```

Do not treat the preposition in an Italian title of nobility used as an entry element (see 12.6A) as a prefix.

Norwegian: See Scandinavian languages.

Portuguese: Enter under the part of the name following the prefix.

```
Fonseca, Martinho Augusto da

Santos, João Adolpho dos
```

Romanian: Enter under the prefix unless it is *de*. In that case, enter under the part of the name following the prefix.

```
A Mariei, Vasile
```

Scandinavian languages: Enter under the part of the name following the prefix if the prefix is of Scandinavian, German, or Dutch origin (except for the Dutch *de*). If the prefix is the Dutch *de* or is of another origin, enter under the prefix.

```
Hallström, Gunnar Johannes af

Linné, Carl von

De Geer, Gerard

De la Gardie, Magnus Gabriel

La Cour, Jens Lassen
```

Slovak: See Czech and Slovak.

Spanish: If the prefix consists of an article only, enter under it.

```
Las Heras, Manuel Antonio
```

Enter all other names under the part following the prefix.

```
Figueroa, Francisco de

Casas, Bartolomé de las

Río, Antonio del
```

Swedish: See Scandinavian languages.

12.5D2. Other Prefixes. If the prefix is neither an article, nor a preposition, nor a combination of the two, enter under the prefix.

```
À Beckett, Gilbert Abbott

Āl Yāsīn, Muhammad Hasan

Ap Rhys Price, Henry Edward

Ben Maÿr, Berl

Ó Faoláin, Seán

Mac Muireadach, Niall Mór
```

12.5E. Prefixes Hyphenated or Combined with Surnames
12.5E1. If the prefix is regularly or occasionally hyphenated or combined with the surname, enter the name under the prefix. As required, refer from the part of the name following the prefix.

```
FitzGerald, David

MacDonald, William

Debure, Guillaume
  x Bure, Guillaume de

Fon-Lampe, A. A.
  x Lampe, A. A.  Fon-
```

12.5F. Members of Royal Houses Entered under Surname, etc.
12.5F1. Enter the name of a member of a royal house no longer reigning or of a royal house that has lost or renounced its throne, and who is no longer identified as royalty, under the surname or the part of the name by which he or she is identified in his or her published works, in his or her papers, or in reference sources (in that order of preference), if there is no surname (e.g., name of the house or dynasty, territorial title). Add titles that the person still uses as instructed in 12.12. Refer from the given name followed by the title as instructed in 12.16A1–12.16A4.

```
Bernadotte, Folke
  x Bernadotte af Wisborg, Folke, greve
  x Folke, Count Bernadotte of Wisborg
  x Wisborg, Folke Bernadotte, greve af

Habsburg, Otto
  x Otto, Archduke of Austria

Hohenzollern, Franz Joseph, Fürst von
  x Franz Joseph, Prince of Hohenzollern
```

```
Paris, Henri, comte de
  x Henri, Count of Paris

Wied, Maximilian, Prinz von
  x Maximilian, Prince of Wied
```

12.6. ENTRY UNDER TITLE OF NOBILITY

12.6A. General Rule

12.6A1. Enter under the proper name in a title of nobility (including courtesy titles) if the person is known by that title. Apply this rule to those persons who

a) use their titles rather than their surnames in their published or distributed works; or

b) are listed under their titles in reference sources.[55]

Follow the proper name in the title by the personal name (excluding unused forenames) in direct order and the term of rank[56] in the vernacular. Omit the surname and term of rank if the person does not use a term of rank or a substitute for it. Refer from the surname unless the proper name in the title is the same as the surname.

```
Byron, George Gordon Byron, Baron

Nairne, Carolina Nairne, Baroness

Bolingbroke, Henry St. John, Viscount
  x St. John, Henry, Viscount Bolingbroke

Cavour, Camillo Benso, conte di
  x Benso, Camillo, conte di Cavour

Willoughby de Broke, Richard Greville Verney, Baron
  x Broke, Richard Greville Verney, Baron Willoughby de
  x Verney, Richard Greville, Baron Willoughby de Broke

Winchilsea, Anne Finch, Countess of
  x Finch, Anne, Countess of Winchilsea

Monluc, Blaise de
  (Name appears as: Blaise de Monluc)
  x Lasseran Massencome, Blaise de, seigneur de Monluc
  x Massencome, Blaise de Lasseran, seigneur de Monluc
```

12.6B. Special Rules

12.6B1. Some titles in the Great Britain peerage include a territorial designation that may or may not be an integral part of the title. If the territorial designation is an integral part of the title, include it.

---

[55] Disregard reference sources that list members of the nobility either all under title or all under surname.

[56] The terms of rank in the Great Britain peerage are *duke, duchess, marquess (marquis), marchioness, earl, countess, viscount, viscountess, baron,* and *baroness.* The heir of a British peer above the rank of baron usually takes the next to highest title of the peer during the peer's lifetime.

```
        Russell of Liverpool, Edward Frederick Langley Russell,
           Baron
```

If it is not an integral part of the title, or if there is doubt that it is, omit it.

```
        Bracken, Brendan Bracken, Viscount
   not  Bracken of Christchurch, Brendan Bracken, Viscount
```

12.6B2. Apply 12.6A1 to judges of the Scottish Court of Session bearing a law title beginning with *Lord*.

```
        Kames, Henry Home, Lord
          x Home, Henry, Lord Kames
```

12.6B3. If a person acquires a title of nobility, disclaims such a title, or acquires a new title of nobility, follow the instructions in 12.2C in choosing the name to be used as the basis for the heading.

```
        Caradon, Hugh Foot, Baron
          (Previously Hugh Foot)

        George-Brown, George Brown, Baron
          (Previously George Brown)

        Grigg, John
          (Previously Baron Altrincham; peerage disclaimed)

        Hailsham of St. Marylebone, Quintin Hogg, Baron
          (Originally Quintin Hogg; became Viscount Hailsham, 1950; peerage disclaimed,
          1963; became Baron Hailsham of St. Marylebone, 1970)
```

12.7. ENTRY UNDER ROMANIAN PATRONYMIC

12.7A. If a name of a person whose language is Romanian contains a patronymic with the suffix *ade*, enter under that patronymic.

```
        Heliade Rădulescu, Ion
```

12.8. ENTRY UNDER GIVEN NAME, ETC.

12.8A. General Rule

12.8A1. Enter a name that does not include a surname and that is borne by a person who is not identified by a title of nobility under the part of the name under which the person is listed in reference sources. In case of doubt, enter under the last element, following the instructions in 12.5B. Include in the name any words or phrases denoting place of origin, domicile, occupation, or other characteristics that are commonly associated with the name in that person's published works, in his or her papers, or in reference sources (in that order of preference). Precede such words or phrases by a comma unless the name cannot be broken down into "name" and "phrase" components. Refer, as appropriate, from the associated words or phrases, from variant forms of the name and from other names by which the person is known.

```
John, the Baptist

Leonardo, da Vinci
  x Vinci, Leonardo da

Alexander, of Aphrodisias
  x Aphrodisias, Alexander of
  x Alexander, Aphrodisiensis
  x Alexander, von Aphrodisias
  x Alexandre, d'Aphrodise

Judas Iscariot
  x Iscariot, Judas

John of the Cross
```

12.8A2. If a person with such a name is listed in reference sources by a part of the name other than the first, follow the instructions in 12.5B.

```
Planudes, Maximus

Helena, Maria
```

12.8B. Names Including a Patronymic

12.8B1. If a name consists of one or more given names and a patronymic, enter it under the first given name, followed by the rest of the name in direct order. If the patronymic precedes the given name(s), transpose the elements to bring the first given name into first position. Refer from the patronymic. For Icelandic names, see 12.9B.

```
Solomon Gebre Christos
  (Given name: Solomon)
  (Patronymic: Gebre Christos)
  x Gebre Christos, Solomon

Isaac ben Aaron
  (Given name: Isaac)
  (Patronymic: ben Aaron)
  x Aaron, Isaac ben
```

12.8C. Names of Royal Persons

12.8C1. If the name by which a royal person is known includes the name of a royal house, dynasty, territorial designation, etc., or a surname, enter the name in direct order. Add titles as instructed in 12.16A.

```
John II Comnenus ...

Louis Bonaparte ...

Chandragupta Maurya ...

Eleanor, of Aquitaine ...

Daulat Rao Sindhia ...
```

```
Ming T'ai-tsu ...
```

12.9. ENTRY OF OTHER NAMES
12.9A. Roman Names
12.9A1. Enter a Roman active before, or mostly before, A.D. 476 under the part of the name most commonly used as entry element in reference sources.

```
Caesar, Gaius Julius

Antoninus Pius
```

In case of doubt, enter the name in direct order.

```
Martianus Capella
```

12.9B. Icelandic Names
12.9B1. Enter an Icelandic name under the first given name, followed by the other given names (if present), by the patronymic, and by the family name, in direct order. If a phrase naming a place follows the given name(s), patronymic, or family name, treat it as an integral part of the name. Refer from the patronymic and from the family name.

```
Svava Jakobsdóttir
```
   (*Given name*: Svava)
   (*Patronymic*: Jakobsdóttir)
   ```
   x Jakobsdóttir, Svava
   ```

```
Halldór Laxness
```
   (*Given name*: Halldór)
   (*Family name*: Laxness)
   ```
   x Laxness, Halldór
   ```

```
Bjarni Benediktsson frá Hofteigi
```
   (*Given name*: Bjarni)
   (*Patronymic:* Benediktsson)
   (Words denoting place: frá Hofteigi)
   ```
   x Benediktsson frá Hofteigi, Bjarni
   x Benediktsson, Bjarni
   ```
      (To be made only when warranted in a particular catalog)

```
Jóhannes úr Kötlum
```
   (*Given name*: Jóhannes)
   (Words denoting place: úr Kötlum)

12.10. ENTRY UNDER INITIALS, LETTERS, OR NUMERALS
12.10A. Enter a name consisting of initials, or separate letters, or numerals, or consisting primarily of initials, under those initials, letters, or numerals in direct order. Include any typographic devices that appear as part of multiletter abbreviations of a name, but omit them when they follow single-letter initials. Include any words or phrases associated with the initials, letters, or numerals.

```
H. D.
  x D., H.

A. de O.
  x O., A. de

B., abbé de
  (Name appears as abbé de B...)

i.e., Master
  x e., i., Master
  x Master i.e.

110908
  x One Hundred and Ten Thousand, Nine Hundred and Eight
  x One, One, Zero, Nine, Zero, Eight
```

12.11. ENTRY UNDER PHRASE

12.11A. Enter in direct order a name that consists of a phrase or appellation that does not contain a forename.

```
Dr. X

Father Time

Pan Painter
```

Also enter in direct order a phrase that consists of a forename or forenames preceded by words other than a term of address or a title of position or office. Make a reference from the forename(s) followed by the initial word(s).

```
Poor Richard
  x Richard, Poor

Buckskin Bill
  x Bill, Buckskin

Calamity Jane
  x Jane, Calamity

Boy George
  x George, Boy
```

If, however, such a name has the appearance of a forename, forenames, or initials, and a surname, enter under the pseudosurname. Refer from the name in direct order.

```
Other, A. N.
  x A. N. Other
```

If such a name does not convey the idea of a person, add in parentheses a suitable designation in English.

```
River (Writer)

Taj Mahal (Musician)
```

12.11B. If a phrase consists of a forename preceded by a term of address (e.g., a word indicating relationship) or a title of position or office (e.g., a professional appellation), enter under the forename. Treat other word(s) as additions to the forename(s) (see 12.8A1). Refer from the name in direct order.

```
Fannie, Cousin
  x Cousin Fannie

Jemima, Aunt
  x Aunt Jemima

Pierre, Chef
  x Chef Pierre
```

Additions To Names: General

12.12. TITLES OF NOBILITY AND TERMS OF HONOR
12.12A. Titles of Nobility. To the name of a nobleman or noblewoman not entered under title (see 12.6), add the title of nobility in the vernacular if the title or part of the title or a substitute for the title[57] appears with the name in the person's published works, in his or her papers, or in reference sources (in that order of preference).[58] In case of doubt, add the title.

```
        Bismarck, Otto, Fürst von

        Sévigné, Marie Rabutin-Chantal, marquise de
but
        Buchan, John
          (Title Baron Tweedsmuir not used in the majority of his works)

        Visconti, Luchino
          (Title conte de Modrone not used in his works)
```

12.13. SAINTS
12.13A. Add "Saint" after the name of a Christian saint, unless the person was a pope, emperor, empress, king, or queen, in which case follow 12.16A–12.16B.

```
        Alban, Saint

        Teresa, of Avila, Saint

        Francis, of Assisi, Saint
```

---

[57] Great Britain peers (other than dukes and duchesses) usually use the terms of address *Lord* or *Lady* in place of their titles. For example, George Gordon, Baron Byron, is almost invariably referred to as Lord Byron.
[58] Disregard, in this context, reference sources dealing with the nobility.

```
More, Thomas, Sir Saint

Seton, Elizabeth Ann, Saint
```

12.13B. Add any other suitable word or phrase necessary to distinguish between two saints.

```
Augustine, Saint, Archbishop of Canterbury

Augustine, Saint, Bishop of Hippo
```

12.14. Spirits
12.14A. Add "(Spirit)" to a heading established for a spirit communication.

```
Parker, Theodore (Spirit)

Beethoven, Ludwig van (Spirit)

Espirito Universal (Spirit)
```

12.15. ADDITIONS TO NAMES ENTERED UNDER SURNAME
12.15A. If the name by which a person is known consists only of a surname, add the word or phrase associated with the name in the person's published works, in his or her papers, or in reference sources (in that order of preference). As required, refer from the name in direct order.

```
Deidier, abbé

Moses, Grandma
  x Grandma Moses

Read, Miss
  x Miss Read

Seuss, Dr.
  x Dr. Seuss
```

If no such word or phrase exists, make additions to surnames alone only when they are needed to distinguish two or more persons with the same name (see 12.19B).

12.15B. Terms of Address of Married Women
12.15B1. Add the term of address of a married woman if she is identified only by her husband's name. Add the term after the last element of the husband's name.

```
Ward, Humphry, Mrs.
```

12.15B2. Include the enclitic *né* attached to the names of some Hungarian married women.

```
Magyary, Zoltánné
```

12.15C. Do not add other titles or terms associated with names entered under surname unless they are required to distinguish between two or more persons with the same name and neither dates nor fuller forms of name are available (see 12.19B).

12.16. ADDITIONS TO NAMES ENTERED UNDER GIVEN NAME, ETC.
12.16A. Royalty
12.16A1. To the name of the person with the highest royal status within a state or people,[59] add a phrase consisting of a person's title (in English if there is a satisfactory English equivalent) and the name of the state or the people in English.

> Clovis, *King of the Franks*
>
> Anne, *Queen of Great Britain*
>
> Elizabeth I, *Queen of England*
>
> Ferdinand I, *Holy Roman Emperor*
>
> Feisal II, *King of Iraq*
>
> Victor Emmanuel II, *King of Italy*
>
> Robert III, *Duke of Burgundy*
>
> Hirohito, *Emperor of Japan*
>
> Alfonso XIII, *King of Spain*
>
> Gustaf I Vasa, *King of Sweden*
>
> Shuja-ud-daulah, *Nawab Wazir of Oudh*

12.16A2. Do not add other epithets associated with the name of such a person. Refer from the name with the epithet(s).

> Catherine II, *Empress of Russia*
>   x Catherine, *the Great*
>
> Constantine I, *Emperor of Rome*
>   x Constantine, *Saint*
>
> Edward, *King of the English*
>   x Edward, *the Confessor, Saint*
>
> Suleiman I, *Sultan of the Turks*
>   x Suleiman, *the Magnificent*

---

[59] Persons with such highest status are kings and queens, persons of imperial rank (emperors and empresses), and persons with other titles that denote such a status within a state or a people (grand-dukes, grand-duchesses, princes, princesses, etc.). Rank is the only determining factor in applying these rules, not the degree of authority or power wielded by the person.

```
Frederick I, Holy Roman Emperor
    x Frederick, Barbarossa
```

12.16A3. Consorts of Royal Persons. To the name of a consort of a person with the highest royal status within a state or a people, add his or her title (in English if there is a satisfactory English equivalent) followed by "consort of" [the name of the royal person as prescribed in 11.16A1].

```
Philip, Prince, consort of Elizabeth II, Queen of Great
    Britain

Anne, Queen, consort of Louis XIII, King of France

Albert, Prince Consort, consort of Victoria, Queen of Great
    Britain
    (His title was Prince Consort)

Eleanor, of Aquitaine, consort of Henry II, King of England
    x Eleanor, Queen, consort of Henry II, King of England
```

12.16A4. Children and Grandchildren of Royal Persons. To the name of a child or grandchild of a person with the highest royal status within a state or people, add the title (in English if there is a satisfactory English equivalent) borne by him or her.

```
Carlos, Prince of Asturias

Eulalia, Infanta of Spain
```

If such a child or grandchild is known only as *Prince* or *Princess* (or a similar title in English or another language) without a territorial designation, add that title (in English if there is a satisfactory equivalent) followed by

a) another title associated with the name; or
b) "daughter of ...," "son of ...," "granddaughter of ...," or "grandson of..."
[the name and title of the parent or grandparent as prescribed in 11.16A1].

```
Mary, Princess Royal, Countess of Harewood

Arthur, Prince, son of Victoria, Queen of Great Britain

Alexis Petrovich, Prince, son of Peter I, Emperor of Russia

Anne, Princess Royal, daughter of Elizabeth II, Queen of
    Great Britain
```

12.16B. Popes
12.16B1. Add "Pope" to a name identifying a pope.

```
Pius XII, Pope
```

```
                Gregory I, Pope
        not     Gregory, Saint, Pope Gregory I
        not     Gregory, the Great, Pope
```

Add "*Antipope*" to a name identifying an antipope.

```
        Clement VII, Antipope
```

12.16C. Bishops, etc.

12.16C1. If a bishop, cardinal, archbishop, metropolitan, abbot, abbess, or other high ecclesiastical official is identified by a given name, add the title (in English if there is a satisfactory English equivalent). If the person has borne more than one such title, give the one of highest rank.

Use "Archbishop" for all archbishops other than cardinals. Use "Bishop" for all bishops other than cardinals. Use "Chorepiscopus" for persons so designated. Use "Cardinal" for cardinal-bishops, cardinal-priests, and cardinal-deacons. To the title of a diocesan bishop or archbishop or of a patriarch, add the name of the latest see, in English if there is an English form.

```
        Bessarion, Cardinal

        Dositheos, Patriarch of Jerusalem

        Platon, Metropolitan of Moscow

        John, Abbot of Ford

        Joannes, Bishop of Ephesus

        Ruricius I, Bishop of Limoges
```

If the name is of an ecclesiastical prince of the Holy Roman Empire, add "Prince-Bishop," "Prince-Archbishop," "Archbishop and Elector," etc., as appropriate, along with the name of the see. Add "Cardinal" also if appropriate.

```
        Neithard, Prince-Bishop of Bamberg

        Albert, of Brandenburg, Archbishop and Elector of Mainz,
           Cardinal
```

12.16D. Other Persons of Religious Vocation

12.16D1. Add the title, term of address, etc., in the vernacular to all other names of persons of religious vocation entered under given name, etc. If there is more than one such term, use the one that is most often associated with the name or is considered to be more important. Use spellings found in English-language dictionaries. For Thai names in religion, see also 22.28D in *AACR2*, 2002 revision.

```
        Angelico, fra
```

```
        Claude, d'Abbeville, père

        Mary Loyola, Mother

        Vivekananda, Swami
```

If such a title, term of address, etc. has become an integral part of the name, treat it as such.

```
        Kakushin-ni
  not   Kakushin, Ni
```

Add also the initials of a Christian religious order if they are regularly used by the person.

```
        Anselm, Brother, F.S.C.

        Mary Jeremy, Sister, O.P.
```

12.17. Dates

12.17A. Add a person's dates (birth, death, etc.), if known, in the form given below as the last element of a heading.

Give dates in terms of the Christian era. Add "B.C." when appropriate. Give dates from 1582 on in terms of the Gregorian calendar.[60]

Optionally, add date(s) to any personal name, even if there is no need to distinguish between headings.

---

[60] Direction for converting dates from 1582 on from the Julian calendar to the Gregorian calendar is provided in *AACR2* rule 22.17A n. 16.

```
Smith, John, 1924-                              Living person
Smith, John, 1900 Jan.  10-  ⎫                  Same name, same year
Smith, John, 1900 Mar.   2-  ⎭
Smith, John, 1837-1896                          Both years known
Smith, John, 1836 or 7-1896                     Year of birth uncertain; known to be
                                                  one of two years
Smith, John, 1837?-1896                         Probable year of birth
Smith, John, 1837-ca.  1896                     Approximate year of death
Smith, John, ca.  1837-ca.  1896                Both years approximate
Smith, John, b.  1825                           Year of death unknown
Smith, John, d.  1859                           Year of birth unknown
Johnson, Carl F., fl.  1893-1940  ⎫
Joannes, Diaconus, fl.  1226-1240 ⎭
                                                Years of birth and death unknown.
                                                  Some years of activity known.  Do not
                                                  use fl. dates within the twentieth
                                                  century.
Joannes, Diaconus, 12th cent.                   Years of birth and death unknown,
                                                  years of activity unknown, century
                                                  known.  Do not use for the twentieth
                                                  century.
Joannes, Actuarius, 13th/14th cent.            Years of birth and death unknown.
                                                  Years of activity unknown, but active in
                                                  both centuries.  Do not use for the
                                                  twentieth century.
Lin, Li, chin shih 1152                        Date at which a Chinese literary degree
                                                  was conferred.
```

12.18. FULLER FORMS

12.18A. If a fuller form of a person's name is known and if the heading as prescribed by the preceding rules does not include all of that fuller form, use the fuller form. Add all the fuller form of the inverted part of the heading or the fuller form of the entry element, as appropriate. Enclose the addition in parentheses.

The most common instances of such additions occur when the heading as prescribed by the preceding rules contains initials and the spelled-out form is known. Less common instances occur when known forenames, surnames, or initials are not part of the heading as prescribed.

Refer from the fuller form of the name when appropriate.

```
        Smith, Russell E. (Russell Edgar)
          x Smith, Russell Edgar

        Smith, Russell E. (Russell Eugene)
          x Smith, Russell Eugene

        Johnson, A. H. (Allison Heartz)
          x Johnson, Allison Heartz

        Johnson, A. H. (Arthus Henry)
          x Johnson, Arthus Henry
```

```
        Johnson, Barbara (Barbara A.)

        Johnson, Barbara (Barbara E.)

        Miller, J. (Anna), Mrs.
          x Miller, Anna

        Miller, J. (Dorothea), Mrs.
          x Miller, Dorothea
```

Optionally, make the additions specified above even if they are not needed to distinguish between headings. However, when following this option, do not add

- unused forenames to headings that contain forenames;
- initials of names that are not part of the heading;
- unused parts of surnames to headings that contain surnames.

```
        Lawrence, D. H. (David Herbert)
          x Lawrence, David Herbert

        H. D. (Hilda Doolittle)
          x Doolittle, Hilda

        Wanner, Joh. (Johann)

        Beeton, Mrs. (Isabella Mary)
          x Beeton, Isabella Mary
but
        Welch, Denton
not     Welch, Denton (Maurice Denton)

        Dickens, Charles
not     Dickens, Charles (Charles John Huffam)

        Wilson, Angus
not     Wilson, Angus (Angus Frank Johnstone-Wilson)
```

12.19. DISTINGUISHING TERMS
12.19A. Names in which the entry element is a given name, etc.
12.19A1. To distinguish between identical headings of which the entry element is a given name, etc., devise a suitable brief term and add it in parentheses.

```
        Johannes (Notary)

        Thomas (Anglo-Norman poet)
```

12.19B. Names in which the Entry Element Is a Surname
12.19B1. To distinguish between identical headings of which the entry element is a surname, add a qualifier (e.g., term of honor, term of address, title of position or office, initials of an academic degree, initials denoting membership in an organization) that appears with the name in the person's works, in reference sources, in his or her papers, in

administrative acquisition records, or in other archival records (in that order of preference). Add the qualifier after the last element of the name.

```
Brown, George, Captain

Brown, George, F.I.P.S.

Brown, George, Rev.

Valmer, capitaine

Saur, Karl-Otto

Saur, Karl-Otto, Jr.

Baker, Miss, of Falls Church, Va.
```

Do not use such a term if dates are available for one person and it seems likely that dates will eventually be available for the other(s).

```
Mudge, Lewis Seymour, 1868-1945

Mudge, Lewis Seymour
  (Name appears as:  Lewis Seymour Mudge, Jr.)
```

12.20. UNDIFFERENTIATED NAMES
12.20A. If no suitable addition (fuller form of name, dates, or distinguishing term) is available, use the same heading for all persons with the same name.

```
Smith, Donald
  Donald Smith papers

Smith, Donald
  Petition

Smith, Donald
  A prospectus...
```

Special Rules

12.21. NAMES IN CERTAIN LANGUAGES: INTRODUCTORY RULE
12.21A. The preceding rules in this chapter give general guidance for personal names not written in the roman alphabet and for names in a non-European language written in the roman alphabet. For more detailed treatment of names in certain of these languages, follow the special rules given in *AACR2* (rules 22.22–22.28). For more detailed treatment of names in other languages, see the IFLA UBCIM Programme's survey of personal names.[61]

---

[61] *Names of Persons : National Usages for Entries in Catalogues*, IFLA Universal Bibliographic Control and International MARC Programme, 4th ed., rev.and enl (München : K.G. Saur, 1996).

12.22-12.28 *DACS* does not have rules that correspond to 22.22-22.28 in *AACR2*, but the corresponding numbers (12.22-12.28) have been included as place-holders. The *DACS* rule for family names, which has no equivalent in *AACR2*, has been given the next consecutive number, 12.29.

12.29. FAMILY NAMES
12.29A. General Rule
The heading for a family consists of the family surname followed by the term "family."[62]

12.29B. Entry Element
In general, choose as the basis of the heading for a family, the name by which it is commonly known.

```
Giroux family

Taylor family

Charron-Lecorre family

Molina y Vedia de Bastianini family
```

12.29C. Determine the name by which a family is commonly known from the following sources and in the order of preference given:

    a) the name that appears most frequently in the published works about the family (if any);
    b) the name that appears most frequently in the archival materials being described;
    c) the latest name;
    d) the name that appears in reference sources.[63]

If the name does not appear on a prescribed source of information, determine the name by which the family is known from reference sources issued in its language or country of residence or activity.

---

[62] For further information on the use of family names as creators see Chapter 9 Identifying Creators.
[63] The term *reference sources,* as used in this chapter, includes books and articles written about a person.

Form of Geographic Names

Commentary: The purpose of this chapter is to provide rules for the standardized form of the names of geographic entities that may also be the name of corporate bodies. The sources of information are indicated within the rules themselves.

For the most part, the numbering system in Chapter 13 follows that of Chapter 23 of *AACR2*, except that the *DACS* chapter number is substituted for *AACR2* chapter number; for example, rule 23.174F2 in *AACR2* is 13.174F2 in *DACS*. There are no significant differences between the numbering of Chapter 23 of *AACR2* and Chapter 13 of *DACS*.

13.1. INTRODUCTORY NOTE

13.1A. The names of geographic entities (referred to throughout this chapter as *places*) are used to distinguish between corporate bodies with the same name (see 14.4C); as additions to other corporate names (e.g., conference names, see 14.7B4); and, commonly, as the names of governments (see 14.3E) and communities that are not governments.[64]

13.2. GENERAL RULES

13.2A. English Form

13.2A1. Use the English form of the name of a place if there is one in general use. Determine this from gazetteers and other reference sources published in English-speaking countries. In case of doubt, use the vernacular form (see 13.2B).

		Austria
	not	Österreich
		Copenhagen
	not	København
		Florence
	not	Firenze
		Ghent
	not	Gent
	not	Gand
		Sweden
	not	Sverige

If the English form of the name of a place is the English name of the government that has jurisdiction over the place, use that form.

---

[64] Note that the geographic name headings resulting from the application of these rules are not meant to be used for geographic features that cannot act as corporate bodies, e.g., rivers, mountains, deserts, archaeological sites, named monuments and battlefields.

13.2B. Vernacular Form

13.2B1. Use the form in the official language of the country if there is no English form in general use.

>   Buenos Aires
>
>   Gorlovka
>
>   Tallinn
>
>   Livorno
>   *not* Leghorn
>   (*English form no longer in general use*)

If the country has more than one official language, use the form most commonly found in English-language sources.

>   Louvain
>   *not* Leuven
>
>   Helsinki
>   *not* Helsingfors

13.3. CHANGES OF NAME

13.3A. If the name of a place changes, use as many of the names as are required by

>   1) the rules on government names (14.3E) (e.g., *Nyasaland* or *Malawi*, as appropriate);
>
> *or* 2) the rules on additions to corporate names (14.4C4) and conference names (14.7B4) (e.g. use *Léopoldville* or *Kinshasa*, as appropriate);
>
> *or* 3) other relevant rules in Chapter 14.

13.4. ADDITIONS

13.4A. Punctuation

13.4A1. Make all additions to place names used as entry elements (see 14.3E) in parentheses.

>   Budapest (*Hungary*)

If the place name is being used as an addition, precede the name of a larger place by a comma.

>   Magyar Nemzeti Galéria (*Budapest, Hungary*)[65]

---

[65] This example and the one above are included solely to show the punctuation patterns. For the construction of the heading, see the later rules in this chapter and those in Chapter 14.

13.4B. General Rule

13.4B1. Add to the name of a place (other than a country or a state, etc., listed in 13.4C1 or 13.4D1) the name of a larger place as instructed in 13.4C–13.4F. For additional instructions on distinguishing between place names used as the headings for governments, see 14.6.

13.4C. Places in Australia, Canada, Malaysia, or United States

13.4C1. States, etc. Do not make any addition to the name of a state, province, territory, etc., of Australia, Canada, Malaysia, or the United States.

>   Northern Territory
>
>   Prince Edward Island
>
>   District of Columbia

13.4C2. Other Places. If the place is in a state, province, territory, etc., of one of the countries listed above, add the name of the state, etc., in which it is located.

>   Darwin (*N.T.*)
>
>   Jasper (*Alta.*)
>
>   George Town (*Penang*)
>
>   Cook County (*Ill.*)
>
>   Alexandria (*Va.*)
>
>   Washington (D.C.)

13.4D. Places in the British Isles

13.4D1. Do not make any addition to the names of the following parts of the British Isles: England, the Republic of Ireland, Northern Ireland, Scotland, Wales, the Isle of Man, the Channel Islands.

13.4D2. If a place is located in England, the Republic of Ireland, Northern Ireland, Scotland, Wales, the Isle of Man, or the Channel Islands, add "England," "Ireland," "Northern Ireland," "Scotland," "Wales," "Isle of Man," or "Channel Islands," as appropriate.

>   Dorset (*England*)
>
>   Clare (*Ireland*)
>
>   Bangor (*Northern Ireland*)
>
>   Strathclyde (*Scotland*)
>
>   Powys (*Wales*)

```
        Ramsey (Isle of Man)

        Jersey (Channel Islands)
```

13.4E. Other Places
13.4E1. Add to the name of a place not covered by 13.4C–13.4D the name of the country in which the place is located.

```
        Formosa (Argentina)

        Luanda (Angola)

        Lucca (Italy)

        Madras (India)

        Monrovia (Liberia)

        Næsby (Denmark)

        Paris (France)

        Toledo (Spain)
```

13.4F. Further Additions
13.4F1. Distinguishing between Otherwise Identical Place Names. If the addition of a larger place as instructed in 13.4C–13.4E is insufficient to distinguish between two or more places with the same name, include a word or phrase commonly used to distinguish them.

```
        Villaviciosa de Asturias (Spain)

        Villaviciosa de Córdoba (Spain)
```

If there is no such word or phrase, give the name of an appropriate smaller place before the name of the larger place.

```
        Friedberg (Bavaria, Germany)

        Friedberg (Hesse, Germany)

        Tarbert (Strathclyde, Scotland)

        Tarbert (Western Isles, Scotland)

        Saint Anthony (Hennepin County, Minn.)

        Saint Anthony (Stearns County, Minn.)
```

13.4F2. Identifying Places If considered necessary to identify the place (as in the case of a community within a city), give the name of an appropriate smaller place before the name of the larger place specified as an addition by the preceding rules.

DESCRIBING ARCHIVES: A CONTENT STANDARD

```
Hyde Park (Chicago, Ill.)

Chelsea (London, England)

St. Peter Port (Guernsey, Channel Islands)

Hataitai (Wellington, N.Z.)

Palermo (Sicily, Italy)

Swansea (Toronto, Ont.)

11ᵉ Arrondissement (Paris, France)

Minato-ku (Tokyo, Japan)
```

13.5. Place Names Including or Requiring Term Indicating a Type of Jurisdiction

13.5A. If the first part of a place name is a term indicating a type of jurisdiction, and the place is commonly listed under another element of its name in lists published in the language of the country in which it is located, omit the term indicating the type of jurisdiction.

```
        Kerry (Ireland)
   not  County Kerry (Ireland)

        Ostholstein (Germany)
   not  Kreis Ostholstein (Germany)
```

In all other cases, include the term indicating the type of jurisdiction.

```
        Città di Castello (Italy)

        Ciudad Juárez (Mexico)

        District of Columbia

        Distrito Federal (Brazil)

        Mexico City (Mexico)
```

13.5B. If a place name does not include a term indicating a type of jurisdiction, and such a term is required to distinguish that place from another of the same name, follow the instructions in 14.6.

CHAPTER 14

Form of Names for Corporate Bodies

Commentary: Once the name of a corporate body has been chosen as an access point, the form of the name must be standardized. The purpose of this chapter is to provide rules for the standardized form of the names of corporate bodies. Standardization of corporate names, particularly in online environments, is critical to the retrieval of all relevant materials. Therefore it is important for archivists to use the authority form of a name, if one exists, from the Library of Congress Authorities (LCNAF).[66] If there is no authorized form in the Name Authority File, the rules in this chapter should be applied. The sources of information to be used in particular circumstances are indicated at various places within the rules themselves. Where a rule in this chapter contains an instruction to make a reference, do so in accordance with the rules in section 11.1.

In the examples in this chapter, variant names (i.e., names that are not authorized names or forms of the name) are indicated by the letter *x* in front of them. This means that the variant name would be included in an authority record as instructed in Chapter 11.

For the most part, the numbering system in Chapter 14 follows that of Chapter 24 of *AACR2*, except that the *DACS* chapter number is substituted for *AACR2* chapter number; for example, Rule 24.13A in *AACR2* is 14.13A in *DACS*. Where the rules in *DACS* are different, as in the expanded rules for the treatment of variant names of corporate bodies (14.2B–14.2E), the numbering has been slightly adjusted.

14.1. GENERAL RULE

14.1A. Enter a corporate body[67] directly under the name by which it is identified, except when the rules that follow provide for entering it under the name of a higher or related body (see 14.13) or under the name of a government (see 14.18).

Determine the name by which a corporate body is identified from the following sources and in the order of preference given:

  a) the name that appears in published items issued by the corporate body in its language (see also 14.3A);
  b) the name that appears in reference sources;[68]
  c) the name that appears in the corporate body's records;
  d) the name that appears in administrative records relating to the acquisition of the materials being described;
  e) the name that appears in other archival records.

If the name of a corporate body consists of or contains initials, omit or include periods and other marks of punctuation according to the predominant usage of the body. In case

---

[66] The authorized form of the corporate body is given in the 110 field in a MARC 21 record.

[67] For definition, see glossary.

[68] *Reference sources*, as used in this chapter, include official publications such as gazettes, registers, statutes, orders, regulations and, also, books and articles written about the corporate body.

of doubt, omit the periods, etc. Do not leave a space between such punctuation and a following initial. Do not leave spaces between the letters of an initialism written without periods, etc. Make references from other forms of the name of a corporate body as instructed in section 11.1.

```
Aslib

Breitkopf & Härtel

British Museum

Light Fantastic Players

Radio Society of Great Britian

Royal Aeronautical Society

Symposium on Cognition…⁶⁹

Carnegie Library of Pittsburgh

Challenger Expedition

Chartered Insurance Institute

G. Mendel Memorial Symposium, 1865-1965 ...

MEDCOM

Museum of American Folk Art

United States Catholic Conference

University of Oxford

W.H. Ross Foundation for the Study of Prevention of
Blindness

Yale University
```

---

[69] For additions to the name of a conference, congress, expedition, etc., see 14.7B.

14.1B. Romanization[70]

14.1B1. If the name of the corporate body is in a language written in a nonroman script, romanize the name according to the table for that language adopted by the institution. Refer from other romanizations as necessary.

```
Chung-kuo wen tzu kai ko wei yuan hui[71]
    x Zhongguo wenzi gaige weiyuanhui
```

14.1C. Changes of Name

14.1C1. If the name of a corporate body has changed (including a change from one language to another), establish an authorized form of the name to be used in the title in accordance with rule 2.3.17 and consider other names to be variant names (see 10.32–10.34, 11.B16–B17).

```
American Material Handling Society
      changed its name to
International Material Management Society
   (Make a see also reference under each name)
```

```
Pennsylvania State University (authorized name)
   (The authority record for this corporate body would contain the following:
Administrative history:  ...The name of the Farmers' High School
was changed in 1862 to Agricultural College of Pennsylvania; in
1874 to Pennsylvania State College; in 1953 to Pennsylvania State
University....)
Variant names:
   Farmers' High School (earlier name, ? -1862)
   Agricultural College of Pennsylvania (earlier name, 1862-1874)
   Pennsylvania State College (earlier name, 1874-1953)
```

14.1C2. Records of More than One Corporate Body within the Same Unit Being Described. If the records of more than one corporate body are included in the unit being described, establish a heading for each corporate body and record their relationships as instructed in rules 11.13–11.17.

---

[70] Alternative rule. Romanization. If the name of the body is in a language written in a nonroman script and a romanized form appears in published items issued by the body or in its records, use that romanized form. Refer as necessary from other romanizations. If more than one romanized form is found, use the form resulting from romanization according to the table adopted by the institution for the language.

```
Zhongguo wenzi gaige weiyuanhui
    x Chung-kuo wen tzu kai ko wei yuan hui
```

[71] Systematic romanizations used in the examples in this chapter follow the tables (published by the Library of Congress in *Cataloging Service*, bulletin 118) adopted jointly by the American Library Association, the Canadian Library Association, and the Library of Congress.

14.2. Variant Forms[72] of Names: General Rules

14.2A. Apply the following rules if variant forms of names for a corporate body appear or are used in the following sources respectively: published items issued by it, reference sources, or the records. Also apply the special rules in 14.3 when they are appropriate.

14.2B. Variant Forms of Names Found in Published Sources

14.2B1. If variant forms of the name are found in published items issued by the corporate body, use the name as it appears in the chief source of information[73] as opposed to forms found elsewhere in the items.

14.2B2. If variant forms of the name appear in the chief sources of information for published items, use the name that is presented formally as indicated by layout or typography. If no name is presented formally, or if all names are presented formally, use the predominant form of name.

If there is no predominant form, use a brief form (including an initialism or an acronym) that would differentiate the corporate body from others with the same or similar brief names.

> **AFL-CIO**
> *not* American Federation of Labor and Congress of Industrial
>   Organizations
>
> **American Philosophical Society**
> *not* American Philosophical Society Held at Philadelphia for
>   Promoting Useful Knowledge
>
> **Canadian Joker Society**
> *not* Canadian Joker Society for Promoting Humour in Canadian
>   Life
>
> **Unesco**
> *not* United Nations Educational, Scientific, and Cultural
>   Organization
>
> **Euratom**
> *not* European Atomic Energy Community
>
> **Maryknoll Sisters**
> *not* Congregation of the Maryknoll Sisters

If the variant forms do not include a brief form that would differentiate two or more bodies with the same or similar brief names, use the form found in reference sources.

> Metropolitan Applied Research Center
> *(Official name. Brief form sometimes used by the center, MARC Corporation, is the same as the name of another body located in New York)*

---

[72] *Variant forms of names* do not include names that result from a name change. For these, see 14.1C.
[73] For published items, the chief source of information is the title page or its equivalent.

14.2C. Variant Forms of Names Found in Reference Sources

14.2C1. If variant forms of the name are found in reference sources, use the name as it appears in the most appropriate reference source.[74]

14.2D. Variant Forms of Names Found in the Records

14.2D1. If variant forms of the name are found in the records, use the name as it appears in the following categories of material and in the order of preference given:

    a) records legally establishing the corporate body (e.g., acts of incorporation, letters patent);

    b) records of administrative regulations (e.g., executive orders, constitutions, by-laws);

    a) other records of policy (e.g., minutes, policy and procedures manuals).

14.2D2. If the corporate body's records do not include materials that fall into the categories listed above, use the form of name that appears most frequently in other materials in the records.

14.2E. Variant Spellings

If variant spellings of the name are found, use the form resulting from an official change in orthography or, if this does not apply, use the predominant spelling. In case of doubt, use the spelling that seems most appropriate.

14.3 VARIANT FORMS OF NAMES: SPECIAL RULES
14.3A. Language[75]

14.3A1. If the name appears in different languages, use the form in the official language of the corporate body.

```
        Société historique franco-américaine
  not   Franco-American Historical Society
```

If there is more than one official language and one of these is English, use the English form.

```
        Canadian Committee on Cataloguing
  not   Comité canadien de catalogage
```

If English is not one of the official languages or if the official language is not known, use the form in the language used predominantly in items issued by the corporate body.

---

[74] Institutions should establish a policy for determining the form of name to be used when variant forms of names are found in reference sources.

[75] Alternative rule. Language. Use a form of name in a language suitable to the users of the institution's retrieval system if the body's name is in a language that is not familiar to those users.

```
          Japan Productivity Center
  if not  Nihon Seisansei Hombu
```

```
                Schweizerische Landesbibliothek
    not         Biblioteca nazionale svizzera
    not         Bibliothèque nationale Suisse
                (German is the language used predominantly by the body in its publications)
```

In case of doubt, use the English, French, German, Spanish, or Russian form, in that order of preference. If there is no form in any of these languages, use the form in the language that comes first in English alphabetic order. Refer from form(s) in other languages.

14.3B. Language: International Bodies

14.3B1. If the name of an international corporate body appears in English in published items issued by the body, in reference sources, or in its records (in that order of preference), use the English form. In other cases, follow the instructions in 14.3A.

```
                Arab League
    not         Union des états arabes
    not         Jami'at al-Duwal al-'Arabīyah

                European Economic Community
    not         Communauté économique européenne
    not         Europese Economische Gemeenschap
                [etc.]

                International Federation of Library Associations and
                    Institutions
    not         Federation internationale des associations de
                    bibliothécaires et des bibliothèques
    not         Internationaler Verband der Bibliothekarischen Vereine und
                    In-situtionen
                [etc.]

                Nordic Association for American Studies
    not         Nordisk selskap for Amerikastudier
    not         Nordiska sällskapet för Amerikastudier
                [etc.]
```

14.3C. Conventional Name

14.3C1. General Rule. If a corporate body is frequently identified by a conventional form of name in reference sources in its own language, use this conventional name.

```
                Westminster Abbey
    not         Collegiate Church of St. Peter in Westminster

                Kunstakademiet
    not         Det Kongelige Danske kunstakademi

                Killam Trust
    not         Izaak Walton Killam Memorial Fund for Advanced Studies
    not         Killam Scholarship Program
```

14.3C2. Ancient and International Bodies.[76] If the name of a corporate body of ancient origin or of one that is international in character has become firmly established in an English form in English-language usage, use this English form.

```
        Benedictines

        Cluniacs

        Coptic Church

        Franciscans

        Freemasons

        Knights of Malta

        Poor Clares

        Royal Arch Masons

        Paris Peace Conference...

        Vatican Council ...
```

14.3C3. Autocephalous Patriarchates, Archdiocese, etc. Enter an ancient autocephalous patriarchate, archdiocese, etc., of the Eastern Church under the place by which it is identified. Add a word or phrase designating the type of ecclesiastical jurisdiction.

```
        Antioch (Jacobite patriarchate)

        Constantinople (Ecumenical patriarchate)
```

14.3D. Religious Orders and Societies

14.3D1. Use the best-known form of name, in English, if possible, for a religious order or society. In case of doubt, follow this order of preference:

a) the conventional name by which its members are known in English;
b) the English form of name used by units of the order or society located in English-speaking countries;
c) the name of the order or society in the language of the country of its origin.

```
        Franciscans
not     Ordo Fratrum Minorum
not     Order of St. Francis
not     Minorites
```

---

[76] Apply this rule, for example, to religious bodies, fraternal and knightly orders, church councils, and diplomatic conferences. If it is necessary to establish a heading for a diplomatic conference that has no formal name and has not yet acquired a conventional name, use the name found most commonly in periodical articles and newspaper accounts in English. If another name becomes established later, change the heading to that name.

```
          Jesuits
not       Societas Jesu
not       Compañía de Jesús
not       Society of Jesus

          Poor Clares
not       Order of St. Clare
not       Second Order of St. Francis
not       Fanciscans.  Second Order

          Brothers of Our Lady of the Fields

          Community of the Resurrection

          Dominican Nuns of the Second Order of Perpetual Adoration
not       Dominicans.  Second Order of Perpetual Adoration

          International Society for Krishna Consciousness
not       Hare Krishna Society
```

14.3E. Governments

14.3E1. Use the conventional name of a government,[77] unless the official name is in common use. The conventional name of a government is the geographic name (see Chapter 13) of the area (e.g., country, province, state, county, municipality) over which the government exercises jurisdiction. See also 14.6.

```
          France
not       République française

          Massachusetts
not       Commonwealth of Massachusetts

          Nottinghamshire (England)
not       County of Nottingham

          Arlington (Mass.)
not       Town of Arlington
```

If the official name of the government is in common use, use it.

```
          Greater Anchorage Borough (Alaska)
```

14.3F. Conferences, Congresses, Meetings, etc.

14.3F1. If, among the variant forms of a conference name appearing in published items issued by the corporate body, in reference sources, or in its records, there is a form that includes the name or abbreviation of the name of a corporate body associated with the meeting to which the meeting is not subordinate, use this form.

---

[77] *Government* is used here to mean the totality of corporate bodies (executive, legislative, and judicial) exercising the powers of a jurisdiction. Treat as a government agency a corporate body known as *government*, or its equivalent in other languages, or a term with similar meaning, that is an executive element of a particular jurisdiction (see 14.18).

```
FAO Hybrid Maize Meeting ...
```

If, however, the name is of a corporate body to which the meeting is subordinate (e.g., the annual meeting of an association), see 14.13A, type 6.

14.3F2. If a conference has both a specific name of its own and a more general name as one of a series of conferences, use the specific name. Refer from the general name to the specific name(s).

```
        Symposium on Protein Metabolism ...
not     Nutrition Symposium ...

        Symposium on Endocrines and Nutrition
not     Nutrition Symposium
```

14.3G. Places of Worship
14.3G1. If variant forms of the name of a local church, cathedral, monastery, convent, abbey, temple, mosque, synagogue, etc., appear in published items issued by the corporate body, in reference sources, or in its records, use the predominant form. If there is no predominant form, follow this order of preference:

    a)   a name containing the name of the person(s), object(s), place(s), or event(s) to which the place of worship is dedicated or after which it is named;

```
        All Saints Church ...

        Chapelle Saint-Louis ...

        Church of the Holy Sepulchre ...

        Duomo di Santa Maria Matricolare ...

        St. Clement's Church ...

        St. Paul's Cathedral ...

        Temple Emanu-El ...
```

    b)   a name beginning with a word or phrase descriptive of a type of place of worship;

```
        Abtei Reichenau

        Great Synagogue ...

        Jüdische Reformgemeinde in Berlin

        Monasterio de Clarisas ...

        Parish Church of Limpsfield
```

```
                Unitarian Universalist Church ...
```

   c) a name beginning with the name of the place in which the place of worship is situated.

```
        Anerly Society of the New Church

        Beechen Grove Baptist Church ...

        English River Congregation of the Church of the Brethren

        Kölner Dom

        Tenafly Presbyterian Church

        Westover Church ...

        Winchester Cathedral
```

For additions to the name of a place of worship, see 14.10.

14.4. ADDITIONS
14.4A. General Rule
14.4A1. Make additions to the name of a corporate body as instructed in 14.4B–14.4C. For additions to special types of corporate bodies (e.g., governments, conferences), see 14.6–14.11. Enclose in parentheses all additions required by rules in this chapter.

14.4B. Names Not Conveying the Idea of a Corporate Body
14.4B1. If the name alone does not convey the idea of a corporate body, add a general designation in English.

```
            Apollo II (Spacecraft)

            Bounty (Ship)

            Elks (Fraternal order)

            Monty Python (Comedy troupe)

            Alabama (Musical group)

            Friedrich Witte (Firm)
```

14.4C. Two or More Bodies with the Same or Similar Names
14.4C1. General Rule. If two or more bodies have the same name, or names so similar that they may be confused, add a word or phrase to each name as instructed in 14.4C2–14.4C7. Add such a word or phrase to any other name if the addition assists in the understanding of the nature or purpose of the corporate body. Do not include the additions to names of places prescribed in 14.6 when the names of these places are used to indicate the location of corporate bodies.

14.4C2. Names of Countries, States, Provinces, etc. If a corporate body has a character that is national, state, provincial, etc., add the name of the country, state, province, etc., in which it is located.

```
Republican Party (Ill.)

Republican Party (Mo.)

Sociedad Nacional de Minería (Chile)

Sociedad National de Minería (Peru)

National Measurement Laboratory (U.S.)

Midlands Museum (Zimbabwe)
```

If such an addition does not provide sufficient identification or is inappropriate (as in the case of national, state, provincial, etc., universities of the same name serving the same country, state, province, etc.), follow the instructions in 14.4C3–14.4C7.

14.4C3. Local Place Names. In the case of any other corporate body, add the name of the local place, whether it is a jurisdiction or not, that is commonly associated with its name, unless the name of an institution, the date(s) of the corporate body, or other designation (see 14.4C5–14.4C7) provides better identification.

```
Salem College (Salem, W. Va.)

Salem College (Winston-Salem, N.C.)

Washington County Historical Society (Washington County,
    Ark.)

Washington County Historical Society (Washington County,
    Md.)

St. Peter's Church (Hook Norton, England)

St. Peter's Church (Sudbury, England)

Red Lion Hotel (Newport, Wales)

Red Lion Hotel (Newport, Isle of Wright, England)

Red Lion Hotel (Newport, Shropshire, England)
```

If further distinction is necessary, give the name of a particular area within that jurisdiction before the name of the jurisdiction.

```
St. John's Church (Georgetown, Washington, D.C.)

St. John's Church (Lafayette Square, Washington, D.C.)
```

14.4C4. Changes of Name of Jurisdiction or Locality. If the name of the local jurisdiction or geographic locality changes during the lifetime of the corporate body, add the latest name in use in the lifetime of the corporate body.

>   St. Paul Lutheran Church *(Skokie, Ill.)*
> *not* St. Paul Lutheran Church *(Niles Center, Ill.)*
>   (*Church founded in 1881. Place name changed in 1940*)

> *but* Historisk samfund (Christiania, *Norway*)
>   (*Ceased to exist before Christiania became Oslo*)

14.4C5. Institutions. Add the name of an institution instead of the local place name if the institution's name is commonly associated with the name of the corporate body. Give the name of the institution in the form and language used for it as a heading.

>   Newman Club *(Brooklyn College)*
> *not* Newman Club *(Brooklyn, New York, N.Y.)*

>   Center for Radiation Research *(National Measurement Laboratory (U.S.))*

14.4C6. Year(s). If the name has been used by two or more corporate bodies that cannot be distinguished by place, add the year of founding or the inclusive years of existence.

>   Scientific Society of San Antonio *(1892-1894)*

>   Scientific Society of San Antonio *(1904-)*

14.4C7. Other Additions. If none of the place name, name of institution, or date(s) is sufficient or appropriate for distinguishing between two or more corporate bodies, add an appropriate general designation in English.

>   Church of God *(Adventist)*

>   Church of God *(Apostolic)*

14.5. OMISSIONS
14.5A. Initial Articles
14.5A1. Omit an initial article unless the heading is to file under the article (e.g., a corporate name that begins with an article that is the first part of the name of a person or place).

>   Francais de Grande-Bretagne *(Association)*
> *not* Le Francais de Grande-Bretagne *(Association)*

>   Library Association
> *not* The Library Association

> *but* Le Corbusier Sketchbook Publication Committee

>   Los Angeles Symphony *(Orchestra)*

14.5B. Citations of Honors
14.5B1. Omit a phrase citing an honor or order awarded to the corporate body.

14.5C. Terms Indicating Incorporation and Certain Other Terms
14.5C1. Omit an adjectival term or abbreviation indicating incorporation (e.g., *Incorporated, E.V., Ltd.*) or state ownership of a corporate body, and a word or phrase, abbreviated or in full, designating the type of incorporated entity (*e.g., Aktiebolaget, Gesellschaft mit beschränkter Haftung, Kabushiki Kaisha, Società per azione*), unless it is an integral part of the name or is needed to make it clear that the name is that of a corporate body.

> American Ethnological Society
>   (*Without* Inc.)
>
> Automobiltechnische Gesellschaft
>   (*Without E.V., i.e., Eingetranger Verein*)
>
> Compañía Internacional Editora
>   (*Without S.a.*)
>
> Henry Birks and Sons
>   (*Without* Ltd.)
>
> *but*
>
> Films Incorporated
>
> Peter Davies Limited
>
> Vickers (Aviation) Limited

14.5C2. If such a term is needed to make it clear that the name is that of a corporate body and it occurs at the beginning of the name, transpose it to the end.

> Elektrometall, Aktiebolaget
> *not*   Aktiebolaget Elektrometall
>
> Hochbauprojektierung Karl-Marx-Stadt, VEB
> *not*   VEB Hochbauprojektierung Karl-Marx-Stadt

14.5C3. Omit an initial word or phrase in an Asian language indicating the private character of a corporate body (e.g., *Shiritsu, Ssu li*), unless the word or phrase is an integral part of the name.

> Tan-chiang Ying yü chuan k`o hsüeh hsiao
> *not*   Ssu li Tan-chiang Ying yü chuan k`o hsüeh hsiao

14.5C4. Omit abbreviations (e.g., *U.S.S., H.M.S.*) occurring before the name of a ship.

> Ark Royal (*Ship*)
> *not*   H.M.S. Ark Royal

14.6. GOVERNMENTS: ADDITIONS

14.6A. Scope

14.6A1. Apply this rule to the names of governments that are not differentiated by the application of 13.4. Make the further additions prescribed here following a space, colon, space, and within the same parentheses that enclose the additions prescribed by 13.4.

14.6B. Add the type of jurisdiction in English if other than a city or a town. If there is no English equivalent for the vernacular term, or in case of doubt, use the vernacular term.

```
Cork (Ireland)

Cork (Ireland : County)

Darmstadt (Germany)

Darmstadt (German : Landkreis)

Darmstadt (Germany : Regierungsbezirk)

Guadalajara (Mexico)

Guadalajara (Spain)

Guadalajara (Spain : Province)

New York (N.Y.)

New York (State)

Québec (Province)

Québec (Québec)

Québec (Québec : County)
```

14.6C. If the type of jurisdiction does not provide a satisfactory distinction, add an appropriate word or phrase.

```
Germany (Democratic Republic)

Germany (Federal Republic)
```

14.6D. If two or more governments lay claim to jurisdiction over the same area (e.g., as with occupying powers and insurgent governments), add a suitable designation to one or each of the governments, followed by the inclusive years of its existence.

```
France

France (Territory under German occupation, 1940-1944)

Algeria

Algeria (Provisional government, 1958-1962)
```

14.7. Conferences, Congresses, Meetings, etc.
14.7A. Omissions
14.7A1. Omit from the name of a conference, etc. (including that of a conference entered subordinately, see 14.13), indications of its number, frequency, or year(s) of convocation.

	Conference on Co-ordination of Galactic Research...
not	Second Conference on Co-ordination of Galactic Research...

	Louisiana Cancer Conference...
not	Biennial Louisiana Cancer Conference...

	Analogies Symposium
not	1986 Analogies Symposium

14.7B. Additions
14.7B1. General Rule. Add to the name of a conference, etc. (including that of a conference entered subordinately, see 14.13), its number (if appropriate), the year(s), and the place(s) in which it was held. Separate these elements by a space, colon, space.

14.7B2. Number. If a conference, etc., is stated or inferred to be one of a series of numbered meetings of the same name, add the ordinal numeral in its English form.

> Conference of British Teachers of Marketing at Advanced
>   Level   (*3ʳᵈ :   *)

If the numbering is irregular, do not add it. Optionally, provide an explanation of the irregularities in a note or an explanatory reference.

14.7B3. Date. If the heading is for a single meeting, add the year or years in which the conference, etc., was held.

> Conference on Library Surveys (*1965 : ...*)
>
> Conference of Technical Information Center Administration
>   (*3ʳᵈ : 1966 :   *)
>
> Study Institute on Special Education (*1969-1970 : ...*)

Add specific dates if necessary to distinguish between two or more meetings held in the same year.

> Conférence agricole interalliée (*1st : 1919 Feb.
>   11-15 : ...*)
>
> Conférence agricole interalliée (*2nd : 1919 Mar.
>   17-19 : ...*)

14.7B4 Location. Add the name of the local place or other location (institution, etc.) in which the conference, etc., was held. Give a local place name in the form prescribed in Chapter 12. Give any other location in the nominative case in the language and form in which it is found in the unit being described.

>   Symposium on Glaucoma *(1966 : New Orleans, La.)*
>
>   Regional Conference on Mental Measurements of the Blind
>   *(1st : 1951 : Perkins Institution)*
>
>   Louisiana Cancer Conference *(2nd : 1958: New Orleans, La.)*
>
>   International Conference on the Biology of Whales
>   *(1971 : Shenandoah National Park)*
>
>   Conference on Cancer Public Education *(1973 : Dulles
>   Airport)*

If the heading is for a series of conferences, etc., do not add the location unless all were held in the same place.

>   Hybrid Corn Industry Research Conference

If the location is part of the name of the conference, etc., do not repeat it.

>   Arden House Conference on Medicine and Anthropology *(1961)*
>
>   Paris Symposium on Radio Astronomy *(1958)*

If the sessions of a conference, etc., were held in two locations, add both names.

>   World Peace Congress *(1st : 1949 Paris, France, and Prague,
>   Czechoslovakia)*
>
>   Institute on Diagnostic Problems in Mental Retardation
>   *(1957 : Long Beach State College and San Francisco State
>   College)*

If the sessions of a conference, etc., were held in three or more locations, add the first named place followed by "etc."

>   International Conference on Alternatives to War *(1982 : San
>   Francisco, Calif., etc.)*

14.8. EXHIBITIONS, FAIRS, FESTIVALS, ETC.
14.8A. Omissions
14.8A1. As instructed in 14.7A1, omit from the name of an exhibition, fair, festival, etc., word(s) that denote its number.

14.8B. Additions

14.8B1. As instructed in 14.7B, add to the name of an exhibition, fair, festival, etc., its number, date, and location. Do not add the date or location if they are integral parts of the name.

```
Biennale de Venezia (36th : 1972)

World's Columbian Exposition (1893 : Chicago, Ill.)

Expo 67 (Montréal, Québec)
```

14.9. CHAPTERS, BRANCHES, ETC.

14.9A. If a chapter, branch, etc., entered subordinately (see 14.13) carries out the activities of a corporate body in a particular locality or within a particular institution, add the name of the locality or institution, unless it is part of the name of the chapter, branch, etc.

```
        Freemasons.  Concordia Lodge, No.  13 (Baltimore, Md.)

        Freemasons.  United.  Grand Lodge (England)

        Knights Templar (Masonic Order).  Grand Commandery (Me.)

        Scottish Rite (Masonic Order).  Supreme Council (Canada)

        Psi Upsilon (Fraternity).  Gamma Chapter (Amherst College)
but
        American Heart Association.  Illinois Affiliate

        American Red Cross.  Champaign County Chapter
```

14.10. PLACES OF WORSHIP

14.10A. If the name of a place of worship does not convey the idea of a place of worship, add a general designation in English.

```
Monte Cassino (Monastery)
```

14.10B. Add to the name of a place of worship the name of the place or local ecclesiastical jurisdiction (e.g., parish, Pfarrei) in which it is located (see 14.4C3–14.4C4), unless the location is clear from the name itself.

```
St. Mary (Church : Aylesbury Vale, England)

Westover Church (Charles City County, Va.)

St. James' Church (Bronx, New York, N.Y.)

Twin City Bible Church (Silver Spring, Md.)

Finnish Lutheran Church of Canberra
```

If there are two or more places of worship with the same name in the same locality, add a further suitable designation.

> Saint James' Church (*New York, N.Y. : Episcopal*)
>
> Saint James' Church (*New York, N.Y. : Catholic*)

14.11. RADIO AND TELEVISION STATIONS

14.11A. If the name of a radio or television station consists solely or principally of its call letters or if its name does not convey the idea of a radio or television station, add "Radio station" or "Television station" and the name of the place in which the station is located.

> HVJ (*Radio station : Vatican City*)
>
> WCIA (*Television station : Champaign, Ill.*)

14.11B. Add to the name of any other radio or television station the place in which it is located unless the name of the place is an integral part of the name of the station.

> Radio Maroc (*Rabat, Morocco*)
>
> *but* Radio London

Subordinate and Related Corporate Bodies

14.12. GENERAL RULE

14.12A. Enter a subordinate corporate body (other than a government agency entered under jurisdiction, see 14.18) or a related body directly under its own name (see 14.1–14.3) unless its name belongs to one or more of the types listed in 14.13. Refer to the name of a subordinate body entered directly from its name in the form of a subheading of the higher body.

> Ansco
>   x General Aniline and Film Corporation. *Ansco*
>
> Association of College and Research Libraries
>   x American Library Association. *Association of College and Research Libraries*
>
> BBC Symphony Orchestra
>   x British Broadcasting Corporation. *Symphony Orchestra*
>
> Bodleian Library
>   x University of Oxford. *Bodleian Library*
>
> Congregation of the Most Holy Name of Jesus
>   x Dominican Sisters. *Congregation of the Most Holy Name of Jesus*
>
> Crane Theological School
>   x Tufts University. *Crane Theological School*

```
Friends of IBBY
     x International Board on Books for Young People.   Friends

Harvard Law School
     x Harvard University.   Law School
```

14.13. SUBORDINATE AND RELATED CORPORATE BODIES ENTERED SUBORDINATELY

14.13A. Enter a subordinate or related corporate body as a subheading of the name of the body to which it is subordinate or related if its name belongs to one or more of the following types.[78] Make it a direct or indirect subheading as instructed in 14.14. Omit from the subheading the name or abbreviation of the name of the higher or related body in noun form unless the omission would result in a heading that does not make sense.

TYPE 1. A name containing a term that by definition implies that the corporate body is part of another (e.g., *Department, Division, Section, Branch*).

```
British Broadcasting Corporation.  Engineering Division

International Federation of Library Associations and
     Institutions.  Section on Cataloguing

Stanford University.  Department of Civil Engineering
```

TYPE 2. A name containing a word that normally implies administrative subordination (e.g., *Committee, Commission*) provided that the name of the higher corporate body is required for the identification of the subordinate body.

```
Association of State Universities and Land-Grant Colleges.
     Committee on Traffic Safety, Research and Education

Society of American Archivists.  National Information
     Systems Task Force

Timber Trade Federation of the Great Britain.  Statistical
     Co-ordinating Committee

National Association of Insurance Commissioners.
     Securities Valuation Office

University of Wales.  University Commission
     (Name: University Commission)
```

but   ```National Commission on United Methodist Higher Education```

TYPE 3. A name that is general in nature or that does no more than indicate a geographic, chronological, numbered, or lettered subdivision of a parent body.

---

[78] Distinguish cases in which the subordinate body's name includes the names of higher bodies from cases in which the names of higher bodies appear only in association with the subordinate body's name.

American Dental Association. *Research Institute*
   (*Name: Research Institute*)

Bell Telephone Laboratories. *Technical Information Library*
   (*Name:* Technical Information Library)

Sondley Reference Library. *Friends of the Library*
   (*Name:* Friends of the Library)

American Institute of Architects. *Utah Society*
   (*Name:* Utah Society)

Canadian Jewish Congress. *Central Region*
   (*Name: Central Region*)

California Home Economics Association. *Orange District*
   (*Name:* Orange District)

International Labour Organisation. *European Regional Conference (2nd : 1968 : Geneva, Switzerland)*
   (*Name:* Second European Regional Conference)

Dartmouth College. *Class of 1980*
   (*Name:* Class of 1980)

Knights of Labor. *District Assembly 99*
   (*Name:* District Assembly 99)

U.S. Customs Service. *Region IX*
   (*Name:* Region IX)

In case of doubt, enter the name of the corporate body directly.

Human Resources Centre (*London, England*)
   x Tavistock Institute of Human Relations. *Human Resources Centre*

Research Centre for Management of New Technology
   x Wilfrid Laurier University. *Research Centre for Management of New Technology*

TYPE 4. A name that does not convey the idea of a corporate body.

British Library. *Collection Development*
   (*Name*: Collection Development)

Bell Canada. *Corporate Public Relations*
   (*Name*: Corporate Public Relations)

TYPE 5. A name of a university faculty, school, college, institute, laboratory, etc., that simply indicates a particular field of study.

Princeton University. *Bureau of Urban Research*

```
Syracuse University.  College of Medicine

University College London.  Communication Research Centre

University of London.  School of Pharmacy
```

TYPE 6. A name that includes the entire name of the higher or related corporate body.

```
American Legion.  Auxiliary
```
   (*Name*: American Legion Auxiliary)

```
Auburn University.  Agricultural Experiment Station
```
   (*Name*: Agricultural Experiment Station of Auburn University)

```
Friends of the Earth.  Camden Friends of the Earth
```
   (*Name*: Camden Friends of the Earth)

```
Labour Party (Great Britain).  Conference (72nd : 1972 :
   Blackpool, England)
```
   (*Name:* 72nd Annual Conference of the Labour Party)
   (*Activity of the Labour Party limited to Great Britain*)

```
United Methodist Church (U.S.).  General Conference
```
   (*Name:* General Conference of the United Methodist Church)

```
University of Southampton.  Mathematical Society
```
   (*Name:* Mathematical Society of the University of Southampton)

```
University of Vermont.  Choral Union
```
(*Name:* University of Vermont Choral Union)

```
Yale University.  Library
```
(*Name:* Yale University Library)

```
but   BBC Symphony Orchestra
not   British Broadcasting Corporation.  Symphony Orchestra
```

14.14. DIRECT OR INDIRECT SUBHEADING

14.14A. Enter a corporate body belonging to one or more of the types listed in 14.13 as a subheading of the lowest element in the hierarchy that is entered under its own name. Omit intervening elements in the hierarchy unless the name of the subordinate or related corporate body has been, or is likely to be, used by another body entered under the name of the same higher or related body. In that case, interpose the name of the lowest element in the hierarchy that will distinguish between the bodies.

```
Public Library Association.  Audiovisual Committee
   Hierarchy:      American Library Association
                   Public Library Association
                   Audiovisual Committee
```

American Library Association. *Cataloging and*
Classification Section. Policy and Research Committee
Hierarchy: American Library Association
Resources and Technical Services Division
Cataloging and Classification Section
Policy and Research Committee

Refer from the name in the form of a subheading of the name of its immediately superior body when the heading does not include the name of that superior body.

American Library Association. *Cataloging and*
Classification Section
Hierarchy: American Library Association
Resources and Technical Services Division
Cataloging and Classification Section
x American Library Association. Resources and Technical
Services Division. Cataloging and Classification
Section

Concordia University. *Doctoral Program in Art Education*
Hierarchy: Concordia University
Faculty of Fine Arts
Division of Graduate Studies
Doctoral Program in Art Education
x Concordia University. *Faculty of Fine Arts. Division*
of Graduate Studies. Doctoral Program in Art
Education

Special Rules

14.15. JOINT COMMITTEES, COMMISSIONS, ETC.

14.15A. Enter a corporate body made up of representatives of two or more other bodies directly under its own name.

Joint Committee on Individual Efficiency in Industry
(A joint committee of the Department of Scientific and Industrial Research and the
Medical Research Council)

Canadian Committee on MARC
(A joint committee of the Association pour l'avancement des sciences et des techniques
de la documentation, the Canadian Library Association, and the National Library of
Canada)

Omit the names of the parent bodies when these occur within or at the end of the name and if the name of the joint unit is distinctive without them.

Joint Committee on Bathing Places
(Name: Joint Committee on Bathing Places of the Conference of State Sanitary
Engineers and the Engineering Section of the American Public Health Association)

but   Joint Commission of the Council for Education in World
Citizenship and the London International Assembly

14.15B. If the parent bodies are entered as subheadings of a common higher corporate body, enter the joint unit as instructed in 13.12–13.14.

> American Library Association. *Joint Committee to Compile a*
> *List of International Subscription Agents*
> (*A joint committee of the Acquisitions and Serials sections of the American Library*
> *Association's Resources and Technical Services Division*)

14.16. CONVENTIONALIZED SUBHEADINGS FOR STATE AND LOCAL ELEMENTS OF UNITED STATES POLITICAL PARTIES

14.16A. Enter a state or local unit of a political party in the United States under the name of the party followed by the state or local name in parentheses and then the name of the unit. Omit from the name of the unit any indication of the name of the party or the state or locality.

> Republican Party (*Mo.*). *State Committee*
> (*Name:* Missouri Republican State Committee)

> Republican Party (*Ohio*). *State Executive Committee*
> (*Name:* Ohio State Republican State Executive Committee)

> Democratic Party (*Tex.*). *State Convention (1857 : Waco,*
> *Tex.)*
> (*Name:* State Convention of the Democratic Party of the State of Texas)

Government Bodies and Officials

14.17. GENERAL RULE

14.17A. Enter a corporate body created or controlled by a government directly under its own name (see 14.1–14.3) unless it belongs to one or more of the types listed in 14.18. However, if a body is subordinate to a higher body that is entered under its own name, formulate the heading for the subordinate body according to 14.12–14.14. Refer to the name of a government agency entered directly from its name as a subheading of the name of the government.

> American Battle Monuments Commission
> *x* United States. *American Battle Monuments Commission*

> Arts Council of Great Britain
> *x* Great Britain. *Arts Council*

> Canada Institute for Scientific and Technical Information
> *x* Canada. *Institute for Scientific and Technical*
> *Information*

> Canadian National Railways
> *x* Canada. *Canadian National Railways*

> Consejo Superior de Investigaciones Científicas
> *x* Spain. *Consejo Superior de Investigaciones Científicas*

```
Council on International Economic Policy
    x United States.  Council on International Economic Policy

Dundee Harbour Trust
    x Great Britain.  Dundee Harbour Trust

University of British Columbia
    x British Columbia.  University
```

14.18. GOVERNMENT AGENCIES ENTERED SUBORDINATELY

14.18A. Enter a government agency subordinately to the name of the government if it belongs to one or more of the following types. Make it a direct or indirect subheading of the heading for the government as instructed in 14.19. Omit from the subheading the name or abbreviation of the name of the government in noun form unless such an omission would result in a heading that does not make sense.

```
        Canada.  Agriculture Canada
    not Canada.  Agriculture
```

TYPE 1. An agency with a name containing a term that, by definition, implies that the corporate body is part of another (e.g., *Department, Division, Section, Branch*, and their equivalents in other languages).

```
        Vermont.  Dept. of Water Resources

        Ottawa (Ont.).  Dept. of Community Development

        United States.  Division of Wildlife Services
```

TYPE 2. An agency with a name containing a word that normally implies administrative subordination in the terminology of the government concerned (e.g., *Committee, Commission*), provided that the name of the government is required for the identification of the agency.

```
        Australia.  Bureau of Agricultural Economics

        Canada.  Royal Commission on Banking and Finance.

        Great Britain.  Central Office of Information

        United States.  Commission on Civil Rights

        United States.  Committee on Retirement Policy for Federal
            Personnel

    but Royal Commission on Higher Education in New Brunswick
```

TYPE 3. An agency with a name that is general in nature or that does no more than indicate a geographic, chronological, numbered, or lettered subdivision of the government or of one of its agencies entered subordinately.

```
United States. National Labor Relations Board. Library
   (Name: Library)

Niger. Commissariat général au développement. Centre de
   documentation
   (Name: Centre de documentation)

Malaysia. Royal Customs and Excise Department. Sabah Region
   (Name: Sabah Region)

United States. General Services Administration. Region 5
   (Name: Region 5)

United States. Public Health Service. Region XI
   (Name: Region XI)
```

In case of doubt, enter the name of the corporate body directly.

```
        Governor's Internship Program
   not  Minnesota. Governor's Internship Program

        National Portrait Gallery (Great Britain)
   not  Great Britain. National Portrait Gallery
```

TYPE 4. An agency with a name that does not convey the idea of a corporate body and does not contain the name of the government.

```
Illinois. Bureau of Employment Security. Research and
   Analysis
   (Name: Research and Analysis)

Lower Saxony. (Germany). Landesvermessung
   (Name: Landesvermessung)

United States. Naval Oceanography and Meteorology
   (Name: Naval Oceanography and Meteorology)

Canada. Ocean and Aquatic Sciences
   (Name: Ocean and Aquatic Sciences)
```

TYPE 5. An agency that is a ministry or similar major executive agency (i.e., one that has no other agency above it) as defined by official publications of the government in question.

```
Great Britain. Home Office

Great Britain. Ministry of Defence

Italy. Ministero del bilancio e della programmazione
   economica

United States. National Aeronautics and Space
   Administration
```

TYPE 6. A legislative body (see also 14.21).

> Chicago (*Ill.*). *City Council*
>
> France. *Assemblée nationale*
>
> Great Britain. *Parliament*
>
> United States. *Congress*

TYPE 7. A court (see also 14.23).

> Ontario. *High Court of Justice*
>
> United States. *Supreme Court*

TYPE 8. A principal service of the armed forces of a government (see also 14.24).

> Canada. *Canadian Armed Forces*
>
> Germany. *Heer*
>
> New York (*State*). *Militia*
>
> Great Britain. *Army*

TYPE 9. A head of state or head of government (see also 14.20).

> Great Britain. *Sovereign*
>
> Montréal (*Québec*). *Mayor*
>
> United States. *President*
>
> Virginia. *Governor*

TYPE 10. An embassy, consulate, etc. (see also 14.25).

> Canada. *Embassy (U.S.)*
>
> Great Britain. *Consulate (New York, N.Y.)*

TYPE 11. A delegation to an international or intergovernmental body (see also 14.26).

> Great Britain. *Delegation (United Nations)*

14.19. DIRECT OR INDIRECT SUBHEADING

14.19A. Enter an agency belonging to one or more of the types listed in 14.18 as a direct subheading of the heading for the government unless the name of the agency has been, or is likely to be, used by another agency entered under the name of the same government. In that case, interpose the name of the lowest element in the hierarchy that will distinguish between the agencies.

United States. *Office of Human Development Services*
    Hierarchy: United States
                      Department of Health, Education and Welfare
                      Office of Human Development Services

Quebec (Province). *Service de l'exploration géologique*
    Hierarchy: Québec
                      Ministère des richesses naturelles
                      Direction générale des mines
                      Direction de géologie
                      Service de l'exploration géologique

United States. *Aviation Forecast Branch*
    Hierarchy: United States
                      Department of Transportation
                      Federal Aviation Administration
                      Office of Aviation Policy
                      Aviation Forecast Branch

France. *Commission centrale des marchés*
    Hierarchy: France Ministère d'économie et des finances
                      Commission centrale des marchés

but

Great Britain. *Department of Employment. Solicitors Office*
    Hierarchy: Great Britain
                      Department of Employment
                      Solicitors Office
    (*Other ministries and departments have had subordinate units called* Solicitors Office)

France. *Direction générale des impôts. Service d'administration générale*
    Hierarchy: France
                      Ministère d'économie et des finances
                      Direction générale des impôts
                      Service d'administration generale
    (*Other units within the same ministry are called* Service de l'administration générale)

Refer from the name in the form of a subheading of the name of its immediately superior body when the heading does not include the name of that superior body.

California. *Employment Data and Research Division*
    Hierarchy: California
                      Health and Welfare Agency
                      Employment Development Department
                      Employment Data and Research Division
    x California. Employment Development Department.
      Employment Data and Research Division

France. *Ministère du travail, de l'emploi et de la population. Division de la statistique et des études*
     Hierarchy: France
                              Ministère du travail, de l'emploi et de la population
                              Service des études et prévisions
                              Division de la statistique et des études
   x France. *Ministère du travail, de l'emploi et de la population. Service des études et prévisions. Division de la statistique et des études*

Special Rules

14.20. GOVERNMENT OFFICIALS
14.20A. Scope
14.20A1. Apply this rule only to officials of countries and other states that have existed in postmedieval times and to officials of international intergovernmental organizations.

14.20B. Heads of State, etc.
14.20B1. Enter a sovereign, president, other head of state, or governor acting in an official capacity under the heading for the jurisdiction, followed by the title of the official in English (unless there is no equivalent English term). Add the inclusive years of the reign or incumbency and the name of the person in a brief form and in the language of the heading for that person.

      United States. *President (1953-1961 : Eisenhower)*

      Iran. *Shah (1941-1979 : Mohammed Reze Pahlavi)*

      Canada. *Governor-General (1979-1984 : Schreyer)*

      Papal States. *Sovereign (1846-1870 : Pius IX)*

If the title varies with the gender of the incumbent, use a general term (e.g., *Sovereign* rather than *King* or *Queen*).

      Great Britain. *Sovereign (1837-1901 : Victoria)*

      Russia. *Sovereign (1894-1917 : Nicholas II)*

      Spain. *Sovereign (1886-1931 : Alfonso XIII)*

If there are two or more nonconsecutive periods of incumbency, use separate headings.

      United States. *President (1885-1889 : Cleveland)*

      United States. *President (1893-1997 : Cleveland)*

If the heading applies to more than one incumbent, do not add the dates and names.

      United States. *President*

14.20B2. If a heading is established for an incumbent head of state or other official position as a person in addition to the heading as a head of state, make an explanatory reference under the heading for the head of state.

14.20C. Heads of Governments and of International Intergovernmental Bodies

14.20C1. Enter a head of government acting in an official capacity who is not also a head of state under the heading for the jurisdiction, followed by the title of the official in the vernacular. Add the inclusive years of the incumbency and the name of the person in a brief form and in the language of the heading for that person.

> Great Britain. *Prime Minister (1979-1990 : Thatcher)*
>
> Philadelphia (Pa.). *Mayor (1972-1980 : Rizzo)*
>
> France. *Premier minister (1993-1995 : Balladur)*
>
> New Zealand. *Prime Minister (1999-   : Clark)*

If there are two or more nonconsecutive period of incumbency, use separate headings.

> Canada. *Prime Minister (1968-1979 : Trudeau)*
>
> Canada. *Prime Minister (1980-1984 : Trudeau)*

If the heading applies to more than one incumbent, do not add the dates and names.

> Canada. *Prime Minister*

14.20C2. Enter a head of an international intergovernmental organization acting in an official capacity under the heading for the organization, followed by the title of the official in the language of the heading for the organization. Add the inclusive years of the incumbency and the name of the person in a brief form and in the language of the heading for that person.

> United Nations. *Secretary-General (1972-1981 : Waldheim)*

If the heading applies to more than one incumbent, do not add the dates and names.

> United Nations. *Secretary-General*

14.20D. Governors of Dependent or Occupied Territories

14.20D1. Enter a governor of a dependent territory (e.g., a colony, protectorate) or of an occupied territory (see 14.6D) acting in an official capacity under the heading for the colony, territory, etc., followed by the title of the governor in the language of the governing power.

> Hong Kong. *Governor*
>
> Jersey *(Channel Islands) (Territory under German*
>   *occupation, 1940-1945). Militärischer Befehlshaber.*

Netherlands (*Territory under German occupation, 1940-1945 :*
   Reichskommisar für die Besetzten Niederländischen
   Gebiete).

Germany (*Territory under Allied occupation, 1945-1955 :*
   U.S. Zone). *Military Governor*

14.20E. Other Officials

14.20E1. Enter any other official under the heading for the ministry or agency that the official represents.

United States. *General Accounting Office*
not   United States. *Comptroller General*

14.20E2. Enter an official who is not part of a ministry or agency or who is part of a ministry or agency that is identified only by the title of the official, under the heading for the jurisdiction, followed by the title of the official.

Great Britain. *Lord Privy Seal*

14.21. LEGISLATIVE BODIES

14.21A. Enter a legislature under the name of the jurisdiction for which it legislates.

Iceland. *Alþingi*

British Columbia. *Legislative Assembly*

If a legislature has more than one chamber, enter each as a subheading of the heading for the legislature. Refer from the name of the chamber as a direct subheading of the jurisdiction.

Great Britain. *Parliament. House of Commons*
not   Great Britain. *House of Commons*

Great Britain. *Parliament. House of Lords*
not · Great Britain. *House of Lords*

14.21B. Enter a committee or other subordinate unit (other than a legislative subcommittee of the United States Congress, see 13.21C) as a subheading of the legislature or of a particular chamber, as appropriate.

United States. *Congress. Joint Committee on the Library*

United States. *Congress. House of Representatives. Select
   Committee on Government Organization*

New York (*State*). *Legislature. Assembly. Committee on
   Canals*

> Nova Scotia. *House of Assembly. Select Committee on Trade Negotiations*

14.21C. Enter a legislative subcommittee of the United States Congress as a subheading of the committee to which it is subordinate.

> United States. *Congress. Senate. Committee on Foreign Relations. Subcommittee on Canadian Affairs*
>
> *not*   United States. *Congress. Senate. Subcommittee on Canadian Affairs*

14.21D. Optionally, if successive legislatures are numbered consecutively, add the ordinal numeral and the year or years to the heading for the particular legislature or one of its chambers.

> United States. *Congress (87th : 1961-1962). House of Representatives*
>
> Canada. *Parliament (27th : 1964-1968)*

If, in such a case, numbered sessions are involved, add the session and its number and the year(s) of the session to the number of the legislature.

> United States. *Congress (87th, 2nd session : 1962). House of Representatives*

14.22. CONSTITUTIONAL CONVENTIONS
14.22A. Enter a constitutional convention under the heading for the government that convened it, followed by the name of the convention. Add the year(s) in which it was held.

> Germany. *Nationalversammlung (1919-1920)*
>
> Canada. *Constitutional Conference (1971)*

14.22B. If there is variation in the forms of name of constitutional conventions convened by a jurisdiction using English as an official language, use "Constitutional Convention" as the subheading for each of the conventions.

> New Hampshire. *Constitutional Convention (1781)*
>
> *not*   New Hampshire. *Convention for Framing a New Constitution or Form of Government (1781)*
>
> New Hampshire. *Constitutional Convention (1889)*
>
> New Hampshire. *Constitutional Convention (1912)*
>
> *not*   New Hampshire. *Convention to revise the Constitution (1912)*

If English is not an official language of the jurisdiction, follow the instructions in 14.2 and 14.3.

14.23. COURTS

14.23A. Civil and Criminal Courts

14.23A1. Enter a civil or criminal court under the heading for the jurisdiction whose authority it exercises, followed by the name of the court.

> Vermont. *Court of Chancery*

Omit the name (or abbreviation of the name) of the place in which the court sits or the area that it serves unless the omission would result in objectionable distortion. If the name of the place or the area served is required to distinguish a court from others of the same name, add it in a conventionalized form.

> France. *Cour d'appel (Caen)*
> (*Name:* Cour d'appel de Caen)

> Great Britain. *Crown Court (Manchester)*
> (*Name:* Manchester Crown Court)

> United States. *Court of Appeals (2nd Circuit)*
> (*Name:* United States Court of Appeals for the Second Circuit)

> United States. *Court of Appeals (District of Columbia Circuit)*
> (*Name:* United States Court of Appeals for the District of Columbia Circuit)

> United States. *District Court (North Carolina : Eastern District)*
> (*Name:* United States District Court for the Eastern District of North Carolina)

> United States. *District Court (Illinois : Northern District : Eastern Division)*
> (*Name:* United States District Court for the Eastern Division of the Northern District of Illinois)

> California. *Municipal Court (Los Angeles Judicial District)*
> (*Name:* Municipal Court, Los Angeles Judicial District)

> California. *Superior Court (San Bernadino County)*
> (*Name:* Superior Court for the State of California in and for the County of San Bernadino)

14.23B. Ad hoc Military Courts

14.23B1. Enter an ad hoc military court (e.g., court-martial, court of inquiry) under the heading for the particular military service (see 14.24), followed by the name of the court. Add the surname of the defendant and the year of the trial.

> United States. *Army. Court of Inquiry (Hall : 1863)*

> Virginia. *Militia. Court-martial (Yancey : 1806)*

14.24. ARMED FORCES
14.24A. Armed Forces at the National Level
14.24A1. Enter a principal service of the armed forces of a national government under the heading for the government, followed by the name of the service. Omit the name (or abbreviation of the name) of the government in noun form unless the omission would result in objectionable distortion.

> Canada. *Canadian Armed Forces*
>
> Great Britain. *Royal Navy*
>
> United States. *Marine Corps*
>
> Great Britain. *Royal Marines*

Enter a component branch, command district, or military unit, large or small, as a direct subheading of the heading for the principal service of which it is a part.

> Great Britain. *Army. Royal Gloucestershire Hussars*
>
> Great Britain. *Royal Air Force. Central Interpretation Unit*
>
> Great Britain. Royal Navy. Sea Cadet Corps
>
> United States. *Army. General Staff*
>
> United States. *Army. Corps of Engineers*
>
> United States. *Army. District of Mindanao*

If the component branch is identified by a number, follow the style of numbering found in the name (spelled out, roman numerals, or Arabic numerals) and place the numbering after the name.

> Great Britain. *Army. Infantry Regiment, 57th*
>
> United States. *Army. Infantry Division, 27th*
>
> United States. *Navy. Fleet, 6th*
>
> United States. *Army. Army, First*
>
> United States. *Army. Corps, IV*
>
> United States. *Navy. Torpedo Squadron 8*
>
> Confederate States of America. *Army. Tennessee Regiment, 1st*
>
> France. *Armée. Régiment de dragons, 15ᵉ*
>
> Germany. *Heer. Panzerdivision, 11*

If the name of such a component branch begins with the name, or an indication of the name, of the principal service, enter it as a direct subheading of the heading for the government.

> United States. *Army Map Service*
>
> United States. *Naval Air Transport Service*

If the name of such a component branch contains, but does not begin with, the name or an indication of the name of the principal service, enter it as a direct subheading of the heading for the service and omit the name or indication of the name unless objectionable distortion would result.

> Canada. *Canadian Army. Royal Canadian Army Medical Corps*

14.24B. Armed Forces below the National Level

14.24B1. Enter an armed force of a government below the national level under the heading for the government, followed by the name of the force.

> New York (*State*). *Militia*
>
> New York (*State*). *National Guard*

14.24B2. Enter a component branch of an armed force of a government below the national level as a subheading of the heading for the force as instructed in 14.24A.

> New York (*State*). *Militia. Regiment of Artillery, 9th*
>   (*Name*: 9th Regiment of Artillery, N.Y.S.M.)
>
> New York (*State*). *National Guard. Coast Defense Command, 9th*

14.24B3. Enter a component branch of a force below the national level that has been absorbed into the national military forces as a component branch of the national force (see 14.24A).

> United States. *Army. New York Volunteers, 83rd*
>
> United States. *Army. Regiment Infantry, New York Volunteers, 9th*

14.25. EMBASSIES, CONSULATES, ETC.

14.25A. Enter an embassy, consulate, legation, or other continuing office representing one country in another under the heading for the country represented, followed by the name of the embassy, etc. Give the subheading in the language (see 14.3A) of the country represented and omit from it the name of the country.

If the heading is for an embassy or legation, add the name of the country to which it is accredited.

```
Germany. Gesandschaft (Switzerland)

Great Britain. Embassy (U.S.)

United States. Legation (Bulgaria)

Canada. Embassy (Belgium)
```

If the heading is for a consulate or other local office, add the name of the city in which it is located.

```
France. Consulat (Buenos Aires, Argentina)

Great Britain. Consulate (Cairo, Egypt)
```

14.26. DELEGATIONS TO INTERNATIONAL AND INTERGOVERNMENTAL BODIES
14.26A. Enter a delegation, commission, or other group representing a country in an international or intergovernmental body, conference, undertaking, etc., under the heading for the country represented, followed by the name of the delegation or group. Give the subheading in the language (see 14.3A) of the country represented. Omit from the subheading the name or abbreviation of the name of the government in noun form unless such an omission would result in objectionable distortion. If the name of the delegation or group is uncertain, give "Delegation [Mission, etc.] to ..."(or equivalent terms in the language of the country represented). If considered necessary to distinguish the delegation or group from others of the same name, add the name, in the form and language used for it as a heading, of the international or intergovernmental body, conference, undertaking, etc., to which the delegation or group is accredited. Make explanatory references as necessary from the heading for the international body, etc., followed by an appropriate subheading.

```
United States. Delegation (International Conference on
    Maritime Law (3rd : 1909 : Brussels, Belgium))

United States. Mission (United Nations)
```
  Explanatory reference:
```
United Nations. Missions
   Delegations, missions, etc., from member nations to the
United Nations and to its subordinate units are entered
under the name of the nation followed by the name of the
delegation, mission, etc.; e.g.,
United States. Mission (United Nations)
United States. Delegation (United Nations. General
   Assembly)
```
  Make the same explanatory reference under United Nations. *Delegations, and under*
      United Nations. *General Assembly.* Delegations, *and under other appropriate*
      headings

If it is uncertain that a delegation represents the government of a country, enter it under its own name.

14.27. RELIGIOUS BODIES AND OFFICIALS

14.27A. Councils, etc., of a Single Religious Body

14.27A1. Enter a council, etc., of the clergy or membership (international, national, regional, provincial, state, or local) of a single religious body under the heading for the religious body, followed by the name of the council, etc. When appropriate, make additions to the heading as instructed in 14.7B.

> Catholic Church. *Antilles Episcopal Conference*
>
> Society of Friends. *Philadelphia Yearly Meeting*
>
> United Methodist Church (U.S.). *Northern Illinois Conference*

14.27A2. If the name of a council, etc., of the Catholic Church is given in more than one language, use (in this order of preference) the English, Latin, French, German, or Spanish name and make appropriate references.

> Catholic Church. *Canadian Conference of Catholic Bishops*
>
> Catholic Church. *Plenary Council of Baltimore (2nd : 1866)*
>
> Catholic Church. *Concilium Plenarium Americae Latinae (1899 : Rome, Italy)*

14.27A3. If a council, etc., is subordinate to a particular district of the religious body, enter it under the heading for that district (see 14.27C2–14.27C3), followed by the name of the council, etc. If the name appears in more than one language, use the name in the vernacular of the district.

> Catholic Church. *Province of Baltimore. Provincial Council (10th : 1869)*
>
> Catholic Church. *Diocese of Grand Falls. Council for the Family*

14.27B. Religious Officials

14.27B1. Enter a religious official (e.g., bishop, abbot, rabbi, moderator, mullah, patriarch) acting in an official capacity under the heading for the religious jurisdiction (e.g., diocese, order, rabbinate, synod, denomination, see 14.27C2–14.27C3), followed by the title of the official in English (unless there is no equivalent English term). Add the inclusive years of incumbency and the name of the person in a brief form and in the language of the heading for that person.

> Catholic Church. *Archdiocese of Halifax. Archbishop (1892-1906 : O'Brien)*

```
Franciscans. Minister General (1947-1951 : Perantoni)

Catholic Church. Diocese of Winchester. Bishop
   (1367-1404 : William, of Wykeham)
```

If the heading applies to more than one incumbent, do not add the dates and names.

```
Church of England. Diocese of Winchester. Bishop
```

If a heading is established for the incumbent as a person in addition to the heading as a religious official, make an explanatory reference under the heading for the official.

14.27B2. Popes. Enter a pope acting in an official capacity under "Catholic Church," followed by "Pope." Add the year or inclusive years of the reign and the pontifical name in its catalog- entry form.

```
Catholic Church. Pope (1878-1903 : Leo XIII)

Catholic Church. Pope (1978 : John Paul I)
```

If the heading applies to more than one pope, do not add the dates and names.

```
Catholic Church. Pope
```

If a heading is established for a pope as a person in addition to the heading as a religious official, make an explanatory reference under the heading for the official.

14.27C. Subordinate Bodies
14.27C1. General Rule. Except as provided in 14.27C2–14.27C4, enter subordinate religious bodies according to the instructions in 14.12–14.13. For religious orders and societies, see 14.3D.

14.27C2. Provinces, Dioceses, Synods, etc. Enter a province, diocese, synod, or other subordinate unit of a religious body having jurisdiction over a geographic area under the heading for the religious body, followed by the name of the province, etc.

```
Church of England. Diocese of Ely

Evangelical and Reformed Church. Reading Synod

Evangelische Kirche der Altpreussischen Union.
   Kirchenprovinz Sachsen

Church of England. Archdeaconry of Surrey

United Church of Canada. Manitou Conference

United Methodist Church (U.S.). Northern Illinois
   Conference
```

```
        Protestant Episcopal Church in the U.S.A. Diocese of
          Southern Virginia

        Anglican Church of Canada. Diocesan Synod of
          Fredericton

        Church of England. Woking Deanery
```

14.27C3. Catholic Dioceses, etc. Use an English form of name for a patriarchate, diocese, province, etc., of the Catholic Church.

```
        Catholic Church. Diocese of Ely

        Catholic Church. Patriarchate of Alexandria of the
          Copts

        Catholic Church. Province of Québec

        Catholic Church. Ukrainian Catholic Archeparchy of
          Philadelphia
```

Do not apply this rule to an ecclesiastical principality (often called *Bistum*) of the Holy Roman Empire bearing the same name as a Catholic diocese and ruled by the same bishop.

```
        Catholic Church. Diocese of Fulda
   but  Fulda (Ecclesiastical principality)
```

14.27C4. Central Administrative Organs of the Catholic Church (Roman Curia). Enter a congregation, tribunal, or other central administrative organ (i.e., one that is part of the Roman Curia) of the Catholic Church under "Catholic Church," followed by the Latin form of the name of the congregation, etc. Omit any form of the word *sacer* when it is the first word of the name and make an explanatory reference from the form of the name beginning with it.

```
        Catholic Church. Congregatio Sacrorum Rituum

        Catholic Church. Rota Romana
```

14.27D. Papal Diplomatic Missions, etc.
14.27D1. Enter a diplomatic mission from the pope to a secular power under "Catholic Church," followed by "Apostolic Nunciature" or "Apostolic Internunciature," as appropriate. Add the heading for the government to which the mission is accredited.

```
        Catholic Church. Apostolic Internnunciature (India)

        Catholic Church. Apostolic Nunciature (Flanders)
```

Enter a nondiplomatic apostolic delegation under "Catholic Church" followed by "Apostolic Delegation." Add the name of the country or other jurisdiction in which the delegation functions.

> Catholic Church. *Apostolic Delegation (Canada)*

Enter an emissary of the pope acting in an official capacity (other than a nuncio, internuncio, or apostolic delegate) under "Catholic Church," followed by the title of the emissary (in English if there is an equivalent term; otherwise in Latin). Add the name of the country or region in which the emissary functions.

> Catholic Church. *Legate (Colombia)*

If the country or region cannot be ascertained, add the name of the emissary in brief form.

> Catholic Church. *Commissary Apostolic (Robertus*
>   *Castellensis)*

Appendices

GLOSSARY

This glossary contains definitions of most of the archival terms used in these rules with the exception of specialized terms that are defined in footnotes within a particular chapter. The terms have been defined only within the context of the rules. For definitions of other terms, consult standard glossaries or dictionaries.[79] A "see" reference refers from an unused to a used term. A "see also" reference refers to a related term defined in the glossary.

Where terms are discussed in commentaries, their "definitions" may not be identical to the glossary definitions because they may have been adjusted slightly for explanatory purposes and to fit in with the flow of the sentence. The definitions in the glossary are to be taken as definitive.

Access point A name, term, keyword, phrase, or code that may be used to search, identify, and locate an archival description. See also **Heading.**

Access tools A generic term encompassing all manner of descriptions of archival materials, including finding aids, catalog records, calendars, guides, etc.

Accrual Materials added to an existing body of records or papers; an accretion.

---

[79] The sources consulted in compiling this glossary include:

Anglo-American Cataloguing Rules, prepared under the direction of the Joint Steering Committee for Revision of AACR, 2nd ed., 2002 revision (Chicago: American Library Association; Ottawa: Canadian Library Association; London: Chartered Institute of Library and Information Professionals, 2002)

Lewis J. Bellardo and Lynn Lady Bellardo, comps, *A Glossary for Archivists, Manuscript Curators, and Records Managers*, SAA Archival Fundamentals Series (Chicago: Society of American Archivists, 1992)

The IASA Cataloguing Rules: A Manual for the Description of Sound Recordings and Related Audiovisual Media. (Stockholm: International Association of Sound and Audiovisual Archives, 1999)

ISAAR(CPF): International Standard Archival Authority Record (Corporate Bodies, Persons, and Families), 1st ed. (Ottawa: International Council on Archives, 1996) and draft 2nd ed. (2003)

ISAD(G) : General International Standard Archival Description, 1st ed. (Ottawa: International Council on Archives, 1994) and 2nd ed. (Ottawa: International Council on Archives, (2000)

A Glossary of Archival and Records Terminology, 2004-03-23 draft, used with the kind permission of Richard Pearce-Moses

Keeping Archives, edited by Ann Pederson (Sydney: Australian Society of Archivists, 1993)

Margaret Procter and Michael Cook, eds., *Manual of Archival Description*, 3rd ed. (London: Gower, 2000)

Rules for Archival Description (Ottawa: Bureau of Canadian Archivists, 1996).

Accumulation The naturally occurring process by which archives are created in the conduct of affairs of any kind.

Aggregation 1. Records that accumulated in interrelated groups according to the way that the records creator carried out its activities, or the way that the records were arranged in inter-related groups by the archivist. 2. A fonds, series, or file.

Architectural drawing A sketch, diagram, plan, or schematic used to design, construct, and document buildings and other structures.

Archival series See **Series**.

Arrangement 1. The process of organizing materials with respect to their provenance and original order, to protect their context and to achieve physical and intellectual control over the materials. 2. The organization and sequence of items within a collection.

Artificial collection See **Collection**.

Authority file An organized set of authority records.

Authority record An entry in an authority file that contains the preferred form of a name or subject heading, and, for corporate bodies and persons, relevant administrative history or biographical information related to the entity named in the heading.

Authorized heading See **Authorized name**.

Authorized name A standardized form of a name used in the description of archival materials or as an entry in an authority file.

Bulk dates The dates of the documents that constitute the largest part of the unit being described. See also **Inclusive dates, Predominant dates**.

Calendar A chronological listing of documents in a collection, which may be comprehensive or selective, and which may include details about the writer, recipient, date, place, summary of content, type of document, and page or leaf count. Though common through the first half of the 20th century, the production of calendars by archives has become increasingly rare.

Cartographic materials Materials that use images, numbers, or relief that correlate to physical or cultural features of the earth or celestial body (or portion thereof), such as maps, charts, plans, and related materials including globes, atlases, topographic and hydrographic charts, cartograms, relief models, and aerial photographs.

Catalog A collection of systematically arranged descriptions of materials. Catalogs may be in a variety of formats, including bound volumes, cards, microform, or online databases.

Collection 1. A group of materials with some unifying characteristic. 2. Materials assembled by a person, organization, or repository from a variety of sources. 3. The holdings of a repository.

Collector The person, family, or corporate body that assembled a collection.

Container A housing for an item, a group of items, or part of an item that is physically separable from the material being housed.

Content dates The dates of the intellectual content or subject of the unit being described.

Corporate body An organization or association of persons that is identified by a particular name and that acts, or may act, as an entity. Typical examples of corporate bodies are societies, institutions, business firms, nonprofit enterprises, governments, government agencies, religious bodies, places of worship, and conferences.

Creating entity See **Creator**.

Creator A person, family, or corporate body that created, assembled, accumulated, and/or maintained and used records in the conduct of personal or corporate activity. A creator can also be responsible for the intellectual content of a single item.

Custodian The corporate body, family, or person (other than the creator) responsible for the care of documents based on their ownership or physical possession.

Date(s) of broadcast Date(s) on which sound recordings or moving image materials were broadcast on radio, television, or the Internet.

Date(s) of creation The date(s) on which the documents being described were originally created or the date(s) that an event or image was captured in some material form.

Date(s) of publication, distribution, etc. The date(s) of the various activities involved in making commercially issued, mass-produced items available to the public in some way, including publishing, distributing, releasing, and issuing of items.

Date(s) of record-keeping activity The dates during which the unit being described was created, accumulated, and maintained as an aggregation of records by the creator of the records.

Date(s) of reproduction The date(s) that the unit being described was copied to another support.

Description The creation of an accurate representation of a unit of archival material by the process of capturing, collating, analyzing, and organizing information that serves to identify archival material and explain the context and records system(s) that produced it.

Descriptive record A representation of a unit being described.

Descriptive unit A document or aggregation of documents in any physical form, treated as an entity and forming the basis of a single description.

Discrete item An individual item that is not part of a larger body of materials.

Document Recorded information irrespective of medium. See also **Record**.

Electronic records Data or information that has been captured or encoded and fixed for storage and manipulation in a computer system and that requires the use of the system to render it intelligible by a person.

Entity The corporate body, person, or family associated with the creation, assembly, accumulation, maintenance, and/or use of archival materials.

File 1. An organized unit of documents grouped together either for current use by the creator or in the process of archival arrangement because they relate to the same subject, activity, or transaction. 2. A level of description.

Finding aid A representation of, or a means of access to, archival materials made or received by a repository in the course of establishing administrative or intellectual control over the archival materials.

Fonds 1. The whole of the documents, regardless of form or medium, automatically and organically created and/or accumulated and used by a particular person, family, or corporate body in the course of that creator's activities and functions. 2. In some descriptive systems, a level of description.

Form 1. The physical (e.g., watercolor, drawing) or intellectual (e.g., diary, journal, daybook, minute book) characteristics of a document. 2. A printed document with clearly defined areas left blank that are to be completed later. 3. The materials and structure of an item; format. 4. The overall appearance, configuration, or shape, independent of its intellectual content. 5. A style or convention for expressing ideas in a literary work or document; documentary form, including extrinsic and intrinsic elements.

Formal title A title that appears prominently on or in the material being described.

Graphic materials Documents in the form of pictures, photographs, drawings, watercolors, prints, and other forms of two-dimensional pictorial representations intended to be viewed by reflected or transmitted light.

Guide A broad description of the holdings of one or more archives, typically at the collection level. A guide covering an individual or several repositories' holdings is often called a repository guide. A guide that describes collections relating to a specific subject is often called a subject guide.

Heading A standardized name, word, or phrase that serves as an access point. See also **Access point.**

Immediate source of acquisition The person or organization from whom the unit being described was acquired through donation, purchase, transfer, etc.

Inclusive dates The earliest and latest dates of the materials being described, or of the activity in question as they relate to the materials being described. See also **Bulk dates, Predominant dates**.

Inventory A finding aid that includes contextual information as well as a description of the materials, and frequently a listing of box or folder contents.

Item 1. An object that can be distinguished from a group and that is complete in itself. 2. The lowest level of description.

Medium The material support of a record's content and form.

Moving images Visual images, with or without sound, recorded on any medium, that when viewed, may present the illusion of motion.

Multilevel description 1. The preparation of descriptions that are related to one another in a part-to-whole relationship and that need complete identification of both the parts and the comprehensive whole in multiple descriptive records. 2. A finding aid or other access tool that consists of separate, interrelated descriptions of the whole and its parts, reflecting the hierarchy of the materials being described.

Nominal access point An access point consisting of the name of a person, family, or corporate body.

Original 1. The initial manifestation of something. 2. A prototype from which copies are made.

Original Order The principle that the order of the records that was established by the creator should be retained whenever possible to preserve existing relationships between the documents and the evidential value inherent in their order. See also **Respect des Fonds**.

Parallel name An authorized form of the name in another language for the same entity.

Physical carrier A physical medium in which data, sound, images, etc. are stored, e.g., microfilm or microfiche, computer disks.

Physical characteristics The results of the techniques and physical processes by which an object came into being, including such aspects as color, polarity, base or support, medium, production process, layout, identifying marks, and any other details relating to the physical nature of the material.

Predominant dates The dates of the documents that constitute the largest part of the unit being described. See also **Bulk dates**, **Inclusive dates**.

Provenance The relationships between records and the organizations or individuals that created, assembled, accumulated, and/or maintained and used them in the conduct of personal or corporate activity. See also **Respect des Fonds**.

Pseudonym A name assumed by a personal author to conceal or obscure his or her identity.

Publication 1. A work that expresses some thought in language, signs, or symbols and that is reproduced for distribution. 2. The act of publishing such a work.

Record 1. A document in any form or medium, created or received and maintained by an organization or person in the transaction of business or the conduct of affairs. 2. A written or printed work of a legal or official nature that may be used as evidence or proof; a document. 3. Data or information that has been fixed on some medium; that has content, context, and structure; and that is used as an extension of human memory or to demonstrate accountability. 4. Data or information in a fixed form that is created or received in the course of individual or institutional activity and set aside (preserved) as evidence of that activity for future reference. 5. An entry describing a work in a catalog; a catalog record.

Reference code A unique combination of letters and numbers used to identify an archival entity in order to facilitate storage and retrieval.

Related name The name(s) of other corporate bodies, persons, or families associated in some way with a name in an archival description or in an archival authority record.

Reproduction 1. The process of making copies of all or part of an item(s) in the unit being described. 2. A copy of all or part of an item in the unit being described.

Respect des Fonds The principle that the records created, assembled, accumulated, and/or maintained and used by an organization or individual must be kept together in their original order if it exists or has been maintained, and not be mixed or combined with the records of another individual or corporate body. See also **Original Order**, **Provenance**.

Series 1. Documents arranged in accordance with a filing system or maintained as a unit because they result from the same accumulation or filing process, the same function, or the same activity; have a particular form or subject, or because of some other relationship arising out of their creation, receipt, or use. 2. A level of description.

Sound recordings Sounds that, when fixed on a medium, can be reproduced.

Supplied title A title provided by the archivist when there is no formal title for the unit being described, or where the formal title is misleading or inadequate.

Technical drawing A graphic using lines and symbols that follows precise conventions of scale and projection, typically used in architecture, construction, engineering, or mapping.

Textual materials Documents in which information is represented as text (handwritten, typed, printed, or displayed words or numbers) readable by the eye, with or without the mediation of a machine.

Title A word, phrase, character, or group of characters that names the unit being described.

Title proper The chief name of the unit being described, whether formal or supplied, including any alternate title but excluding parallel titles and other title information appearing in conjunction with a title proper.

Unit being described See **Descriptive unit.**

Variant name A name or form of name other than that established as the authorized form of name.

APPENDIX B

Companion Standards

As indicated in the Overview, *DACS* includes basic rules for the types of holdings found in many archives, but they do not include all the rules needed to describe every possible type of document. Where further guidance is required, the following standards provide more detailed rules for describing published materials and particular types of non-textual materials. Listed here are the most recent editions at the time of writing; however, where a standard is revised periodically, users are encouraged to use the most recent edition.

Content Standards

Published Materials

Anglo-American Cataloging Rules, 2nd edition, 2002 revision. Chicago: American Library Association; Ottawa: Canadian Library Association; London: Chartered Institute of Library and Information Professionals, 2002.

Graphic Materials

Parker, Elisabeth Betz. *Graphic materials: rules for describing original items and historical collections.* Washington, D.C.: Library of Congress, 1982.

Cartographic Materials

Cartographic Materials: A Manual of Interpretation for AACR2. Edited by Hugo Stibbe, Vivien Cartmell, and Velma Parker. Chicago: American Library Association, Ottawa: Canadian Library Association, London: The Library Association, 1982.

Geomatic data sets: cataloguing rules. Edited by Velma Parker. Ottawa: Canadian General Standards Board, 1992.

Architectural Materials

Vicki Porter and Robin Thornes. *A Guide to the Description of Architectural Drawings.* New York: Published on behalf of the Getty Art History Information Program [by] G.K. Hall, c1994.

Moving Image Materials

The FIAF Cataloguing Rules for Film Archives. Munich: K.G. Saur, 1991.

Archival Moving Image Materials: A Cataloging Manual. 2nd ed. The AMIM Revision Committee, Motion Picture, Broadcasting, and Recorded Sound Division. Washington, D.C.: Library of Congress, Cataloging Distribution Service, 2000.

The IASA Cataloguing Rules: A Manual for the Description of Sound Recordings and Related Audiovisual Media. Stockholm: International Association of Sound and Audiovisual Archives, 1999, or on-line at <http://www.iasa-web.org/icat/icat001.htm>.

Sound Recordings

The IASA Cataloguing Rules: A Manual for the Description of Sound Recordings and Related Audiovisual Media. Stockholm: International Association of Sound and Audiovisual Archives, 1999, or on-line at <http://www.iasa-web.org/icat/icat001.htm>.

Marion Matters, comp. *Oral History Cataloging Manual.* Chicago: Society of American Archivists, 1995.

Objects

Cataloging Cultural Objects: A Guide to Describing Cultural Works and Their Images. Visual Resources Association, draft available online at <http://www.vraweb.org/CCOweb/index.html> (accessed June 2004)

Thesauri

Art & Architecture Thesaurus, Version 3.0. Los Angeles: The J. Paul Getty Trust, 2000. Available online at: <http://www.getty.edu/research/conducting_research/vocabularies/aat/> (accessed April 2004)

Categories for the Description of Works of Art. Version 2.0. Los Angeles: The J. Paul Getty Trust and College Art Association, Inc., 2000. Available online at: <http://www.getty.edu/research/conducting_research/standards/cdwa/> (accessed April 2004)

Dictionary of Occupational Titles, 4th ed., rev. Washington, DC: U.S. Department of Labor, Employment and Training Administration, U.S. Employment Service, 1991. Available online at: <http://www.wave.net/upg/immigration/dot_index.html> (accessed April 2004)

Library of Congress Authorities. Washington, DC: The Library of Congress. Available online at: <http://authorities.loc.gov/>. This resource covers subjects, names (both personal and corporate), and titles. (accessed April 2004)

Medical Subject Headings. Bethesda, MD: National Library of Medicine, 2003. Available online at: <http://www.nlm.nih.gov/mesh/meshhome.html> (accessed April 2004)

The Moving Image Genre-Form Guide. Compiled by Brian Taves, Judi Hoffman, and Karen Lund. Coordinated by Motion Picture, Broadcasting, and Recorded Sound Division, Library of Congress, 1998. Available online at: <http://www.loc.gov/rr/mopic/migintro.html> (accessed April 2004)

Revised Nomenclature for Museum Cataloging: A Revised and Expanded Version of Robert G. Chenhall's System for Classifying Man-made Objects. Edited by James R. Blackaby and Patricia Greeno. Nashville, Tenn.: AASLH Press, 1989.

Thesaurus for Graphic Materials I: Subject Terms (TGM I). Compiled by the Prints and Photographs Division, Library of Congress. Washington, D.C.: Cataloging Distribution Service, Library of Congress, 1995. Available online at: <http://www.loc.gov/rr/print/tgm1/> (accessed April 2004)

Thesaurus for Graphic Materials II: Genre and Physical Characteristics Terms (TGM II). Compiled by the Prints and Photographs Division, Library of Congress. Washington, D.C.: Cataloging Distribution Service, Library of Congress, 1995. Available online at: <http://www.loc.gov/rr/print/tgm2/> (accessed April 2004)

Getty Thesaurus of Geographic Names, Version 3.0. Los Angeles: The J. Paul Getty Trust, 2000. Available online at : <http://www.getty.edu/research/conducting_research/vocabularies/tgn/> (accessed April 2004)

Unesco Thesaurus: A Structured List of Descriptors for Indexing and Retrieving Literature in the Fields of Education, Science, Social and Human Science, Culture, Communication and Information. Paris: Unesco Publishing, 1995. Available online at: <http://www.ulcc.ac.uk/unesco/> (accessed April 2004)

Union List of Artists' Names, Version 3.0. Los Angeles: The J. Paul Getty Trust, 2000. Available online at : <http://www.getty.edu/research/conducting_research/vocabularies/ulan/> (accessed April 2004)

USMARC Code List for Countries. Prepared by Network Development and MARC Standards Office. Washington: Library of Congress Cataloging Distribution Service, 2003. Available online at: <http://www.loc.gov/marc/countries/cou_home.html> (accessed April 2004)

USMARC Code List for Languages. Prepared by Network Development and MARC Standards Office. Washington: Library of Congress Cataloging Distribution Service, 2003. Available online at: <http://www.loc.gov/marc/languages/langhome.html> (accessed April 2004)

USMARC Code List for Organizations. Prepared by Network Development and MARC Standards Office. Washington: Library of Congress Cataloging Distribution Service, 2004. Available online at: <http://www.loc.gov/marc/organizations/orgshome.html> (accessed April 2004)

Data Structure Standards

Encoded Archival Description Tag Library, Version 2002. Prepared and Maintained by the Encoded Archival Description Working Group of the Society of American Archivists and the Network Development and MARC Standards Office of the Library of Congress. Chicago, IL: Society of American Archivists, 2002. Available online at: <http://www.loc.gov/ead/tglib/index.html> (accessed April 2004)

MARC 21 Format for Bibliographic Data: Including Guidelines for Content Designation. Prepared by the Network Development and MARC Standards Office, Library of Congress, in cooperation with Standards and Support, National Library of Canada. Washington, DC: Library of Congress, Cataloging Distribution Service, 1999. *MARC 21 Concise Format for Bibliographica Data* available online at: <http://www.loc.gov/marc/bibliographic/ecbdhome.html> (accessed April 2004)

APPENDIX C

CROSSWALKS

The following tables present the relationships between the rules in *DACS* and the corresponding rules in its immediate antecedent (*APPM*), related structure standards (EAD and MARC), and international standards (*ISAD(G)* and *ISAAR(CPF)*).

Table C1: *APPM* to *DACS*
Table C2: *ISAD(G)* to *DACS*
Table C3: *ISAAR(CPF)* to *DACS*
Table C4: *DACS* to *APPM*
Table C5: *DACS* to EAD and MARC
Table C6: *DACS* to *ISAD(G)*
Table C7: *DACS* to *ISAAR(CPF)*

Abbreviations used:

DACS: *Describing Archives: A Content Standard* (Society of American Archivists, 2004)
APPM: *Archives, Personal Papers, and Manuscripts*, 2nd edition (Society of American Archivists, 1989)
ISAD(G): General International Standard Archival Description, 2nd edition, 1999 (http://www.ica.org)
ISAAR(CPF): International Standard Archival Authority Record, Final English Language Version of the second edition of as circulated by the secretary of the Committee on Descriptive Standards, 2004 (http://www.ica.org)
MARC 21: MARC 21 (machine-readable cataloguing), 2002 concise edition (http://www.loc.gov/marc)
EAD: Encoded Archival Description, version 2002 (http://www.loc.gov/ead)

Table C1: *APPM* to *DACS*

APPM	DACS
1.1 Title and Statement of Responsibility Area	
1.1B Title proper	2.3 Title
1.1B5 Date	2.4 Date
1.1C General material designation	
1.1D Parallel titles	
1.1E Other title information	
1.1F Statements of responsibility	
1.1G Items without a collective title	
1.2 Edition Area	
1.5 Physical Description Area	2.5 Extent
1.5B Extent	2.5.1-2.5.9 Extent
1.5C Other physical details	
1.5D Dimensions	
1.7 Note Area	
1.7B1 Biographical/Historical	2.7, Chapter 10 Admin/Biographical history
1.7B2 Scope and content/Abstract	3.1 Scope and content
1.7B3 Linking entry complexity	
1.7B4 Additional physical form available	6.2.3 Existence/location of copies
1.7B5 Reproduction	6.1 Existence/location of originals
1.7B6 Location of originals/duplicates	6.1 Existence/location of originals / 6.2.5 Existence/location of copies
1.7B7 Organization and arrangement	3.2 System of arrangement
1.7B8 Language	4.5 Languages/scripts of the material
1.7B9 Provenance	5.1 Custodial history
1.7B10 Immediate source of acquisition	5.2 Immediate source of acquisition
1.7B11 Restrictions on access	4.1 Conditions governing access/ 4.2 Physical access/4.3 Technical access
1.7B12 Terms governing use and reproduction	4.4 Conditions governing reproduction and use
1.7B13 Cumulative index/Finding aids	4.6 Finding aids
1.7B14 Citation	
1.7B15 Preferred citation	
1.7B16 Publications	6.4 Publication note
1.7B17 General note	7 Notes

2 *Choice of access points*	Overview of Archival Description, Chapter 9 Identifying Creators
3 *Headings for Persons*	12 Form of Names for People and Families
4 *Geographic Names*	13 Form of Geographic Names
5 *Headings for Corporate Bodies*	14 Form of Names for Corporate Bodies
6 *Uniform Titles*	

Table C2: *ISAD(G)* to *DACS*

ISAD(G)	*DACS*
3.1 Identity Statement Area	
3.1.1 Reference code(s)	2.1 Reference code
3.1.2 Title	2.3 Title
3.1.3 Dates	2.4 Date
3.1.4 Level of description	1 Levels of Description
3.1.5 Extent and medium of the unit	2.5 Extent
3.2 Context Area	
3.2.1 Name of creator	2.6, Chapter 9 Identifying Creators
3.2.2 Administrative/ Biographical history	2.7, 10 Admin/Biographical history
3.2.3 Archival history	5.1 Custodial history
3.2.4 Immediate source of acquisition	5.2 Immediate source of acquisition
3.3 Context and Structure Area	
3.3.1 Scope and content	3.1 Scope and content
3.3.2 Appraisal, destruction and scheduling	5.3 Appraisal/destruction/scheduling information
3.3.3 Accruals	5.4 Accruals
3.3.4 System of arrangement	3.2 System of arrangement
3.4 Conditions of Access and Use Area	
3.4.1 Conditions governing access	4.1 Conditions governing access
3.4.2 Conditions governing reproduction	4.4 Conditions governing reproduction and use
3.4.3 Language/scripts of material	4.5 Language/script
3.4.4 Physical characteristics and technical requirements	4.2 Physical access/4.3 Technical access
3.4.5 Finding aids	4.6 Finding aids
3.5 Allied Materials Area	
3.5.1 Existence and location of originals	6.1 Existence/location of originals
3.5.2 Existence and location of copies	6.2 Existence/location of copies
3.5.3 Related units of description	6.3 Related archival materials
3.5.4 Publication note	6.4 Publication note
3.6 Notes Area	
3.6.1 Note	7 Notes
3.7 Description Control Area	
3.7.1 Archivist's note	8.1.5 Archivist and date
3.7.2 Rules or conventions	8.1.4 Rules or conventions
3.7.3 Date(s) of descriptions	8.1.5 Archivist and date

Table C3: *ISAAR(CPF)* to *DACS*

ISAAR(CPF)	*DACS*
5.1 Identity Area	
5.1.1 Type of entity	11.6 Type of entity
5.1.2 Authorized form of name	11.5 Standardized form of name
5.1.3 Parallel forms of name	11.7 Parallel forms of name
5.1.4 Standardized forms of name according to other rules	11.9 Standardized form of name according to other rules
5.1.5 Other forms of name	11.10 Other forms of names
5.1.6 Identifiers for corporate bodies	11.11 Identifiers for corporate names
5.2 Description Area	
5.2.1 Dates of existence	10.18, 10.27 Dates
5.2.2 History	10.14, 10.25 Biographical/Administrative history
5.2.3 Places	10.19, 10.28 Places
5.2.4 Legal status	10.29 Mandate
5.2.5 Functions, occupations and activities	10.21, 10.29 Occupation, life, activities, Functions
5.2.6 Mandates/Sources of authority	10.29 Mandate
5.2.7 Internal structures/Genealogy	10.23, 10.31 Family relationships, Administrative Structure
5.2.8 General context	10.14, 10.25 Biographical/Administrative history
5.3 Relationships Area	
5.3.1 Name/Identifiers of the related corporate bodies, persons or families	11.13 Names of related entities
5.3.2 Category of relationship	11.15 Nature of relationship
5.3.3 Description of relationship	11.14 Description of relationship
5.3.4 Dates of the relationship	11.16 Dates of relationship
5.4 Control Area	
5.4.1 Authority record identifier	11.19 Authority record identifier
5.4.2 Institution identifiers	11.18 Repository code
5.4.3 Rules and/or convention	11.20 Rules or conventions
5.4.4 Status	11.22 Status
5.4.5 Level of detail	11.23 Level of detail
5.4.6 Dates of creation and revision	11.24 Dates
5.4.7 Languages and scripts	11.25 Language or scripts
5.4.8 Sources	11.26 Sources
5.4.9 Maintenance notes	11.27 Maintenance information

6 Relating corporate bodies, persons and families to archival materials and other resources	
6.1 Identifies and titles of related resources	11.28 Identifiers and titles of related resources
6.2 Types of related resource	11.29 Types of related resources
6.3 Nature of relationships	11.30 Nature of relationships
6.4 Dates of related resources and/or relationships	11.31 Dates of related resources and/or relationships

Table C4: *DACS* to *APPM*

DACS	APPM
1 Levels of Description	
2 Identity Elements	
2.1 Reference code	
2.3 Title	1.1B Title proper
2.4 Date	1.1B5 Date
2.5 Extent	1.5 Physical description area
2.6 Name of creator(s)	2 Choice of access points
2.7 Admin/Biographical history	1.7B1 Biographical/Historical
3 Content and Structure Elements	
3.1 Scope and content	1.7B2 Scope and content/Abstract
3.2 System of arrangement	1.7B7 Organization and arrangement
4 Access Elements	
4.1 Conditions governing access	1.7B11 Restrictions on access
4.2 Physical access	1.7B11 Restrictions on access
4.3 Technical access	
4.4 Conditions governing reproduction and use	1.7B12 Terms governing use and reproduction
4.5 Languages/scripts of the material	1.7B8 Language
4.6 Finding aids	1.7B13 Cumulative index/Finding aids
5 Acquisition and Appraisal Elements	
5.1 Custodial history	1.7B9 Provenance
5.2 Immediate source of acquisition	1.7B10 Immediate source of acquisition
5.3 Appraisal/destruction/scheduling information	
5.4 Accruals	
6 Related Materials Elements	
6.1 Existence/location of originals	1.7B5 Reproduction
6.2 Existence/location of copies	1.7B4 Additional physical form available
6.3 Related archival materials	
6.4 Publication note	1.7B16 Publications
7 Notes	1.7B17 General note
8 Description control	
9 Identifying creators	2 Choice of access points
10 Admin/Biographical history	1.7B1 Biographical/Historical
11 Authority records	
12 Form of Names for People and Families	3 Headings for Persons
13 Form of Geographic Names	4 Geographic Names
14 Form of Names for Corporate Bodies	5 Headings for Corporate Bodies

Table C5: *DACS* to EAD and MARC

DACS	EAD	MARC
1. Level of description	<archdesc> and <c> LEVEL attribute	351$c
2. Identity Elements		
2.1.3 Local identifier	<unitid>	099
2.1.4 Repository identifier	<unitid> REPOSITORYCODE attribute	040$a
2.1.5 Country identifier	<unitid> COUNTRYCODE attribute	The MARC21 format does not contain a straightforward mapping for this *DACS* subelement value.
2.2 Name and Location of Repository	<repository>	852, 524 (if the preferred citation indicates both the name and location of the repository)
2.3 Title	<unittitle>	245$a
2.4 Date	<unitdate>	245$f ($g for bulk dates), 260$c if recording data about formal publication
2.5 Extent	<physdesc> and subelements <extent>, <dimensions>, <genreform>, <physfacet>	300$a and potentially other subfields
2.6 Name of creator(s)	<origination>	100, 110, or 111; 700, 710, or 711 for names in addition to that of the predominant creator
2.7 Admin/Biog history	<bioghist>	545
3. Content and Structure Elements		
3.1 Scope and content	<scopecontent>	520
3.2 System of arrangement	<arrangement>	351
4. Access Elements		
4.1 Conditions governing access	<accessrestrict>	506
4.2 Physical access	<accessrestrict>, <phystech>, <physloc>	340, 506
4.3 Technical access	<phystech>	340, 538

4.4 Conditions governing reproduction and use	\<userestrict\>	540
4.5 Languages/scripts of the material	\<langmaterial\>	546
4.6 Finding aids	\<otherfindaid\>	555
5. Acquisition and Appraisal Elements		
5.1 Custodial history	\<custodhist\>	561
5.2 Immediate source of acquisition	\<acqinfo\>	541
5.3 Appraisal/destruction/ scheduling information	\<appraisal\>	583
5.4 Accruals	\<accruals\>	584
6. Related Materials Elements		
6.1 Existence/location of originals	\<originalsloc\>	535
6.2 Existence/location of copies	\<altformavail\>	530
6.3 Related archival materials	\<relatedmaterial\> \<separatedmaterial\>	544
6.4 Publication note	\<bibliography\>\<p\> or \<bibliography\>\<bibref\>	581
7. Notes[80]	\<odd\>, \<note\>	500
8. Description control	\<processinfo\>	583
8.1.4 Rules or conventions	\<descrules\>	040$e
8.1.5 Archivist and date	\<processinfo\>\<p\>\<date\>	583
9. Identifying creators	See 2.6	
10. Admin/Biographical history	See 2.7	

---

[80] Notes should only be encoded using the more generic \<odd\> and \<note\> elements (EAD) or 500 field (MARC21) when they do not correspond to a more specific EAD element or MARC21 field.

Table C6: *DACS* to *ISAD(G)*

DACS	ISAD(G)
1 Levels of Description	3.1.4 Level of description
2 Identity Elements	
2.1 Reference code	3.1.1 Reference code(s)
2.3 Title	3.1.2 Title
2.4 Date	3.1.3 Dates
2.5 Extent	3.1.5 Extent and medium of the unit
2.6 Name of creator(s)	3.2.1 Name of creator
2.7 Administrative/Biographical history	3.2.2 Administrative/Biographical history
3 Content and Structure Elements	
3.1 Scope and content	3.3.1 Scope and content
3.2 System of arrangement	3.3.4 System of arrangement
4 Access Elements	
4.1 Conditions governing access	3.4.1 Conditions governing access
4.2 Physical access	3.4.4 Physical characteristics and technical requirements
4.3 Technical access	3.4.4 Physical char. and technical req.
4.4 Conditions governing reproduction and use	3.4.2 Conditions governing reproduction
4.5 Languages/scripts of the material	3.4.3 Language/scripts of material
4.6 Finding aids	3.4.5 Finding aids
5 Acquisition and Appraisal Elements	
5.1 Custodial history	3.2.3 Archival history
5.2 Immediate source of acquisition	3.2.4 Immediate source of acquisition
5.3 Appraisal/destruction/scheduling	3.3.2 Appraisal, destruction, scheduling
5.4 Accruals	3.3.3 Accruals
6 Related Materials Elements	
6.1 Existence/location of originals	3.5.1 Existence and location of originals
6.2 Existence/location of copies	3.5.2 Existence and location of copies
6.3 Related archival materials	3.5.3 Related units of description
6.4 Publication note	3.5.4 Publication note
7 Notes	3.6.1 Note
8 Description control	3.7.1 Archivist's note
8.1.4 Rules or conventions	3.7.2 Rules or conventions
8.1.5 Archivist and date	3.7.3 Date(s) of descriptions
9 Identifying creators	3.2.1 Name of creator
10 Admin/Biographical history	3.2.2 Administrative/Biographical history
11 Authority control	
12-14 Form of Names	

Table C7: DACS to *ISAAR(CPF)*

DACS	ISAAR(CPF)
Chapter 10 Administrative/Biographical History	
10.14 Biographical History	5.2.2 History
10.16 Names	5.1.2 Authorized form(s) of name
10.17 Family information	5.2.7 Internal structure/Genealogy
10.18 Dates	5.2.1 Dates of existence
10.19 Place of residence	5.2.3 Places
10.20 Education	5.2.2 History
10.21 Occupation, life, activities	5.2.5 Functions, occupations, and activities
10.22 Other relationships	5.2.8 General context
10.23 Family relationships	5.2.7 Internal structure/Genealogy
10.24 Other significant information	5.2.9 Other significant information
10.25 Administrative history	5.2.2 History
10.27 Dates of founding and/or dissolution	5.2.1 Dates of existence
10.28 Geographical areas	5.2.3 Places
10.29 Mandate	5.2.6 Mandates/Sources of authority
10.30 Functions	5.2.5 Functions, occupations, and activities
10.31 Administrative structure	5.2.7 Internal structure/Genealogy
10.32 Predecessor and successor bodies	5.2.2 History
10.33 Amalgamations and mergers	5.2.2 History
10.34 Name changes	5.2.2 History
10.35 Names of officers	5.2.2 History
10.36 Other significant information	5.2.8 General context
Chapter 11 Authority records	
11.5 Authorized form	5.1.2 Authorized form(s) of name
11.6 Type of entity	5.1.1 Type of entity
11.7 Parallel forms of the name	5.1.3 Parallel forms of name
11.9 Standardized form of the name according to other rules	5.1.4 Standardized forms of name according to other rules
11.10 Other forms of name	5.1.5 Other forms of name
11.11 Identifiers for corporate bodies	5.1.6 Identifiers for corporate bodies
11.12 Description of the person, family or corporate body	5.2.2 History
11.13 Related entities	5.3.1 Names/identifiers of related corporate bodies, persons or families
11.14 Description of the relationship	5.3.3 Description of the relationship
11.15 Nature of the relationship	5.3.2 Category of the relationship
11.16 Dates	5.3.4 Dates of the relationship

11.17 Explanation of the relationship	5.3.3 Description of the relationship
11.18 Repository codes	5.4.2 Institution identifiers
11.19 Authority record identifier	5.4.1 Authority record identifier
11.20, 11.21 Rules or conventions	5.4.3 Rules and/or conventions
11.22 Status	5.4.4 Status
11.23 Level of detail	5.4.5 Level of detail
11.24 Date(s) of authority record creation	5.4.6 Dates of creation, revision, or deletion
11.25 Languages or scripts	5.4.7 Languages and scripts
11.26 Sources	5.4.8 Sources
11.27 Maintenance information	5.4.9 Maintenance notes
11.28 Identifiers and titles of related resources	6.1 Identifiers and titles of related resources
11.29 Types of resource resources	6.2 Types of related resources
11.30 Nature of relationships	6.3 Nature of relationships
11.31 Dates of related resources and/or relationships	6.4 Dates of related resources and/or relationships

APPENDIX D

Full EAD and MARC 21 Examples

The following examples represent short finding aids, all multilevel descriptions and fully encoded using *Encoded Archival Description, Version 2002* (EAD). Following the finding aids are MARC 21 records for the same materials. Examples are provided for:

- Personal papers—Mildred Davenport Dance Programs and Dance School Materials.
- Family papers—Bacot Family Papers.
- Organizational records—Swine Influenza Immunization Program Records.
- Collection—Herndon-Weik Collection of Lincolniana.

The presentation of these examples is intended only to assist in understanding how descriptive data, created according to *DACS* rules, can be encoded in EAD for online output. The examples are not meant to be prescriptive and should not be used as a reference for encoding. Archivists seeking more information on encoding should consult the *Encoded Archival Description Tag Library, Version 2002* (see Appendix B).

In these examples, *DACS* element numbers are provided to the left of specific data elements whose content was formulated according to *DACS* rules. *DACS* elements noted in Chapter 1 as minimum requirements for a multilevel description are indicated in **bold** in these examples.

At the highest level of description, the EAD examples use all of the "multilevel added value" elements from Chapter 1. Subsequent levels of description in the finding aids (series, subseries, file, and item) use only "multilevel added value" elements from which information is not inherited from higher levels. At the lowest level of description in each of these examples, the *DACS* element numbers are only indicated until the pattern is established.

EAD Examples

Mildred Davenport Dance Programs and Dance School Materials

```
<?xml version="1.0" encoding="UTF-8" standalone="no"?>
<!DOCTYPE ead PUBLIC "+//ISBN 1-931666-00-8//DTD ead.dtd (Encoded
Archival Description (EAD) Version 2002)//EN" "ead.dtd" [
<!NOTATION GIF PUBLIC "+//ISBN 0-7923-9432-1::Graphic Notation//NOTATION
CompuServe Graphic Interchange Format//EN" "">
<!ENTITY ucseal PUBLIC "-//University of California, Berkeley::Library//NONSGML
(University of California seal)//EN" "ucseal.gif" NDATA GIF>
]>
<?filetitle Davenport (Mildred) Dance Programs and Dance School Materials?>
<ead>
<eadheader langencoding="iso639-2b" audience="internal"
countryencoding="iso3166-1" dateencoding="iso8601"
repositoryencoding="iso15511" scriptencoding="iso15924">
<eadid type="SGML catalog">PUBLIC "-//University of California,
Irvine::Library::Special Collections and Archives//TEXT (US::CU-I::MS-
P29::Mildred Davenport Dance Programs and Dance School Materials)//EN"
"p29.xml"
</eadid>
<filedesc>
<titlestmt><titleproper>Guide to the Mildred Davenport Dance Programs and Dance
School Materials</titleproper><author>Processed by Adrian Turner; machine-
readable finding aid created by Adrian Turner</author></titlestmt>
<publicationstmt>
<publisher>Special Collections and Archives, The UC Irvine
Libraries</publisher>
<address><addressline>P.O. Box 19557</addressline>
<addressline>Irvine, California, 92623-9557</addressline>
<addressline>Phone: (949) 824-7227</addressline>
<addressline>Fax: (949) 824-2472</addressline>
<addressline>E-mail: spcoll@uci.edu</addressline>
<addressline>Web site: http://special.lib.uci.edu/</addressline></address>
<date>&#x00A9; 2001</date>
<p>The Regents of the University of California. All rights reserved.</p>
</publicationstmt>
</filedesc>
<profiledesc><creation>Machine-readable finding aid derived from MS Word.
Date of source: <date>2001.</date></creation><langusage>Description is in
<language langcode="eng">English.</language></langusage>
</profiledesc>
</eadheader>
<archdesc level="collection" relatedencoding="MARC21">
<did>
<head>Descriptive Summary</head>
```

2.3	...	`<unittitle>Mildred Davenport dance programs and dance school materials</unittitle>`
2.4	...	`<unitdate type="inclusive" datechar="creation" normal="1934/1942">1934-1942</unitdate>`
2.1	...	`<unitid countrycode="US" repositorycode="CUI">MS-P29</unitid>`
2.6	...	`<origination><persname role="creator" source="aacr2">Davenport, Mildred, 1900-1990</persname></origination>`
2.5	...	`<physdesc><extent>0.3 linear feet (1 box and 1 oversize folder)</extent></physdesc>`
2.2	...	`<repository>`
		`<address>`

```
              <addressline>Irvine, California 92623-9557</addressline>
              </address>
              </repository>
4.5   ...     <langmaterial>Collection materials entirely in <language
              langcode="eng">English</language>.</langmaterial>
<abstract>This collection comprises dance programs, dance school materials,
photographs, and ephemera documenting the early career of the Boston-based
African American dancer, dance instructor, and civic official Mildred
Davenport.</abstract>
</did>
<descgrp>
<head>Information for Researchers</head>
4.1   ...     <accessrestrict>
              <head>Access</head>
              <p>Collection is open for research.</p>
              </accessrestrict>
4.4   ...     <userestrict>
              <head>Publication Rights</head>
              <p>Property rights reside with the University of California. Literary
              rights are retained by the creators of the records and their heirs.
              For permissions to reproduce or to publish, please contact the Head
              of Special Collections and Archives.</p>
              </userestrict>
7.1   ...     <prefercite>
              <head>Preferred Citation</head>
              <p>Mildred Davenport Dance Programs and Dance School Materials. MS-
              P29. Special Collections and Archives, The UC Irvine Libraries,
              Irvine, California.</p>
              </prefercite>
5.2   ...     <acqinfo>
              <head>Acquisition Information</head>
              <p>Purchased from rare materials dealer, 1998.</p>
              </acqinfo>
8.1   ...     <processinfo>
              <head>Processing History</head>
              <p>Processed and finding aid prepared using DACS by Adrian Turner,
              2001.</p>
              </processinfo>
</descgrp>
2.7   ...     <bioghist>
              <head>Biography</head>
              <p>Mildred Ellen Davenport was a noted civic official and military
              officer with an extensive career as a dancer and dance instructor in
              Boston in the 1930s and 1940s. She was born in Boston on November 12,
              1900. She began her dance studies at C.C. Perkins Grade School and
              Prince School as a teenager, and graduated from Boston Girls' High
              School in 1918. In the 1920s she studied at the Sargent School for
              Physical Culture and at Harvard, and opened her first dance school,
              the Davenport School of Dance. Over the next ten years she studied
              under Ted Shawn and taught dance in Boston. She was also
              progressively more involved in road show performances such as Hot
              Chocolates. From 1930 to 1935 she performed in a number of African-
              American musical productions on Broadway, including Fast and Furious,
              Flying Colors, and Black Birds. In 1932 she established her second
              dance school, the Silver Box Studio, in the South End of Boston. She
              became the first African American woman to perform with the Arthur
              Fiedler Pops unit of the Boston Symphony Orchestra at this time.</p>
              <p>During World War II, Davenport enlisted in the Army as a captain.
              She produced musical shows for military bases and later served as a
              special service officer, library officer, and advisor in the Office
              of Racial Affairs. In 1950, she served as an executive board member
              for the N.A.A.C.P. office in Boston. From 1947 to 1968 she worked for
              the Massachusetts Commission Against Discrimination, founded in 1944
```

```
                    to enforce fair employment practices. Davenport died in Boston in
                    1990.</p>
                    </bioghist>
3.1  ...            <scopecontent>
                    <head>Collection Scope and Content Summary</head>
                    <p>This collection comprises dance programs, dance school materials,
                    photographs, and ephemera documenting the early career of the Boston-
                    based African American dancer, dance instructor, and civic official
                    Mildred Davenport. The bulk of this collection consists of dance
                    programs and dance school materials. The collection also contains 29
                    photographs of Davenport, her students in various performances, and
                    friends or individual students. Dance programs from 1925 to 1942
                    feature her solo performances and group performances with her
                    students. The collection includes a complete run of programs for
                    Bronze Rhapsody, an annual performance series choreographed, staged,
                    and directed by Davenport. Her personal copy of a typescript of stage
                    directions for a 1934 performance is included with these programs.
                    Her dance schools, Davenport School of the Dance and Silver Box
                    Studio, are documented in course brochures and applications.
                    Biographical and academic materials include a 1939 newspaper article
                    on Davenport.</p>
                    </scopecontent>
3.2  ...            <arrangement>
                    <head>Collection Arrangement</head>
                    <p>Files in this collection are arranged topically, and then
                    chronologically within each topical grouping whenever possible.</p>
                    </arrangement>
Access...           <controlaccess>
Points              <head>Indexing Terms</head>
                    <p>The following terms have been used to index the description of
                    this collection in the library's online public access catalog.</p>
                    <controlaccess>
                    <head>Subjects</head>
                    <persname encodinganalog="600" source="aacr2"
                    role="subject">Davenport, Mildred, 1900-1990--Archives.</persname>
                    <subject encodinganalog="650" source="lcsh">Dance schools--
                    Massachusetts--Boston--Archives.</subject>
                    <subject encodinganalog="650" source="lcsh">Dance--
                    Archives.</subject>
                    <subject encodinganalog="650" source="lcsh">Modern dance--United
                    States--Archives.</subject>
                    <subject encodinganalog="650" source="lcsh">Dance, Black--
                    Archives.</subject>
                    <subject encodinganalog="650" source="lcsh">African American dancers-
                    -Archives.</subject>
                    </controlaccess>
                    <controlaccess>
                    <head>Genres and Forms of Materials</head>
                    <genreform encodinganalog="655" source="local">Dance
                    programs.</genreform>
                    <genreform encodinganalog="655" source="gmgpc">Photographic
                    prints.</genreform>
                    <genreform encodinganalog="655" source="gmgpc">Posters.</genreform>
                    </controlaccess>
                    <controlaccess>
                    <head>Occupations</head>
                    <occupation encodinganalog="656" source="aat">Dancers.</occupation>
                    <occupation encodinganalog="656" source="lcsh">Dance
                    teachers.</occupation>
                    </controlaccess>
                    </controlaccess>
```

```
<dsc type="combined">
<head>Collection Contents</head>
<c01 level="file"><did>
2.5 ... <container type="Box : Folder">1 : 1 </container>
2.3 ... <unittitle>Biographical and academic materials</unittitle>
</did>
<c02 level="file"><did>
2.5 ... <container type="Box : Folder">FB-21 : 1 </container>
2.3 ... <unittitle>Boston Girls' High School, commencement program,
        </unittitle>
2.4 ... <unitdate datechar="creation" normal="1918">1918</unitdate>
</did></c02>
<c02 level="file"><did>
2.5 ... <container type="Box : Folder">1 : 1 </container>
2.3 ... <unittitle>George Peabody College for Teachers, School of the Dance,
        schedule of courses offered by Ted Shawn, </unittitle>
2.4 ... <unitdate datechar="creation" normal="1938">1938</unitdate>
</did></c02>
<c02 level="file"><did><container type="Box : Folder">1 : 1 </container>
<unittitle>"Boston teacher called evangelist of the dance," newspaper clipping,
</unittitle>
<unitdate datechar="creation" normal="1939">1939</unitdate></did></c02></c01>
<c01 level="file"><did><container type="Box : Folder">1 : 2-4 </container>
<unittitle>Dance programs</unittitle></did>
<c02 level="file"><did><container type="Box : Folder">1 : 4 </container>
<unittitle>The Feast of Apollo, Brattle Hall, Massachusetts, </unittitle>
<unitdate datechar="creation" normal="1925">1925</unitdate></did></c02>
<c02 level="file"><did><container type="Box : Folder">1 : 4 </container>
<unittitle>Mildred Davenport and her pupils, Brattle Hall, Massachusetts,
</unittitle>
<unitdate datechar="creation" normal="1928">1928</unitdate></did></c02>
<c02 level="file"><did><container type="Box : Folder">1 : 4 </container>
<unittitle>Recital of dance poems and songs, Allied Art Studio, Boston,
</unittitle>
<unitdate datechar="creation" normal="1928">1928</unitdate></did></c02>
<c02 level="file"><did><container type="Box : Folder">1 : 4 </container>
<unittitle>Mildred Davenport and Sepia Beauties in revue, Challengers Club,
Boston, </unittitle>
<unitdate datechar="creation" normal="1933">1933</unitdate></did></c02>
<c02 level="file"><did><container type="Box : Folder">1 : 2-3 </container>
<unittitle>Bronze rhapsody</unittitle></did>
<c03 level="file"><did><container type="Box : Folder">1 : 2 </container>
<unittitle><unitdate datechar="creation" normal="1934">1934</unitdate>
</unittitle></did>
<c04 level="file"><did><container type="Box : Folder">1 : 2 </container>
<unittitle>Typescript of stage directions, with holograph note "Miss Davenport
(personal)" on first leaf, </unittitle>
<unitdate datechar="creation" normal="1934">1934</unitdate></did></c04></c03>
<c03 level="file"><did><container type="Box : Folder">1 : 3 </container>
<unittitle><unitdate type="inclusive" datechar="creation"
normal="1935/1941">1935-1941</unitdate></unittitle>
<physdesc><extent>7 items</extent></physdesc></did></c03>
<c03 level="file"><did><container type="Box : Folder">1 : 3 </container>
<unittitle><unitdate datechar="creation" normal="1942">1942</unitdate>
</unittitle></did>
<c04 level="file"><did><container type="Box : Folder">FB-21 : 1 </container>
<unittitle>Hand-colored poster (partial), </unittitle>
<unitdate datechar="creation" normal="1942">1942</unitdate></did>
</c04></c03></c02>
<c02 level="file"><did><container type="Box : Folder">1 : 4 </container>
<unittitle>Classic, John Hancock Hall, Boston, </unittitle>
<unitdate datechar="creation" normal="1938">1938</unitdate></did></c02>
```

```
<c02 level="file"><did><container type="Box : Folder">1 : 4 </container>
<unittitle>Shadowland Ball Room performances, Boston, undated.</unittitle>
<physdesc><extent>2 items.</extent></physdesc></did></c02></c01>
<c01 level="file"><did><container type="Box : Folder">1 : 5 </container>
<unittitle>Dance school materials</unittitle></did>
<c02 level="file"><did><container type="Box : Folder">1 : 5 </container>
<unittitle>Davenport School of the Dance application,
undated</unittitle></did></c02>
<c02 level="file"><did><container type="Box : Folder">1 : 5 </container>
<unittitle>Silver Box Studio</unittitle></did>
<c03 level="file"><did><container type="Box : Folder">1 : 5 </container>
<unittitle>Course brochures and applications, undated.</unittitle>
<physdesc><extent>3 items.</extent></physdesc></did></c03>
<c03 level="file"><did><container type="Box : Folder">1 : 5 </container>
<unittitle>Event invitation and greeting card, </unittitle>
<unitdate datechar="creation" normal="1939">1939 and undated.</unitdate>
<physdesc><extent>2 items.</extent></physdesc></did></c03></c02></c01>
<c01 level="file"><did><container type="Box : Folder">1 : 6-11 </container>
<unittitle>Photographs</unittitle></did>
<c02 level="file"><did><container type="Box : Folder">1 : 6-7 </container>
<unittitle>Personal</unittitle></did>
<c03 level="file"><did><container type="Box : Folder">FB-21 : 1 </container>
<unittitle>Prince School class, </unittitle>
<unitdate datechar="creation" normal="1914">1914</unitdate></did></c03>
<c03 level="file"><did><container type="Box : Folder">1 : 6 </container>
<unittitle>Teenage performances, undated.</unittitle> <physdesc><extent>5
items.</extent></physdesc></did></c03>
<c03 level="file"><did><container type="Box : Folder">1 : 7 </container>
<unittitle>Portraits, undated.</unittitle> <physdesc><extent>3
items.</extent></physdesc></did></c03></c02>
<c02 level="file"><did><container type="Box : Folder">1 : 8-10 </container>
<unittitle>Performances by students</unittitle></did>
<c03 level="file"><did><container type="Box : Folder">1 : 8 </container>
<unittitle>Piggilly wiggily, </unittitle>
<unitdate datechar="creation" normal="1941/1943">circa 1942</unitdate>
</did></c03>
<c03 level="file"><did><container type="Box : Folder">1 : 8 </container>
<unittitle>Top hat, </unittitle>
<unitdate datechar="creation" normal="1941/1943">circa 1942</unitdate>
</did></c03>
<c03 level="file"><did><container type="Box : Folder">1 : 8-10 </container>
<unittitle>Unidentified, undated.</unittitle> <physdesc><extent>15
items.</extent></physdesc></did></c03></c02>
<c02 level="file"><did><container type="Box : Folder">1 : 11 </container>
<unittitle>Other individuals</unittitle></did>
<c03 level="file"><did><container type="Box : Folder">1 : 11 </container>
<unittitle>Hall, Tom, </unittitle>
<unitdate datechar="creation" normal="1930">1930</unitdate></did></c03>
<c03 level="file"><did><container type="Box : Folder">1 : 11 </container>
<unittitle>Purcell, Barbara, </unittitle>
<unitdate datechar="creation" normal="1941/1943">circa 1942</unitdate>
</did></c03>
<c03 level="file"><did><container type="Box : Folder">1 : 11 </container>
<unittitle>Stokes, Bernice, </unittitle>
<unitdate datechar="creation" normal="1941/1943">circa 1942</unitdate>
</did></c03>
<c03 level="file"><did><container type="Box : Folder">1 : 11 </container>
<unittitle>Roberts, Francine, </unittitle>
<unitdate datechar="creation" normal="1941/1943">circa 1942</unitdate>
</did></c03></c02></c01>
</dsc>
</archdesc>
</ead>
```

Bacot Family Papers

```
<?xml version="1.0" encoding="UTF-8" standalone="no"?>
<?xml-stylesheet type="text/xsl" href="./styles/uncxmlmenu.xsl" ?>
<!DOCTYPE ead PUBLIC "+//ISBN 1-931666-00-8//DTD ead.dtd (Encoded Archival
Description (EAD) Version 2002)//EN" "./dtds/ead.dtd" [
<!ENTITY uncseal PUBLIC "-//University of North Carolina at Chapel
Hill::Manuscripts Department//NONSGML (uncseal)//EN" "./seals/uncseal.gif"
NDATA gif>
<!ENTITY hdruncmss PUBLIC "-//University of North Carolina at Chapel
Hill::Manuscripts Department//TEXT (hdruncmss)//EN"
"./addresses/hdruncmss.xml">
]>
<ead>
<eadheader audience="internal" countryencoding="iso3166-1"
dateencoding="iso8601" langencoding="iso639-2b" repositoryencoding="iso15511">
<eadid countrycode="us" mainagencycode="ncu" publicid="-// University of North
Carolina at Chapel Hill::Manuscripts Department//TEXT (US::NCU::OFC$::Bacot
Family Papers, (916-z))//EN"
url="http://www.lib.unc.edu/mss/inv/ead2002/00916.xml">00916</eadid>
<filedesc>
<titlestmt><titleproper encodinganalog="title">Inventory of the Bacot Family
Papers, <date normal="1767/1887">1767-1887</date>916-z</titleproper>
<author encodinganalog="creator">Processed by: Roslyn Holdzkom; machine-
readable finding aid created by: Roslyn Holdzkom</author>
</titlestmt>
<publicationstmt>
&hdruncmss;
</publicationstmt>
</filedesc>
<profiledesc>
<creation>Machine-readable finding aid derived from NoteTab Pro Software.<lb/>
<date>Date of source: July 1990</date><lb/>
Processed by Roslyn Holdzkom, July 1990; finding aid encoded by Roslyn
Holdzkom, Manuscripts Department, University of North Carolina at Chapel Hill,
<date>May 2004</date>
</creation>
<langusage>Finding aid written in <language langcode="eng">English</language>
</langusage>
</profiledesc>
</eadheader>
<frontmatter>
<titlepage>
<titleproper>Inventory of the Bacot Family Papers, <date normal="1767/1887"
type="inclusive">1767-1887</date>
</titleproper><num>916-z</num>
<publisher>Manuscripts Department,
<extptr show="embed" entityref="uncseal"/><lb/>
Library of the University of North Carolina at Chapel Hill</publisher>
</titlepage>
</frontmatter>
<archdesc level="collection" relatedencoding="MARC">
<did>
<head>Descriptive Summary</head>
```

2.2 ...   `<repository label="Repository">`
       `<corpname>Southern Historical Collection</corpname>`
       `</repository>`

2.6 ...   `<origination label="Creator">`
       `<famname encodinganalog="100">Bacot family.</famname>`
       `</origination>`

```
2.3 ...    <unittitle label="Title" encodinganalog="245">Bacot family papers,
2.4 ...    <unitdate type="inclusive" normal="1767/1887">1767-1887</unitdate>;
           <unitdate type="bulk" normal="1845/1866">bulk 1845-1866</unitdate>
           </unittitle>
2.1 ...    <unitid countrycode="us" repositorycode="ncu" label="Call Number"
           encodinganalog="099">916-z</unitid>
4.5 ...    <langmaterial label="Language of Materials" encodinganalog="546">
           Materials in <language langcode="eng">English</language>
           </langmaterial>
2.5 ...    <physdesc label="Extent">
           <extent unit="items" encodinganalog="300">Items: About 90</extent>
           <extent unit="linear feet" encodinganalog="300">Linear Feet:
           0.5</extent>
           </physdesc>
<abstract label="Abstract">Bacot family members were cotton planters of Mars
Bluff Plantation near Florence, Darlington District, S.C., and, beginning in
1865, partners in the Jarrot &amp; Bacot Drug Store in Florence. The Bacots
were related to the Brockinton family and descended from South Carolina
Huguenots. The collection includes correspondence, financial and legal
materials, and other items of Bacot family members and their Brockinton family
relatives. Correspondence chiefly relates to business dealings of Peter Samuel
Bacot, who managed the plantation, and to family and social activities. Some
letters are from cotton factors in Charleston, S.C. Also included are slave
lists, and, after the Civil War, contracts relating to the employment of
freedmen on the plantation; a few items relating to the Jarrot &amp; Bacot Drug
Store; currency issued by South Carolina, 1775-1862; and typed transcriptions
of articles published in 1826 about Huguenots in South Carolina.</abstract>
</did>
<descgrp type="admininfo">
<head>Administrative Information</head>
4.1 ...    <accessrestrict encodinganalog="506">
           <head>Restrictions to Access</head>
           <p>No restrictions.</p></accessrestrict>
6.2 ...    <altformavail encodinganalog="530">
           <head>Alternate Form of Material</head>
           <p>Microfilm copy available.
           <list type="simple">
           <item>Reel 1: Folders 1-6</item>
           </list></p>
           </altformavail>
5.2 ...    <acqinfo encodinganalog="541">
           <head>Acquisitions Information</head>
           <p>Received from Emma Bacot of Florence, S.C., in October 1944.</p>
           </acqinfo>
8.1 ...    <processinfo>
           <head>Processing Information</head>
           <p>Processed by: Roslyn Holdzkom, July 1990</p>
           <p>Encoded by: Roslyn Holdzkom, May 2004</p>
           </processinfo>
7.1 ...    <prefercite encodinganalog="524">
           <head>Preferred Citation</head>
           <p>[Identification of item], in the Bacot Family Papers #916-z,
           Southern Historical Collection, Wilson Library, University of North
           Carolina at Chapel Hill.</p>
           </prefercite>
4.4 ...    <userestrict encodinganalog="500">
           <head>Copyright Notice</head>
           <p>Copyright is retained by the authors of items in these papers, or
           their descendants, as stipulated by United States copyright law.</p>
           </userestrict>
</descgrp>
```

```
Access...    <controlaccess>
Points       <head>Online Catalog Headings</head>
             <p>These and related materials may be found under the following
             headings in online catalogs.</p>
             <subject source="lcsh" encodinganalog="650">African American
             agricultural laborers--South Carolina.</subject>
             <subject source="lcsh" encodinganalog="650">Agriculture--South
             Carolina.</subject>
             <famname source="lcnaf" encodinganalog="600">Bacot family.</famname>
             <persname source="lcnaf" encodinganalog="600">Bacot, Peter Samuel,
             1810-1864.</persname>
             <famname source="lcnaf" encodinganalog="600">Brockinton
             family.</famname>
             <geogname source="lcsh" encodinganalog="651">Charleston (S.C.)--
             Economic conditions.</geogname>
             <subject source="lcsh" encodinganalog="650">Commission merchants--
             South Carolina--Charleston.</subject>
             <subject source="lcsh" encodinganalog="650">Cotton growing--South
             Carolina.</subject>
             <geogname source="lcsh" encodinganalog="651">Darlington District
             (S.C.)--History.</geogname>
             <subject source="lcsh" encodinganalog="650">Drugstores--South
             Carolina--History--19th century.</subject>
             <subject source="lcsh" encodinganalog="650">Family--South Carolina--
             Social life and customs.</subject>
             <geogname source="lcsh" encodinganalog="651">Florence (S.C.)--
             Economic conditions.</geogname>
             <subject source="lcsh" encodinganalog="650">Freedmen--South
             Carolina.</subject>
             <subject source="lcsh" encodinganalog="650">Huguenots--South
             Carolina.</subject>
             <corpname source="lcnaf" encodinganalog="610">Jarrot &amp; Bacot Drug
             Store (Florence, S.C.).</corpname>
             <geogname source="lcsh" encodinganalog="651">Mars Bluff Plantation
             (Darlington District, S.C.).</geogname>
             <subject source="lcsh" encodinganalog="650">Merchants--South
             Carolina--History--19th century.</subject>
             <subject source="lcsh" encodinganalog="650">Money--South
             Carolina.</subject>
             <subject source="lcsh" encodinganalog="650">Plantation life--South
             Carolina.</subject>
             <subject source="lcsh" encodinganalog="650">Plantation owners--South
             Carolina.</subject>
             <subject source="lcsh" encodinganalog="650">Slavery--South
             Carolina.</subject>
             </controlaccess>
6.3 ...      <relatedmaterial encodinganalog="544">
             <head>Related Collection</head>
             <list type="simple">
             <item>Peter Brockington Bacot Papers (#2742)</item>
             </list>
             </relatedmaterial>
2.7 ...      <bioghist encodinganalog="545">
             <head>Biographical Note</head>
             <p>The Bacot family, descendants of South Carolina Huguenots and
             related to the Brockington family, owned the Mars Bluff Plantation
             near Florence in the Darlington District of South Carolina. They
             owned a considerable number of slaves and grew cotton and other cash
             crops on the plantation. Chief among the Bacots in the 1840s and
             1850s was Peter Samuel Bacot, who appears to have been responsible
             for managing Mars Bluff. After the Civil War, the Bacots employed
             freedmen to work the plantation and entered into a partnership to
             open the Jarrot &amp; Bacot Drug Store in Florence.</p>
```

```
                    </bioghist>
3.1 ...             <scopecontent encodinganalog="520">
                    <head>Collection Overview</head>
                    <p>The collection includes correspondence, financial and legal
                    materials, and other items relating to the Bacot family of Mars Bluff
                    Plantation, Darlington District, S.C., and to their Brockinton
                    relatives.  Many 1840s letters relating to family and social affairs
                    are to Mary Brockington, who lived at Mars Bluff. Most of the
                    letters, 1850s-1860s, relate to Peter Samuel Bacot's management of
                    the plantation and include several from cotton factors in Charleston,
                    S.C. Financial and legal materials from the 1850s include slave lists
                    and, in 1866 and 1867, contracts and other materials relating to the
                    employment of freedmen on the plantation. Other papers include
                    examples of South Carolina currency, 1775-1862, and a typed
                    transcription of <title render="doublequote">The French
                    Refugees,</title> a series of articles about Huguenots in South
                    Carolina, that appeared in the <title render="italic">City Gazette
                    and Commercial Daily Advertiser</title> of Charleston in May
                    1826.</p>
                    </scopecontent>
3.2 ...             <arrangement encodinganalog="351">
                    <head>Arrangement of Collection</head>
                    <list type="simple">
                    <item>1. Correspondence, 1767, 1845-1866, 1887</item>
                    <item>2. Financial and Legal Materials, 1786, 1851-1887</item>
                    <item>3. Other Items, 1775-1862</item>
                    </list>
                    </arrangement>
<dsc type="combined">
<head>Detailed Description of the Collection</head>
<c01 level="series"><did>
2.1 ...     <unitid>1.</unitid>
2.3 ...     <unittitle>Correspondence,
2.4 ...     <unitdate normal="1767/1887" type="inclusive">1767, 1845-1866,
            1887</unitdate>.
            </unittitle>
2.5 ...     <physdesc><extent>About 30 items.</extent></physdesc>
</did>
3.2 ...     <arrangement><p>Arrangement: chronological.</p></arrangement>
3.1 ...     <scopecontent>
            <p>Correspondence relating to Bacot family members and their
            relatives, friends, and business associates. Letters in the 1840s are
            chiefly to Mary H. Brockinton at Mars Bluff Plantation. They discuss
            social engagements and family affairs. Except for an invitation in
            1850 and an exchange of letters in July 1855 between Peter Samuel
            Bacot and his son Richard at school, all letters in the 1850s relate
            to Peter Samuel Bacot's business accounts with cotton factors in
            Charleston, S.C. Several of the letters after 1865 relate to the
            Jarrot &amp; Bacot Drug Store in Florence, S.C. The 1887 item
            announces an event at the Ashley Phosphate Company in Charleston.</p>
            </scopecontent>
<c02 level="file"><did>
2.5 ...     <container type="folder">1</container>
2.3 ...     <unittitle>1767, 1845-1850</unittitle>
</did></c02>
<c02 level="file"><did>
2.5 ...     <container type="folder">2</container>
2.3 ...     <unittitle>1865-1866, 1887</unittitle>
</did></c02>
</c01>
<c01 level="series"><did>
2.1 ...     <unitid>2.</unitid>
```

```
2.3 ...    <unittitle>Financial and legal materials,
2.4 ...    <unitdate normal="1786/1887" type="inclusive">1786, 1851-
           1887</unitdate>.
           </unittitle>
2.5 ...    <physdesc><extent>About 50 items.</extent></physdesc>
</did>
3.2 ...    <arrangement><p>Arrangement: chronological.</p></arrangement>
3.1 ...    <scopecontent>
           <p>Financial and legal materials relating to Bacot family members and
           their relatives. Early material is about property of Brockinton
           family members and includes a list of slaves and other property owned
           by Mary H. Brockinton on 21 July 1853. Most other items through 1863
           relate to managing the Mars Bluff Plantation. There are several
           items, 1866-1867, that document the work of freedmen at Mars Bluff.
           These include contracts, 18 August 1866, that set out terms of
           employment and a 7 March 1867 medical services contract between the
           freedmen and a local physician. Most items in the 1870s and 1880s are
           routine bills and receipts for food and other purchases.</p>
           </scopecontent>
<c02 level="file"><did>
2.5 ...    <container type="folder">3</container>
2.3 ...    <unittitle>1786, 1851-1863</unittitle>
</did></c02>
<c02 level="file"><did><container type="folder">4</container>
2.3 ...    <unittitle>1865-1887</unittitle>
</did></c02>
</c01>
<c01 level="series"><did>
<unitid>3.</unitid>
<unittitle>Other items,
<unitdate normal="1775/1862" type="inclusive">1775-1862</unitdate>.
</unittitle>
<physdesc><extent>10 items.</extent></physdesc>
</did>
<arrangement><p>Arrangement: by form of material.</p></arrangement>
<scopecontent>
<p>Nine pieces of paper money issued by South Carolina, 1775-1862, and a typed
transcription of <title render="doublequote">The French Refugees,</title> a
series of four articles about Huguenots in South Carolina that appeared in the
<title render="italic">City Gazette and Commercial Daily Advertiser</title> of
Charleston, S.C., 11-15 May 1826. While the Bacots are not mentioned in these
articles, they were descendants of French &eacute;migr&eacute;s and may have
been related to the author of the articles, who is identified only as <emph
render="doublequote">A Descendant of the Refugees.</emph></p>
</scopecontent>
<c02 level="file"><did><container type="folder">5</container>
<unittitle>South Carolina currency</unittitle>
</did></c02>
<c02 level="file"><did><container type="folder">6</container>
<unittitle><title render="doublequote">The French Refugees</title></unittitle>
</did></c02>
</c01>
</dsc>
</archdesc>
</ead>
```

Swine Influenza Immunization Program Records

```
<?xml version="1.0" encoding="UTF-8" standalone="no"?>
<!DOCTYPE ead PUBLIC "+//ISBN 1-931666-00-8//DTD ead.dtd (Encoded Archival
Description (EAD) Version 2002)//EN" "ead.dtd">
<ead relatedencoding="MARC21">
<eadheader langencoding="iso639-2b" audience="internal"
countryencoding="iso3166-1" dateencoding="iso8601"
repositoryencoding="iso15511" scriptencoding="iso15924">
<eadid countrycode="us" mainagencycode="mnhi">hea001</eadid>
<filedesc>
<titlestmt><titleproper>Minnesota. Dept. Of Health</titleproper>
<subtitle>An Inventory of its Swine Influenza Immunization Program Records at
the Minnesota Historical Society </subtitle>
<author>Inventory prepared by Cheri Thies</author>
</titlestmt>
<publicationstmt>
<publisher>Minnesota Historical Society</publisher>
<address>
<addressline>St. Paul, MN 55102</addressline>
</address>
<date> 2004</date>
</publicationstmt>
</filedesc>
<profiledesc>
<creation>Finding aid encoded by Michael Fox<date>23 June 2004</date>
</creation><langusage>Finding aid written in<language>English.</language>
</langusage>
</profiledesc>
</eadheader>
<archdesc level="series" type="inventory">
<did>
<head> Collection Summary</head>
2.2 ...    <repository label="Repository:" encodinganalog="852$a">
           <corpname>Minnesota Historical Society</corpname>
           <address>
           <addressline>St. Paul, MN 55102</addressline>
           </address>
           </repository>
2.6 ...    <origination label="Creator:" encodinganalog="110">
           <corpname>Minnesota. Dept. of Health. </corpname>
           </origination>
2.3 ...    <unittitle label="Title:" encodinganalog="245$a">Swine influenza
           immunization program records</unittitle>
2.4 ...    <unitdate type="inclusive" label="Dates:"
           encodinganalog="245$f">1975-1979 </unitdate>
2.5 ...    <physdesc label="Quantity:" encodinganalog="300$a">1.25 cubic feet (1
           box and 1 partial box)</physdesc>
<abstract label="Abstract:" encodinganalog="520$a">Records of a statewide
program to immunize vulnerable segments of Minnesota's population against swine
influenza. </abstract>
2.1 ...    <unitid label="Identification:" encodinganalog="099"
           repositorycode="mnhi" countrycode="us">hea001</unitid>
4.5 ...    <langmaterial encodinganalog="546$a" label="Language: ">Records are
           in English. </langmaterial>
4.2 ...    <physloc label="Location: ">126.B.16.16F - 126.B.17.1B</physloc>
</did>
3.1 ...    <scopecontent encodinganalog="520">
           <head>Scope and Contents of the Records</head>
           <p>Records of a statewide program to immunize vulnerable segments of
           Minnesota's population against swine influenza, which in the middle
```

```
1970s was epidemic in many parts of the world.  The records include
files on the administration of the program and on public outreach and
informational activities; data on a grant received by the state from
the federal Department of Health, Education, and Welfare as part of
the National Influenza Immunization Program; statistic on vaccine
usage and immunizations; and program evaluations from the majority of
Minnesota's counties.</p>
</scopecontent>
```

3.2 ...
```
<arrangement encodinganalog="351">
<head>Arrangement of the Records</head>
<p>Arranged in 7 subseries</p>
</arrangement>
```

Access...
Points
```
<controlaccess>
<head> Index Terms</head>
<p><emph render="italic">These records are indexed under the
following headings in the catalog of the Minnesota Historical
Society. Researchers desiring materials about related topics, persons
or places should search the catalog using these headings.</emph></p>
<controlaccess>
<head>Organizations:</head>
<corpname source="lcnaf" encodinganalog="710">United States. Dept. of
Health, Education, and Welfare. </corpname>
</controlaccess>
<controlaccess>
<head>Subjects:</head>
<subject source="lcsh" encodinganalog="650">Health promotion--
Minnesota.</subject>
<subject source="lcsh" encodinganalog="650">Influenza--Minnesota--
Vaccination--Statistics. </subject>
<subject source="lcsh" encodinganalog="650">Interstate relations--
Minnesota. </subject>
<subject source="lcsh" encodinganalog="650">Public relations--Health
planning--Minnesota. </subject>
<subject source="lcsh" encodinganalog="650">Swine influenza--
Minnesota. </subject>
<subject source="lcsh" encodinganalog="650"> Vaccination--Minnesota--
Statistics.</subject>
</controlaccess>
</controlaccess>
```

4.1 ...
```
<accessrestrict>
<p>Collection is open for research.</p>
</accessrestrict>
```

7.1 ...
```
<prefercite>
<head>Preferred Citation:</head>
<p><emph render="italic">[Indicate the cited item and folder title
here].</emph>Minnesota. Dept. of Health. Swine influenza immunization
program records.  [Subunit title]. Minnesota Historical Society.
State Archives.</p>
<p><emph render="italic">See the Chicago Manual of Style for
additional examples.</emph></p>
</prefercite>
```

5.2 ...
```
<acqinfo>
<head>Accession Information:</head>
<p>Accession number(s): 1988-110</p>
</acqinfo>
```

8.1 ...
```
<processinfo>
<head>Processing Information:</head>
<p>PALS ID No. 001716763. RLIN ID No.: MNHV92-A429</p>
</processinfo>
```

```
<dsc type="combined">
<head>Detailed Description of the Records</head>
<p>Note to Researchers: To request materials, please note both the location and
box numbers shown below. Box and file numbers are segments of an overall set of
1858-1932 gubernatorial files.</p>
<c01 level="subseries">
<did>
<container type="Box">1</container>
2.3 ...    <unittitle>Correspondence, </unittitle>
2.4 ...    <unitdate type="inclusive">1976-1977</unitdate>
2.5 ...    <physdesc>2 folders</physdesc>
</did>
3.1 ...    <scopecontent>
           <p>Includes correspondence with state and federal agencies, mailings
           to members of the Swine Influenza Program, Advisory Committee, and
           news releases. </p>
           </scopecontent>
</c01>
<c01 level="subseries">
<did>
<container type="Box">1</container>
2.3 ...    <unittitle>Swine influenza originals, </unittitle>
2.4 ...    <unitdate type="inclusive">1976</unitdate>
2.5 ...    <physdesc>1 folder</physdesc>
</did>
3.1 ...    <scopecontent>
           <p>Original copies of various mailings to county program
           coordinators, staff, and physicians, and program information leaflets
           and forms.</p>
           </scopecontent>
</c01>
<c01 level="subseries">
<did>
<container type="Box">1</container>
2.3 ...    <unittitle>Minnesota Influenza Immunization Project grant
           files</unittitle>
2.4 ...    <unitdate type="inclusive">1976-1979</unitdate>
2.5 ...    <physdesc>2 folders</physdesc>
</did>
3.1 ...    <scopecontent>
           <p> Grant application and supporting materials sent to the federal
           Health, Education, and Welfare Dept. (HEW). HEW coordinated the
           National Influenza Immunization Program.</p>
           </scopecontent>
</c01>
<c01 level="subseries">
<did>
<container type="Box">1</container>
2.3 ...    <unittitle>Subject files </unittitle>
2.4 ...    <unitdate type="inclusive">1975-1977</unitdate>
2.5 ...    <physdesc>7 folders</physdesc>
</did>
3.2 ...    <arrangement><p>Files arranged alphabetically.</p></arrangement>
<c02 level="file">
<did>
<container type="Box">1</container>
2.3 ...    <unittitle>Background, </unittitle>
2.4 ...    <unitdate type="inclusive">1976</unitdate>
2.5 ...    <physdesc>1 folder</physdesc>
</did>
</c02>
<c02 level="file">
```

```
<did>
<container type="Box">1</container>
2.3 ...    <unittitle>County plans, </unittitle>
2.4 ...    <unitdate type="inclusive">1976</unitdate>
2.5 ...    <physdesc>1 folder</physdesc>
</did>
</c02>
<c02 level="file">
<did>
<container type="Box">1</container>
2.3 ...    <unittitle>Local involvement, </unittitle>
2.4 ...    <unitdate type="inclusive">1975-1976</unitdate>
2.5 ...    <physdesc>1 folder</physdesc>
</did>
</c02>
<c02 level="file">
<did>
<container type="Box">1</container>
2.3 ...    <unittitle>Phase II, </unittitle>
2.4 ...    <unitdate type="inclusive">1977</unitdate>
2.5 ...    <physdesc>1 folder</physdesc>
</did>
</c02>
<c02 level="file">
<did>
<container type="Box">1</container>
2.3 ...    <unittitle>Program evaluations, </unittitle>
2.4 ...    <unitdate type="inclusive">1977</unitdate>
2.5 ...    <physdesc>1 folder</physdesc>
</did>
</c02>
<c02 level="file">
<did>
<container type="Box">1</container>
2.3 ...    <unittitle>Promotion materials, </unittitle>
2.4 ...    <unitdate type="inclusive">1976-1977</unitdate>
2.5 ...    <physdesc>1 folder</physdesc>
</did>
</c02>
<c02 level="file">
<did>
<container type="Box">1</container>
2.3 ...    <unittitle>Vaccine usage statistics</unittitle>
2.4 ...    <unitdate type="inclusive">1976-1977</unitdate>
2.5 ...    <physdesc>1 folder</physdesc>
</did>
</c02>
</c01>
<c01 level="subseries">
<did>
<container type="Box">1</container>
<unittitle>Radio transcripts, </unittitle>
<unitdate type="inclusive">1976</unitdate>
<physdesc>2 folders</physdesc>
</did>
<scopecontent>
<p>Transcripts of radio announcements about the swine influenza program in
Hennepin County.  </p>
</scopecontent>
</c01>
<c01 level="subseries">
<did>
<container type="Box">1</container>
```

```
<unittitle>Country and district swine influenza program files, </unittitle>
<unitdate type="inclusive">1976-1977.</unitdate>
<physdesc>4 folders</physdesc>
</did>
<c02 level="file">
<did>
<container type="Box">1</container>
<unittitle>Carver County, </unittitle>
<unitdate type="inclusive">1976</unitdate>
<physdesc>1 folder</physdesc>
</did>
</c02>
<c02 level="file">
<did>
<container type="Box">1</container>
<unittitle>Hennepin County, </unittitle>
<unitdate type="inclusive">1976-1977</unitdate>
<physdesc>2 folders</physdesc>
</did>
<scopecontent>
<p>Include program reports, swine influenza committee minutes, and mailings and
guidelines for clinics.</p>
</scopecontent>
</c02>
<c02 level="file">
<did>
<container type="Box">1</container>
<unittitle>Ramsey County, </unittitle>
<unitdate type="inclusive">1976</unitdate>
<physdesc>1 folder</physdesc>
</did>
<scopecontent>
<p> Includes county plan and committee minutes.</p>
</scopecontent>
</c02>
<c02 level="file">
<did>
<container type="Box">1</container>
<unittitle>Central District</unittitle>
<unitdate type="inclusive">1976</unitdate>
<physdesc>1 folder</physdesc>
</did>
<scopecontent>
<p>Includes minutes of the Central District's swine influenza committee.  The
Health Dept.'s Central District office was located in St. Cloud. </p>
</scopecontent>
</c02>
</c01>
<c01 level="subseries">
<did>
<container type="Box">1</container>
<unittitle>County swine influenza program evaluations,</unittitle>
<unitdate type="inclusive">1976</unitdate>
<physdesc>11 folders</physdesc>
</did>
<scopecontent>
<p>Evaluations includes various reports on program planning, activities,
services, clinic organizations, finances, and statistics.  Evaluations were
completed by county program staff and are arranged alphabetically by county.
Some county evaluations are missing. </p>
</scopecontent>
<c02 level="file">
```

```
<did>
<container type="Box">1</container>
<unittitle>Aitkin-Marshall</unittitle>
<physdesc>6 folders</physdesc>
</did>
</c02>
<c02 level="file">
<did>
<container type="Box">2</container>
<unittitle>Martin-Wright</unittitle>
<physdesc>5 folders</physdesc>
</did>
</c02>
</c01>
</dsc>
</archdesc>
</ead>
```

Herndon-Weik Collection of Lincolniana

```
<?xml version="1.0" encoding="utf-8" standalone="no"?>
<!-- Transformed with v1v2002_4.xsl -->
<!DOCTYPE ead PUBLIC "-//Society of American Archivists//DTD ead.dtd (Encoded
Archival Description (EAD) Version 2002)//EN"
"http://lcweb2.loc.gov/xmlcommon/dtds/ead2002/ead.dtd"  [
<!ENTITY lcseal SYSTEM "http://lcweb2.loc.gov/xmlcommon/lcseal.jpg" NDATA jpeg>
]>
<ead>
<eadheader repositoryencoding="iso15511" relatedencoding="MARC21"
countryencoding="iso3166-1" scriptencoding="iso15924" dateencoding="iso8601"
langencoding="iso639-2b">
<eadid mainagencycode="dlc" countrycode="us"
identifier="hdl:loc.gov/loc.mss/eadmss.ms001002"
encodinganalog="856$u">http://hdl.loc.mss/loc.mss/eadmss.ms001002</eadid>
<filedesc>
<titlestmt encodinganalog="245$a">
<titleproper encodinganalog="245$a">The Herndon-Weik Collection of
Lincolniana</titleproper>
<subtitle>A Register of the Collection in the Library of Congress</subtitle>
<author encodinganalog="245$c">Prepared by Mary M. Wolfskill and David Mathisen
<lb/>Revised by T. Michael Womack</author>
</titlestmt>
<publicationstmt>
<publisher>
<extptr href="lcseal" show="embed" actuate="onload"/>Manuscript Division,
Library of Congress</publisher>
<address>
<addressline>Washington, D.C.</addressline>
</address>
<date encodinganalog="260$c" normal="1997">1997</date>
</publicationstmt>
<notestmt><note><p>Contact information: <extref
href="http://lcweb.loc.gov/rr/mss/address.html" show="new"
actuate="onrequest">http://lcweb.loc.gov/rr/mss/address.html</extref>
</p></note></notestmt>
</filedesc>
<profiledesc>
<creation>Finding aid encoded by Library of Congress Manuscript Division,
<date normal="2001">2001</date></creation><langusage encodinganalog="546">
Finding aid written in<language encodinganalog="041" langcode="eng">
English.</language></langusage>
</profiledesc>
<revisiondesc>
<change encodinganalog="583">
<date normal="2004-06-01">2004 June 01</date>
<item>Converted from EAD 1.0 to EAD 2002 </item>
</change>
</revisiondesc>
</eadheader>
<archdesc type="register" level="collection" relatedencoding="MARC21">
<did>
<head>Collection Summary</head>
```

2.3 ...   `<unittitle label="Title" encodinganalog="245$a">Herndon-Weik`
       `collection of Lincolniana`

2.4 ...   `<unitdate label="Span Dates" type="inclusive" normal="1824/1933"`
       `encodinganalog="245$f">circa 1824-1933</unitdate>`
       `</unittitle>`

2.1 ...   `<unitid label="ID No." encodinganalog="590" countrycode="us"`
       `repositorycode="dlc">MSS25791</unitid>`

```
2.6 ...    <origination label="Collector">
           <persname encodinganalog="700" role="collector"
           source="lcnaf">Herndon, William Henry, 1818-1891</persname>
           </origination>
           <origination label="Creator">
           <persname source="lcnaf" encodinganalog="700" role="creator">Lincoln,
           Abraham, 1809-1865</persname>
           </origination>
           <origination label="Collector">
           <persname source="lcnaf" encodinganalog="700" role="collector">Weik,
           Jesse William, 1857-1930</persname>
           </origination>
2.5 ...    <physdesc label="Extent">
           <extent encodinganalog="300">4,600 items</extent>
           </physdesc>
           <physdesc label="Size">
           <extent encodinganalog="300">36 containers</extent>
           </physdesc>
           <physdesc label="Size">
           <extent encodinganalog="300">10 linear feet</extent>
           </physdesc>
           <physdesc label="Size">
           <extent encodinganalog="300">15 microfilm reels</extent></physdesc>
4.5 ...    <langmaterial label="Language">Collection material in <language
           encodinganalog="041" langcode="eng">English</language>
           </langmaterial>
2.2 ...    <repository label="Repository" encodinganalog="852">
           <corpname>
           <subarea>Manuscript Division</subarea> Library of Congress</corpname>
           <address>
           <addressline>Washington, D.C.</addressline>
           </address>
           </repository>
<abstract label="Abstract" encodinganalog="520$a">Collection composed of the
papers of Abraham Lincoln, U.S. president, U.S. representative from Illinois,
and lawyer; William Henry Herndon, Lincoln's law partner, collector, and
biographer from Springfield, Illinois; and Jesse William Weik, lawyer of
Greencastle, Indiana, and coauthor of Herndon <title>Lincoln.</title> Includes
records (1933) of the Weik Manuscript Corporation and miscellaneous material
collected chiefly by Herndon and Weik for use in writing Herndon's
<title>Lincoln: The True Story of a Great Life</title> (1889).</abstract>
</did>
Access...   <controlaccess>
Points      <head>Selected Search Terms</head>
            <note>
            <p>The following terms have been used to index the description of
            this collection in the Library's online catalog. They are grouped by
            name of person or organization, by subject or location, and by
            occupation and listed alphabetically therein.</p>
            </note>
            <controlaccess>
            <head>Names:</head>
            <persname source="lcnaf" encodinganalog="600" role="subject">Bell,
            John, 1797-1869--Correspondence</persname>
            <persname source="lcnaf" encodinganalog="600"
            role="subject">Beveridge, Albert Jeremiah, 1862-1927--
            Correspondence</persname>
            <persname source="lcnaf" encodinganalog="600"
            role="subject">Conkling, James Cook, 1816-1899--
            Correspondence</persname>
            <persname source="lcnaf" encodinganalog="600" role="subject">Dana,
            Richard Henry, 1815-1882--Correspondence</persname>
```

```
<persname source="lcnaf" encodinganalog="600" role="subject">Delahay,
Mark W. (Mark William), 1818?-1879--Correspondence</persname>
<persname source="lcnaf" encodinganalog="600" role="subject">Douglas,
Stephen Arnold, 1813-1861</persname>
<persname source="lcnaf" encodinganalog="600" role="subject">Edwards,
Ninian Wirt</persname>
<persname source="lcnaf" encodinganalog="600" role="subject">Friend,
Charles</persname>
<persname source="lcnaf" encodinganalog="600" role="subject">Gentry,
Kate Roby</persname>
<persname source="lcnaf" encodinganalog="600"
role="subject">Giddings, Joshua R. (Joshua Reed), 1795-1864--
Correspondence</persname>
<persname source="lcnaf" encodinganalog="600" role="subject">Graham,
Mentor, 1800-1886</persname>
<persname source="lcnaf" encodinganalog="600" role="subject">Hanks,
Dennis</persname>
<persname source="lcnaf" encodinganalog="600" role="subject">Hay,
John, 1838-1905</persname>
<persname source="lcnaf" encodinganalog="600" role="subject">Hay,
John, 1838-1905--Correspondence</persname>
<persname source="lcnaf" encodinganalog="600"
role="subject">Haycraft, Samuel, 1795-1878--Correspondence</persname>
<persname source="lcnaf" encodinganalog="600" role="subject">Helm,
John B.</persname>
<persname source="lcnaf" encodinganalog="600"
role="subject">Johnston, John D., b. 1815--Correspondence</persname>
<persname source="lcnaf" encodinganalog="600" role="subject">Judd,
Norman B. (Norman Buel), 1815-1878--Correspondence</persname>
<persname source="lcnaf" encodinganalog="600" role="subject">Lincoln,
Mary Todd, 1818-1882</persname>
<persname source="lcnaf" encodinganalog="600" role="subject">Lincoln,
Sarah Bush Johnston, 1788-1869</persname>
<persname source="lcnaf" encodinganalog="600" role="subject">Logan,
Stephen T. (Stephen Trigg), 1800-1880</persname>
<persname source="lcnaf" encodinganalog="600"
role="subject">McCallen, Andrew--Correspondence</persname>
<persname source="lcnaf" encodinganalog="600" role="subject">Nicolay,
John G. (John George), 1832-1901--Correspondence</persname>
<persname source="lcnaf" encodinganalog="600" role="subject">Pierce,
Edward Lillie, 1829-1897--Correspondence</persname>
<persname source="lcnaf" encodinganalog="600" role="subject">Speed,
Joshua F. (Joshua Fry), 1814-1882--Correspondence</persname>
<persname source="lcnaf" encodinganalog="600" role="subject">Stevens,
Thaddeus, 1792-1868--Correspondence</persname>
<persname source="lcnaf" encodinganalog="600" role="subject">Swett,
Leonard, 1825-1889</persname>
<persname source="lcnaf" encodinganalog="600" role="subject">Swett,
Leonard, 1825-1889--Correspondence</persname>
<persname source="lcnaf" encodinganalog="600" role="subject">Thomas,
Richard S. (Richard Symmes)--Correspondence</persname>
<persname source="lcnaf" encodinganalog="600"
role="subject">Trumbull, Lyman, 1813-1896--Correspondence</persname>
<persname source="lcnaf" encodinganalog="600" role="subject">Wallace,
Frances, b. 1817</persname>
<persname source="lcnaf" encodinganalog="600"
role="subject">Wentworth, John, 1815-1888--Correspondence</persname>
<persname source="lcnaf" encodinganalog="600" role="subject">White,
Horace, 1834-1916--Correspondence</persname>
<persname source="lcnaf" encodinganalog="600" role="subject">Whitney,
Henry Clay, 1831-1905--Correspondence</persname>
```

DESCRIBING ARCHIVES: A CONTENT STANDARD

```
          <persname source="lcnaf" encodinganalog="600"
          role="subject">Williams, Archibald, 1801-1863--
          Correspondence</persname>
          <persname source="lcnaf" encodinganalog="600" role="subject">Wilson,
          R. L. (Robert L.)</persname>
          <persname source="lcnaf" encodinganalog="600" role="subject">Yates,
          Richard, 1815-1873--Correspondence</persname>
          <famname source="lcnaf" encodinganalog="600" role="subject">Lincoln
          family</famname>
          <corpname source="lcnaf" encodinganalog="610"
          role="subject">Illinois. General Assembly</corpname>
          <corpname source="lcnaf" encodinganalog="610"
          role="subject">Republican Party (U.S. : 1854- )</corpname>
          <corpname source="lcnaf" encodinganalog="610">Weik Manuscript
          Corporation</corpname>
          <corpname source="lcnaf" encodinganalog="610" role="subject">Whig
          Party (U.S.)</corpname>
          <corpname source="lcnaf" encodinganalog="610" role="subject">White
          House (Washington, D.C.)</corpname>
          <persname source="lcnaf" encodinganalog="700">Herndon, William Henry,
          1818-1891. Papers (1849-1891)</persname>
          <persname source="lcnaf" encodinganalog="700">Lincoln, Abraham, 1809-
          1865. Papers (1824-1865)</persname>
          <persname source="lcnaf" encodinganalog="700">Weik, Jesse William,
          1857-1930. Papers (1830-1927)</persname>
          </controlaccess>
          <controlaccess>
          <head>Subjects:</head>
          <subject source="lcsh" encodinganalog="650">Lincoln-Douglas debates,
          1858</subject>
          <subject source="lcsh" encodinganalog="650">Practice of law--
          Illinois--Springfield</subject>
          <subject source="lcsh" encodinganalog="650">Presidents--United
          States--Biography</subject>
          <subject source="lcsh" encodinganalog="650">Presidents--United
          States--Election--1856</subject>
          <subject source="lcsh" encodinganalog="650">Presidents--United
          States--Election--1860</subject>
          <subject source="lcsh" encodinganalog="650">Illinois--Politics and
          government--To 1865</subject>
          <subject source="lcsh" encodinganalog="650">Springfield (Ill.)--
          History</subject>
          <geogname source="lcsh" encodinganalog="651">United States--Politics
          and government--19th century</geogname>
          <geogname source="lcsh" encodinganalog="651">United States--Politics
          and government--1861-1865</geogname>
          </controlaccess>
          <controlaccess>
          <head>Occupations:</head>
          <occupation source="itoamc"
          encodinganalog="656">Biographers</occupation>
          <occupation source="itoamc"
          encodinganalog="656">Collectors</occupation>
          <occupation source="itoamc" encodinganalog="656">Lawyers</occupation>
          </controlaccess>
          </controlaccess>
<descgrp type="admininfo">
<head>Administrative Information</head>
5.2 ...    <acqinfo encodinganalog="541">
          <head>Provenance:</head>
          <p>The Herndon-Weik Collection of Lincolniana was purchased by the
          Library of Congress from G. A. Baker and Co. in 1941. Material
```

```
                relating to Abraham Lincoln acquired by the Library from other
                sources between 1929 and 1982 is also included in the collection.</p>
                </acqinfo>
8.1 ...         <processinfo>
                <head>Processing History:</head>
                <p>The Herndon-Weik Collection of Lincolniana was first processed in
                1974; additional material received was incorporated into the
                collection in 1984. This register was revised in 1997.</p>
                </processinfo>
6.3 ...         <separatedmaterial encodinganalog="544 0">
                <head>Transfers:</head>
                <p>Items have been transferred from the Manuscript Division to other
                custodial divisions of the Library. Photographs and etchings have
                been transferred to the Prints and Photographs Division. A broadside
                has been transferred to the Rare Book and Special Collections
                Division.  All transfers are identified in these divisions as part of
                the Herndon-Weik Collection of Lincolniana.</p>
                </separatedmaterial>
4.4 ...         <userestrict encodinganalog="540">
                <head>Copyright Status:</head>
                <p>The status of copyright in the unpublished writings of Abraham
                Lincoln, William Henry Herndon, and Jesse William Weik in these
                papers and in other collections of papers in the custody of the
                Library of Congress is governed by the Copyright Law of the United
                States (Title 17, U.S.C.).</p>
                </userestrict>
4.1 ...         <accessrestrict encodinganalog="506"><head>Restrictions:</head><p>The
                Herndon-Weik Collection of Lincolniana is
                unrestricted.</p></accessrestrict>
                <accessrestrict encodinganalog="506"><head>Access:</head><p>Consult a
                reference librarian in the Manuscript Division before visiting the
                Library to determine whether or not containers should be requested in
                advance.</p></accessrestrict>
6.2 ...         <altformavail encodinganalog="530">
                <head>Microfilm:</head>
                <p>A microfilm edition of these papers is available on fifteen reels.
                Use of the microfilm copy may be required. Consult a reference
                librarian in the Manuscript Division concerning purchase or
                interlibrary loan. </p>
                </altformavail>
7.1 ...         <prefercite encodinganalog="524">
                <head>Preferred Citation:</head>
                <p>Researchers wishing to cite this collection should include the
                following information: Container or reel number, Herndon-Weik
                Collection of Lincolniana, Manuscript Division, Library of Congress,
                Washington, D.C.</p>
                </prefercite>
</descgrp>
2.7 ...         <bioghist encodinganalog="545">
                <head>Biographical Notes</head>
                <bioghist encodinganalog="545">
                <head>William Henry Herndon</head>
                <chronlist>
                <listhead>
                <head01>Date</head01>
                <head02>Event</head02>
                </listhead>
                <chronitem>
                <date>1818 December 25</date>
                <event>Born, Greensburg, Ky.
                </event>
                </chronitem>
```

```
<chronitem>
<date>1820</date>
<event>Moved to Illinois
</event>
</chronitem>
<chronitem>
<date>1821</date>
<event>Moved to Sangamon County, Ill.
</event>
</chronitem>
<chronitem>
<date>1825</date>
<event>Moved to Springfield, Ill.
</event>
</chronitem>
<chronitem>
<date>1836-1837</date>
<event>Student, preparatory department, Illinois College,
Jacksonville, Ill.
</event>
</chronitem>
<chronitem>
<date>1840</date>
<event>Married Mary Maxcy (died 1861)</event>
</chronitem>
<chronitem>
<date>1844</date>
<event>Admitted to bar and formed law partnership with Abraham
Lincoln
</event>
</chronitem>
<chronitem>
<date>1854</date>
<event>Elected mayor of Springfield, Ill.
</event>
</chronitem>
<chronitem>
<date>1862</date>
<event>Married Anna Miles
</event>
</chronitem>
<chronitem>
<date>1889</date>
<event>Coauthored with Jesse W. Weik
<bibref>
<title>Herndon's Lincoln: The True Story of a Great Life</title>
(Chicago: Belford, Clarke. 3 vols.)</bibref>
</event>
</chronitem>
<chronitem>
<date>1891 March 18</date>
<event>Died, Springfield, Ill.
</event>
</chronitem>
</chronlist>
</bioghist>
<bioghist encodinganalog="545">
<head>Jesse William Weik</head>
<chronlist>
<listhead>
<head01>Date</head01>
<head02>Event</head02>
</listhead>
```

```
<chronitem>
<date>1857 August 23</date>
<event>Born, Greencastle, Ind.
</event>
</chronitem>
<chronitem>
<date>1875</date>
<event>A.B., Indiana Asbury (now DePauw) University, Greencastle,
Ind.
</event>
</chronitem>
<chronitem>
<date>1883</date>
<event>A.M., Indiana Asbury University, Greencastle, Ind.
</event>
</chronitem>
<chronitem>
<date>1880</date>
<event>Admitted to bar but never practiced</event>
</chronitem>
<chronitem>
<date>1889</date>
<event>Coauthored with William H. Herndon
<bibref>
<title>Herndon's Lincoln: The True Story of a Great Life</title>
(Chicago: Belford, Clarke. 3 vols.)</bibref>
</event>
</chronitem>
<chronitem>
<date>1892</date>
<event>Published <bibref>
<title>Abraham Lincoln: The True Story of a Great Life</title> (New
York: D. Appleton. 2 vols.),</bibref> a revised edition of
<bibref><title>Herndon's Lincoln: The True Story of a Great
Life</title> (Chicago: Belford, Clarke. 3 vols.)</bibref>
</event>
</chronitem>
<chronitem>
<date>1930 August 18</date>
<event>Died</event>
</chronitem>
</chronlist>
</bioghist>
<bioghist encodinganalog="545">
<head>Abraham Lincoln</head>
<chronlist>
<listhead>
<head01>Date</head01>
<head02>Event</head02>
</listhead>
<chronitem>
<date>1809 February 12</date>
<event>Born, Hardin County, Ky.
</event>
</chronitem>
<chronitem>
<date>1816</date>
<event>Moved to Indiana
</event>
</chronitem>
<chronitem>
<date>1830</date>
```

```
<event>Moved to Macon County, Ill.
</event>
</chronitem>
<chronitem>
<date>1831</date>
<event>Moved to New Salem, Ill.; employed as storekeeper</event>
</chronitem>
<chronitem>
<date>1832</date>
<event>Served in Black Hawk War; became partner in Lincoln &amp;
Berry, a general store</event>
</chronitem>
<chronitem>
<date>1833-1836</date>
<event>Postmaster, New Salem, Ill.
</event>
</chronitem>
<chronitem>
<date>1834-1836</date>
<event>Deputy county surveyor, Sangamon County, Ill.
</event>
</chronitem>
<chronitem>
<date>1834-1841</date>
<event>Member, Illinois state legislature (Whig)
</event>
</chronitem>
<chronitem>
<date>1836</date>
<event>Licensed as.attorney</event>
</chronitem>
<chronitem>
<date>1837</date>
<event>Moved to Springfield and practiced law in partnership with
John T. Stuart and later Stephen T. Logan
</event>
</chronitem>
<chronitem>
<date>1842</date>
<event>Married Mary Todd
</event>
</chronitem>
<chronitem>
<date>1844</date>
<event>Formed law partnership with William H. Herndon
</event>
</chronitem>
<chronitem>
<date>1847-1849</date>
<event>Member, U.S. House of Representatives (Whig) from Illinois,
Thirtieth Congress</event>
</chronitem>
<chronitem>
<date>1849</date>
<event>Resumed law practice</event>
</chronitem>
<chronitem>
<date>1856</date>
<event>Joined Republican party
</event>
</chronitem>
<chronitem>
<date>1858</date>
```

```
<event>Unsuccessful Republican candidate for U.S. Senate in
opposition to Stephen A. Douglas
</event>
</chronitem>
<chronitem>
<date>1860</date>
<event>Elected president</event>
</chronitem>
<chronitem>
<date>1864</date>
<event>Reelected president</event>
</chronitem>
<chronitem>
<date>1865 April 14</date>
<event>Shot by John Wilkes Booth
</event>
</chronitem>
<chronitem>
<date>1865 April 15</date>
<event>Died, Washington, D.C.
</event>
</chronitem>
</chronlist>
</bioghist>
</bioghist>
```

3.1 ...
```
<scopecontent encodinganalog="520">
<head>Scope and Content Note</head>
<p>Shortly after the death of Abraham Lincoln, William Henry Herndon
began gathering material for a biography of his former law partner.
In 1885, Jesse William Weik brought new inspiration and assistance to
the endeavor, and in 1888 Herndon's biography was completed through
their joint effort. This collection of Lincolniana is the product of
their research. The material covers the time period circa 1824-1933
and is divided into six groups: I: Arithmetic Book and Scrapbooks;
II: Correspondence of Lincoln; III: Legal Documents; IV: Papers of
William Henry Herndon; V: Papers of Jesse William Weik; and VI:
Miscellany.</p>
<p>Group I consists of one leaf (two pages) of an arithmetic book,
into which Lincoln, as a young man, entered tables and exercises in
linear measure, and two scrapbooks of newspaper clippings. One
scrapbook contains editorials, news items, letters, and a number of
statistical tables dealing with such subjects as demographics,
slavery, geography, religion, railroads, agriculture, immigration,
and monetary matters. Lincoln is alleged to have gathered the
material for his debates with Stephen Arnold Douglas during their
race for the United States Senate in 1858. The other scrapbook
contains similar clippings and also includes material on the
presidential election of 1860.</p>
<p>Group II, comprised largely of correspondence, is divided into
three sections. Section A consists of twelve letters and a
certificate of survey in Lincoln's hand. These items are listed as
Nos. 3-14 and 770 in the inventory and include six letters from
Lincoln to Mark William Delahay. Section B consists chiefly of
reproductions of letters and papers written by Lincoln. Several
letters from Lincoln to Joshua Speed document the friendship between
the two men and their close communication on personal and public
affairs. Other recipients include Joshua R. Giddings, Samuel
Haycraft, John D. Johnston, Andrew McCallen, Leonard Swett, Richard
S. Thomas, Henry Clay Whitney, and Archibald Williams. Letters to
Lincoln from 1848 through 1861 and listed as Nos. 774-806 in the
inventory constitute Section C of Group II. The campaign of 1856 is
the subject of much of the correspondence. The candidates, Millard
```

DESCRIBING ARCHIVES: A CONTENT STANDARD

Fillmore, John C. Fremont, and James Buchanan; campaign strategy; and the strength of the Democratic, Republican, and Know-Nothing parties are among the topics discussed. The correspondents include John Bell, Joshua R. Giddings, Norman B. Judd, Thaddeus Stevens, John Wentworth, Richard Yates, and others. This section also contains newspaper clippings and miscellaneous printed material.
Group III comprises documents related to Lincoln's legal cases. It contains certificates, petitions, affidavits, notices, abstracts, writs, briefs, depositions, and other papers dealing with such subjects as divorce, slander, assault and battery, and usury. Most of this material is described as Nos. 15-773 and 2000-78 in the inventory.
The largest series in the collection, Group IV, consists of correspondence, interviews, recollections, notes, newspaper clippings, and other material of William Henry Herndon. Included are an interview with Mary Todd Lincoln in 1871, two long interviews with Dennis Hanks, letters from Hanks to Herndon written in 1865 and 1866 mainly on family history, letters to Herndon from Charles Friend on the Enlow story, and letters and notes from Herndon to Weik between 1881 October 1 and 1891 February 27 containing reminiscences of Lincoln's life.
Prominent in this series are Lincoln's family members, schoolmates, neighbors in New Salem and Springfield, Illinois, law partners, colleagues at the bar and in the Illinois legislature, political party allies, and White House associates. Representative names include Ninian Wirt Edwards (brother-in-law), Kate Roby Gentry (schoolmate), Mentor Graham (teacher), John Hay, whose letter of 1866 September 5 discusses Lincoln's daily life in the White House and ends with the statement that he was "the greatest character since Christ," John B. Helm (store clerk), Sarah Bush Johnston Lincoln (stepmother), Stephen T. Logan (law partner), Leonard Swett (lawyer), Frances Wallace (sister-in-law), and Robert L. Wilson (one of the "Long Nine," a group of tall Whigs, including Lincoln, who served together in the Illinois legislature). Also in Group IV are manuscripts by Herndon bearing such titles as "Lincoln's Development," "Lincoln's Courtship with Miss Owens," "The Lincoln-Douglas Debates," "Miss Rutledge and Lincoln," and "Lincoln's Ways."
Group V, the papers of Jesse William Weik, consists of correspondence, notes, extracts, interviews, typed and handwritten copies of documents, and other items. Correspondents include Albert Jeremiah Beveridge, James Cook Conkling, Richard Henry Dana, John Hay, John G. Nicolay, Edward Lillie Pierce, Lyman Trumbull, and Horace White.
Group VI is an assortment of unbound material which includes photostatic copies and facsimiles of documents mostly by Lincoln, a printed sermon and speech by Theodore Parker, newspaper clippings, magazine articles, pamphlets, one chapter of Albert Jeremiah Beveridge's <title>Abraham Lincoln (1928),</title> Charles M. Thompson's report on the "Lincoln Way" investigation, records of the Weik Manuscript Corporation, and negative photographs of documents collected by Herndon and Weik.
</scopecontent>
4.6 ...   <otherfindaid encodinganalog="555">
<head>Other Guides to the Herndon-Weik Collection</head>
An annotated inventory describing each item in the collection, but in an order different from the current arrangement, and a negative photostatic copy of the inventory with fewer annotations may be found in the Manuscript Division Reading Room reference collection. Special card file indexes for the collection exist but are housed separately from the items themselves. A microfilm version of these indexes may be found on reel 15 of the Miscellany series. To use the original

```
                    indexes consult the reference staff in the Manuscript Division
                    Reading Room.</p></otherfindaid>
3.2 ...     <arrangement encodinganalog="351$a">
            <head>Organization of the Papers</head>
            <p>The collection is arranged in six series:</p>
            <list type="simple">
            <item>Group I: Arithmetic Book and Scrapbooks, circa 1824-1860,
            undated</item>
            <item>Group II: Correspondence of Abraham Lincoln, 1833-1865, undated
            </item>
            <item>Group III: Legal Documents, 1834-1860, undated</item>
            <item>Group IV: Papers of William Henry Herndon, 1849-1891, undated
            </item>
            <item>Group V: Papers of Jesse William Weik, 1830-1927, undated
            </item>
            <item>Group VI: Miscellany, circa 1824-1933, undated</item>
            </list>
            </arrangement>
<dsc type="combined">
<head>Container List</head>
<thead valign="bottom">
<row>
<entry morerows="0">Box</entry>
<entry morerows="0">Reel</entry>
<entry morerows="0">Contents</entry>
</row>
</thead>
<c01 level="series">
<did>
<container type="box">1</container>
<container type="reel">1</container>
2.1 ...     <unitid>Group I: </unitid>
2.3 ...     <unittitle>Arithmetic book and scrapbooks,
2.4 ...     <unitdate normal="1824/1860">circa 1824-1860, </unitdate>
            <unitdate>undated</unitdate>
            </unittitle>
</did>
3.1 ...     <scopecontent encodinganalog="520">
            <p>One leaf from Lincoln's arithmetic book and two scrapbooks with
            clippings of statistical tables, articles, editorials, and extracts
            from speeches. </p>
            </scopecontent>
3.2 ...     <arrangement encodinganalog="351$b">
            <p>Arranged by type of material.</p>
            </arrangement>
<c02>
<did>
<container type="box">1</container>
<container type="reel">1</container>
2.3 ...     <unittitle>Lincoln's arithmetic book, one leaf (two pages),
2.4 ...     <unitdate>circa 1824-1826</unitdate>
            </unittitle>
</did>
</c02>
<c02>
<did>
2.3 ...     <unittitle>Scrapbooks</unittitle>
</did>
<c03>
<did>
2.3 ...     <unittitle>Newspaper clippings allegedly used by Lincoln in his
            debates with Stephen A. Douglas in 1858,
```

```
2.4 ...     <unitdate>circa 1850-1858, </unitdate>
            <unitdate>undated</unitdate>
            </unittitle>
</did>
</c03>
<c03>
<did>
2.3 ...     <unittitle>Newspaper clippings,
2.4 ...     <unitdate>circa 1854-1860, </unitdate>
            <unitdate>undated</unitdate>
            </unittitle>
</did>
</c03>
</c02>
</c01>
<c01 level="series">
<did>
<container type="box">2</container>
<container type="reel">1</container>
<unitid>Group II: </unitid>
<unittitle>Correspondence of Abraham Lincoln,
<unitdate normal="1833/1865">1833-1865, </unitdate>
<unitdate>undated</unitdate>
</unittitle>
</did>
<scopecontent encodinganalog="520">
<p>Original correspondence, copies of documents, and other miscellaneous
items.</p>
</scopecontent>
<arrangement encodinganalog="351$b">
<p>Arranged chronologically in three sections. </p>
</arrangement>
<note>
<p>See original index in Manuscript Division Reading Room or microfilm copy in
Group VI, reel no. 15.</p>
</note>
<c02>
<did>
<container type="box">2</container>
<container type="reel">1</container>
<unittitle>Section A, letters and documents in Lincoln's hand, <unitdate
normal="1834-01-14/1861-03-13">1834 January 14-1861 March 13</unitdate>
</unittitle>
</did>
</c02>
<c02>
<did>
<unittitle>Section B, copies of letters and documents mostly by Lincoln,
<unitdate normal="1833-10-19/1865-04-06">1833 October 19-1865 April
6</unitdate>
</unittitle>
</did>
</c02>
<c02>
<did>
<unittitle>Section C, original letters to Lincoln, <unitdate
encodinganalog="1848-09-07/1861-03-11">1848 September 7-1861 March
11</unitdate>
</unittitle>
</did>
</c02>
</c01>
<c01 level="series">
```

```
<did>
<container type="box">3-13</container>
<container type="reel">2-6</container>
<unitid>Group III: </unitid>
<unittitle>Legal documents,<unitdate normal="1834/1860">1834-1860, </unitdate>
<unitdate>undated</unitdate>
</unittitle>
</did>
<scopecontent encodinganalog="520">
<p>Briefs, complaints, petitions, and other legal documents relating to
Lincoln's law cases. </p>
</scopecontent>
<arrangement encodinganalog="351$b">
<p>Arranged alphabetically by name of plaintiff with separate papers for each
case file by the date entered with the clerk of court. </p>
</arrangement>
<note>
<p>See original index in Manuscript Division Reading Room or microfilm copy in
Group VI, reel no. 15.</p>
</note>
<c02>
<did>
<container type="box">3</container>
<container type="reel">2</container>
<unittitle>A-Bro</unittitle>
</did>
</c02>
<c02>
<did>
<container type="box">4</container>
<container type="reel">2</container>
<unittitle>Bru-De</unittitle>
</did>
</c02>
<c02>
<did>
<container type="box">5</container>
<container type="reel">2-3</container>
<unittitle>Do-Gre</unittitle>
</did>
</c02>
<c02>
<did>
<container type="box">6</container>
<container type="reel">3</container>
<unittitle>Gru-Hi</unittitle>
</did>
</c02>
<c02>
<did>
<container type="box">7</container>
<container type="reel">3-4</container>
<unittitle>Ho-La</unittitle>
</did>
</c02>
<c02>
<did>
<container type="box">8</container>
<container type="reel">4</container>
<unittitle>Le-Mal</unittitle>
</did>
</c02>
```

```
<c02>
<did>
<container type="box">9</container>
<container type="reel">4-5</container>
<unittitle>Man-Pad</unittitle>
</did>
</c02>
<c02>
<did>
<container type="box">10</container>
<container type="reel">5</container>
<unittitle>Par-Rob</unittitle>
</did>
</c02>
<c02>
<did>
<container type="box">11</container>
<container type="reel">5</container>
<unittitle>Rog-Spi</unittitle>
</did>
</c02>
<c02>
<did>
<container type="box">12</container>
<container type="reel">5-6</container>
<unittitle>Spr-Van</unittitle>
</did>
</c02>
<c02>
<did>
<container type="box">13</container>
<container type="reel">6</container>
<unittitle>Vau-You</unittitle>
</did>
</c02>
<c02>
<did>
<unittitle>Miscellany</unittitle>
</did>
</c02>
</c01>
<c01 level="series">
<did>
<container type="box">14-27</container>
<container type="reel">7-11</container>
<unitid>Group IV: </unitid>
<unittitle>Papers of William Henry Herndon,
<unitdate normal="1849/1891">1849-1891, </unitdate>
<unitdate>undated</unitdate>
</unittitle>
</did>
<scopecontent encodinganalog="520">
<p>Correspondence, notes, interviews, collections, copies of documents, and
miscellaneous material. </p>
</scopecontent>
<arrangement encodinganalog="351$b">
<p>Arranged chronologically. </p>
</arrangement>
<note>
<p>See original index in Manuscript Division Reading Room or microfilm copy in
Group VI, reel no. 15.</p>
</note>
<c02>
```

```
<did>
<container type="box">14</container>
<container type="reel">7</container>
<unittitle>
<unitdate normal="1849-07-24/1865-07-21">1849 July 24-1865 July 21</unitdate>
</unittitle>
</did>
</c02>
<c02>
<did>
<container type="box">15</container>
<container type="reel">7-8</container>
<unittitle>
<unitdate normal="1865-07-30/1866-01-12">1865 July 30-1866 January
12</unitdate>
</unittitle>
</did>
</c02>
<c02>
<did>
<container type="box">16</container>
<container type="reel">8</container>
<unittitle>
<unitdate normal="1866-01-13/1866-08-10">1866 January 13-1866 August
10</unitdate>
</unittitle>
</did>
</c02>
<c02>
<did>
<container type="box">17</container>
<container type="reel">8</container>
<unittitle>
<unitdate normal="1866-08-11/1866-11-16">1866 August 11-1866 November
16</unitdate>
</unittitle>
</did>
</c02>
<c02>
<did>
<container type="box">18</container>
<container type="reel">8</container>
<unittitle>
<unitdate normal="1866-11-18/1866-12-30">1866 November 18-1866 December 30
</unitdate>
</unittitle>
</did>
</c02>
<c02>
<did>
<container type="box">19</container>
<container type="reel">9</container>
<unittitle>
<unitdate normal="1867-01-05/1874-01-10">1867 January 5-1874 January
10</unitdate>
</unittitle>
</did>
</c02>
<c02>
<did>
<container type="box">20</container>
<container type="reel">9-10</container>
```

```
<unittitle>
<unitdate normal="1874-02-09/1887-01-02">1874 February 9-1887 January
2</unitdate>
</unittitle>
</did>
</c02>
<c02>
<did>
<container type="box">21</container>
<container type="reel">10</container>
<unittitle>
<unitdate normal="1887-01-06/1889-01-04">1887 January 6-1889 January
4</unitdate>
</unittitle>
</did>
</c02>
<c02>
<did>
<container type="box">22</container>
<container type="reel">10</container>
<unittitle>
<unitdate normal="1889-01-05/1891-02-27">1889 January 5-1891 February
27</unitdate>
</unittitle>
</did>
</c02>
<c02>
<did>
<container type="box">23-24</container>
<container type="reel">11</container>
<unittitle>Undated</unittitle>
</did>
</c02>
<c02>
<did>
<container type="box">25-27</container>
<container type="reel">11</container>
<unittitle>Drafts of portions of  <title>Herndon's Lincoln</title>
</unittitle>
</did>
</c02>
</c01>
<c01 level="series">
<did>
<container type="box">28-35</container>
<container type="reel">12-14</container>
<unitid>Group V: </unitid>
<unittitle>Papers of Jesse William Weik, <unitdate normal="1830/1927">1830-
1927, </unitdate><unitdate>undated</unitdate>
</unittitle>
</did>
<scopecontent encodinganalog="520">
<p>Correspondence, notes, interviews, copies of documents, and miscellaneous
material. </p>
</scopecontent>
<arrangement encodinganalog="351$b">
<p>Arranged chronologically. </p>
</arrangement>
<note>
<p>See original index in Manuscript Division Reading Room or microfilm copy in
Group VI, reel no. 15.</p>
</note>
<c02>
```

```
<did>
<container type="box">28</container>
<container type="reel">12</container>
<unittitle>
<unitdate normal="1830-02-20/1886-02-04">1830 February 20-1886 February
4</unitdate>
</unittitle>
</did>
</c02>
<c02>
<did>
<container type="box">29</container>
<container type="reel">12</container>
<unittitle>
<unitdate normal="1886-03-15/1889-01-03">1886 March 15-1889 January
3</unitdate>
</unittitle>
</did>
</c02>
<c02>
<did>
<container type="box">30</container>
<container type="reel">12-13</container>
<unittitle>
<unitdate normal="1889-01-11/1898-12-15">1889 January 11-1898 December
15</unitdate>
</unittitle>
</did>
</c02>
<c02>
<did>
<container type="box">31</container>
<container type="reel">13</container>
<unittitle>
<unitdate normal="1898-12-27/1913-11-20">1898 December 27-1913 November
20</unitdate>
</unittitle>
</did>
</c02>
<c02>
<did>
<container type="box">32</container>
<container type="reel">13</container>
<unittitle>
<unitdate normal="1913-11-25/1918-02-15">1913 November 25-1918 February
15</unitdate>
</unittitle>
</did>
</c02>
<c02>
<did>
<container type="box">33</container>
<container type="reel">14</container>
<unittitle>
<unitdate normal="1918-03-05/1927-12-04">1918 March 5-1927 December 4,
</unitdate>
<unitdate>undated</unitdate>
</unittitle>
</did>
</c02>
<c02>
<did>
```

```
<container type="box">34-35</container>
<container type="reel">14</container>
<unittitle>Undated</unittitle>
</did>
</c02>
</c01>
<c01 level="series">
<did>
<unitid>Group VI: </unitid>
<unittitle>Miscellany, <unitdate normal="1824/1933">circa 1824-1933,
</unitdate>
<unitdate>undated</unitdate>
</unittitle>
</did>
<c02 level="subseries">
<did>
<container type="reel">15</container>
<unittitle>Microfilmed material.</unittitle>
</did>
<scopecontent encodinganalog="520">
<p>Microfilm of indexes not physically housed with collection; to use original
indexes, consult reference staff in Manuscript Division Reading Room.</p>
</scopecontent>
<c03><did><container type="reel">15</container>
<unittitle>Special indexes</unittitle>
<note>
<p>Not physically housed with collection; to use original indexes, consult
reference staff in Manuscript Division Reading Room.</p>
</note></did></c03></c02>
<c02 level="subseries">
<did>
<container type="box">36</container>
<container label="not filmed"/>
<unittitle>Unfilmed material.</unittitle>
</did>
<scopecontent encodinganalog="520">
<p>Photocopies and facsimiles, newspaper clippings, pamphlets, magazine
articles, report, sermon, speech, Weik Manuscript Corp. records, and other
items. </p>
</scopecontent>
<note><p>See original index in Manuscript Division Reading Room or microfilm
copy in Group VI, reel no. 15.</p></note><c03>
<did>
<container type="box">36</container>
<unittitle>Herndon family genealogy, <unitdate>undated</unitdate>
</unittitle>
</did>
</c03>
<c03>
<did>
<unittitle>
<emph>Herndon v. Smith</emph> praecipe, <unitdate normal="1837-06-09">1837 June
9</unitdate>
</unittitle>
</did>
</c03>
<c03>
<did>
<unittitle>Lincoln, Abraham, duplicate holograph transcription of letter to
Abraham Jonas, <unitdate normal="1860-02-04">1860 February 4</unitdate>
</unittitle>
</did>
</c03>
```

```
<c03>
<did>
<unittitle>Newspaper and magazine clippings, <unitdate normal="1856/1921">1856-
1921,</unitdate> <unitdate>undated</unitdate>
</unittitle>
</did>
</c03>
<c03>
<did>
<unittitle>Photocopies and facsimiles, <unitdate normal="1824-1888">circa 1824-
1888</unitdate>
</unittitle>
</did>
</c03>
<c03>
<did>
<unittitle>Proceedings of the first annual meeting and dinner of the Lincoln
Fellowship, <unitdate normal="1908-02-12">1908 February 12</unitdate>
</unittitle>
</did>
</c03>
<c03>
<did>
<unittitle>Weik, Jesse William, photocopy of pages from diary, <unitdate
normal="1876-07-04/1876-07-05">1876 July 4-5</unitdate>
</unittitle>
</did>
</c03>
<c03>
<did>
<unittitle>Weik, Jesse William and Mary (daughter), photocopies of photographs,
<unitdate normal="1910">1910, </unitdate>
<unitdate>undated</unitdate>
</unittitle>
</did>
</c03>
<c03>
<did>
<unittitle>Weik Manuscript Corp.</unittitle>
</did>
<c04>
<did>
<c05>
<did>
<unittitle>"The Effect of Slavery on the American People," <unitdate
normal="1858">1858</unitdate>
</unittitle>
</did>
</c05>
<c05>
<did>
<unittitle>"The Relation of Slavery to a Republican Form of Government,"
<unitdate normal="1858">1858</unitdate>
</unittitle>
</did>
</c05>
</c04>
<c04>
<did>
<unittitle>Rugg, Arthur P., "Abraham Lincoln in Worcester,"
<unitdate normal="1914">1914</unitdate>
</unittitle>
```

```
</did>
</c04>
<c04>
</c04>
<c04>
<did>
<unittitle>Thompson, Charles M., report on "Lincoln Way,"
<unitdate>undated</unitdate>
</unittitle>
</did>
</c04>
<c04>
<did>
<unittitle>Weik, Mary Hays, "My Father and Lincoln,"
<unitdate>undated</unitdate>
</unittitle>
</did>
</c04>
</c03>
</c02>
</c01>
</dsc>
</archdesc>
</ead>
```

MARC 21 Record Examples

The following examples represent single-level descriptions that are fully encoded using MAchine-Readable Cataloging (MARC 21). Examples are provided for the following archival materials:

- Personal papers—Mildred Davenport Dance Programs and Dance School Materials
- Family papers—Bacot Family Papers
- Organizational records—Swine Influenza Immunization Program Records
- Collection—Herndon-Weik Collection of Lincolniana
- Item—Field book of James C. Duane

The presentation of these examples is intended only to assist in understanding how descriptive data, created according to *DACS* rules, can be encoded in MARC 21 for output in MARC-based public access catalogs. The examples are not meant to be prescriptive. Archivists seeking more information on MARC 21 coding should consult the *MARC 21 Format for Bibliographic Data: Including Guidelines for Content Designation* (see Appendix B).

DACS element numbers are provided in **bold** for specific data elements whose content was formulated according to *DACS* rules. These single-level descriptions use a variation of the "single-level added value" elements from Chapter 1.

Mildred Davenport Dance Programs and Dance School Materials

```
                001        47267296
2.1...          008        010710i19341942cau | eng d
                035    bb  ‡a .b28303544
2.1/8.1...      040    bb  ‡a CUI ‡e dacs ‡c CUI
2.1 ...         099    bb  ‡a MS-P 29
2.6/12.1A       100    1b  ‡a Davenport, Mildred, ‡d 1900-1990.
2.3/2.4...      245    10  ‡a Mildred Davenport dance programs and dance
                           school materials, ‡f 1914-1942.
2.5 ...         300    bb  ‡a 0.3 linear feet (1 box and 1 oversize folder).
3.1 ...         520    bb  ‡a This collection comprises dance programs,
                           dance school materials, photographs, and ephemera
                           documenting the early career of the Boston-based
                           African-American dancer, dance instructor, and
                           civic official Mildred Davenport. ‡b The bulk of
                           this collection consists of dance programs and
                           dance school materials. The collection also
                           contains 29 photographs of Davenport, her
                           students in various performances, and friends or
                           individual students. Dance programs from 1925 to
                           1942 feature her solo performances and group
                           performances with her students. The collection
                           includes a complete run of programs for Bronze
```

<table>
<tr><td></td><td></td><td></td><td>Rhapsody, an annual performance series choreographed, staged, and directed by Davenport. Her personal copy of a typescript of stage directions for a 1934 performance is included with these programs. Her dance schools, Davenport School of the Dance and Silver Box Studio, are documented in course brochures and applications.</td></tr>
<tr><td>4.5 ...</td><td>546</td><td>bb</td><td>‡a Materials in English.</td></tr>
<tr><td>4.1 ...</td><td>506</td><td>bb</td><td>‡a Collection open for research.</td></tr>
<tr><td>7.1 ...</td><td>524</td><td>bb</td><td>‡a Cite as: Mildred Davenport Dance Programs and Dance School Materials. MS-P29. Special Collections and Archives, The UC Irvine Libraries, Irvine, California</td></tr>
<tr><td>5.2 ...</td><td>541</td><td>bb</td><td>‡a Acquired, ‡d 1998</td></tr>
<tr><td>2.7/10.9</td><td>545</td><td>bb</td><td>‡a Mildred Ellen Davenport was a noted civic official and military officer with an extensive career as a dancer and dance instructor in Boston in the 1930s and 1940s. ‡b She was born in Boston in 1900. In the 1920s, she studied at the Sargent School for Physical Culture and at Harvard, and opened her first dance school, the Davenport School of Dance. Over the next ten years she studied under Ted Shawn and taught dance in Boston. From 1930 to 1935, she performed in a number of African American musical productions on Broadway, including Fast and Furious, Flying Colors, and Black Birds. In 1932, she established her second dance school, the Silver Box Studio. During World War II, Davenport enlisted in the Army as a captain. From 1947 to 1968, she worked for the NAACP office in Boston and the Massachusetts Commission Against Discrimination. Davenport died in Boston in 1990.</td></tr>
<tr><td>4.6 ...</td><td>555</td><td>bb</td><td>‡a Electronic finding aid available via the Internet in the Online Archive of California; ‡c folder-level control</td></tr>
<tr><td></td><td>600</td><td>10</td><td>‡a Davenport, Mildred, ‡d 1900-1990 ‡v Archives.</td></tr>
<tr><td></td><td>650</td><td>b0</td><td>‡a Dance schools ‡z Massachusetts ‡z Boston ‡v Archives.</td></tr>
<tr><td></td><td>650</td><td>b0</td><td>‡a Dance ‡v Archives.</td></tr>
<tr><td></td><td>650</td><td>b0</td><td>‡a Modern dance ‡z United States ‡v Archives.</td></tr>
<tr><td></td><td>650</td><td>b0</td><td>‡a Dance, Black ‡v Archives.</td></tr>
<tr><td></td><td>650</td><td>b0</td><td>‡a African American dancers ‡v Archives.</td></tr>
<tr><td></td><td>655</td><td>b7</td><td>‡a Dance programs. ‡2 local</td></tr>
<tr><td></td><td>655</td><td>b7</td><td>‡a Photographic prints. ‡2 gmgpc</td></tr>
<tr><td></td><td>655</td><td>b7</td><td>‡a Posters. ‡2 gmgpc</td></tr>
<tr><td></td><td>656</td><td>b7</td><td>‡a Dancers. ‡2 aat</td></tr>
<tr><td></td><td>656</td><td>b7</td><td>‡a Dance teachers. ‡2 lcsh</td></tr>
<tr><td></td><td>710</td><td>2b</td><td>‡a Online Archive of California</td></tr>
<tr><td>2.2 ...</td><td>852</td><td>bb</td><td>‡a Special Collections and Archives, ‡e The UC Irvine Libraries, Irvine, California</td></tr>
<tr><td>4.6 ...</td><td>856</td><td>42</td><td>‡3 OAC finding aid: ‡u http://www.oac.cdlib.org/findaid/ark:/13030/tf4s200680</td></tr>
</table>

Bacot Family Papers

	001		AFJ-0133
2.1 ...	008		901130i17671887scu | eng d
2.1/8.1 ...	040	bb	‡a NOC ‡e dacs ‡c NOC
2.1 ...	099	b9	‡a 916-z
2.6/12.29	100	3b	‡a Bacot family.
2.3/2.4 ...	245	10	‡a Bacot family papers, ‡f 1767-1887 ‡g (bulk 1845 1866).
2.5 ...	300	bb	‡a 90 ‡f items ‡a (0.5 linear feet).
3.2 ...	351	bb	‡a Arranged in three series: Series 1. Correspondence, 1767, 1845-1866, 1887; Series 2. Financial and legal materials, 1786, 1861-1887; Series 3. Other items. 1775-1862.
4.1 ...	506	bb	‡a No restrictions.
3.1 ...	520	bb	‡a Correspondence, financial and legal materials, and other items of Bacot family members and their Brockinton family relatives. Correspondence chiefly relates to business dealings of Peter Samuel Bacot, who managed the plantation, and to family and social activities. Some letters are from cotton factors in Charleston, S.C. Also included are slave lists, and, after the Civil War, contracts relating to the employment of freedmen on the plantation; a few items relating to the Jarrot & Bacot Drug Store; currency issued by South Carolina, 1775-1862; and typed transcriptions of articles published in 1826 about Huguenots in South Carolina.
4.5 ...	546	bb	‡a Materials in English.
6.2 ...	530	bb	‡a Microfilm copy available.
5.2 ...	541	1b	‡a Acquired ‡d 1944
6.3 ...	544	bb	‡d See also Peter Brockington Bacot papers (#2742) in the ‡a Southern Historical Collection, University of North Carolina at Chapel Hill.
2.7/10.9...	545	bb	‡a Bacot family members were cotton planters at Mars Bluff Plantation near Florence, Darlington District, S.C., and, beginning in 1865, partners in the Jarrot & Bacot Drug Store in Florence. The Bacots were related to the Brockinton family and descended from South Carolina Huguenots.
	600	10	‡a Bacot, Peter Samuel, ‡d 1810-1864.
	600	30	‡a Bacot family.
	600	30	‡a Brockinton family.
	610	20	‡a Jarrot & Bacot Drug Store (Florence, S.C.)
	650	b0	‡a African American agricultural laborers ‡z South Carolina.
	650	b0	‡a Agriculture ‡z South Carolina.
	650	b0	‡a Commission merchants ‡z South Carolina ‡z Charleston.
	650	b0	‡a Cotton growing ‡z South Carolina.
	650	b0	‡a Drugstores ‡z South Carolina ‡x History ‡y 19th century.

	650	b0	‡a Family ‡z South Carolina ‡ Social life and customs ‡y 18th century.
	650	b0	‡a Family ‡z South Carolina ‡ Social life and customs ‡y 19th century.
	650	b0	‡a Freedmen ‡z South Carolina.
	650	b0	‡a Huguenots ‡z South Carolina.
	650	b0	‡a Merchants ‡z South Carolina.
	650	b0	‡a Money ‡z South Carolina.
	650	b0	‡a Plantation life ‡z South Carolina.
	650	b0	‡a Plantation owners ‡z South Carolina.
	650	b0	‡a Slavery ‡z South Carolina.
	651	b0	‡a Charleston (S.C.) ‡x Economic conditions.
	651	b0	‡a Darlington District (S.C.) ‡x History.
	651	b0	‡a Mars Bluff Plantation (Darlington District, S.C.)
12.29 ...	700	3b	‡a Brockinton family.
2.2 ...	852	bb	‡a University of North Carolina at Chapel Hill ‡b Southern Historical Collection ‡e CB#3926, Wilson Library, Chapel Hill, N.C. 27514-8890 ‡n ncu
4.6 ...	856	42	‡3 Finding aid ‡u http://www.lib.unc.edu/mss/inv/b/Bacot%5FFamily.html

Swine Influenza Immunization Program Records

	001	bb	001716763
2.1 ...	008	bb	921027i19751979mnu | eng d
	035	bb	‡a (MnHi-Ar)State
2.1/8.1 ...	040	bb	‡a MnHi-Ar ‡c MnHi-Ar ‡e dacs ‡d hf
	043	bb	‡a n-us-mn
2.6/14.18..	110	1b	‡a Minnesota. ‡b Dept. of Health.
2.3/2.4 ...	245	10	‡a Swine influenza immunization program records, ‡f 1975-1979.
2.5 ...	300	bb	‡a 1.25 cubic feet (1 box and 1 partial box).
3.1 ...	520	bb	‡a Records of a statewide program to immunize vulnerable segments of Minnesota's population against swine influenza, which in the middle 1970s was epidemic in many parts of the world. The records include files on the administration of the program and on public outreach and informational activities; data on a grant received by the state from the federal Department of Health, Education, and Welfare as part of the National Influenza Immunization Program; statistics on vaccine usage and immunizations; and program evaluations from the majority of Minnesota's counties.
4.1 ...	506	bb	‡a Records available for research.
5.2 ...	541	bb	‡e 1988-110
4.6 ...	555	0b	‡a Folder list available in repository; filed under Health Department. An electronic version is also available online. ‡u http://www.mnhs.org/library/findaids/hea001.html
5.2 ...	583	bb	‡a Accessioned ‡c 02/05/88
	610	10	‡a United States. ‡b Dept. of Health, Education, and Welfare.
	650	b0	‡a Swine influenza ‡z Minnesota.
	650	b0	‡a Influenza ‡z Minnesota ‡x Vaccination ‡v Statistics.
	650	b0	‡a Vaccination ‡z Minnesota ‡v Statistics.
	650	b0	‡a Interstate relations ‡z Minnesota.
	650	b0	‡a Health promotion ‡z Minnesota.
	650	b0	‡a Health planning ‡x Public relations ‡z Minnesota.
2.2 ...	852	bb	‡a Minnesota Historical Society, ‡c St. Paul, MN.
	852	bb	‡a MnHi

Herndon-Weik Collection of Lincolniana

2.1 ...	008		741029i18241933dcu | eng
2.1/8.1 ...	040	bb	‡a DLC ‡e dacs ‡c DLC
2.3/2.4 ...	245	04	‡a The Herndon-Weik collection of Lincolniana, ‡f circa 1824-1933.
2.5 ...	300	bb	‡a 4,600 ‡f items.
	300	bb	‡a 36 ‡f containers.
	300	bb	‡a 15 ‡f microfilm reels.

	300	bb	‡a 10 ‡f linear feet.
3.2 ...	351	bb	‡a Arranged in 6 series: 1. Arithmetic book and scrapbooks, circa 1824-1860. 2. Correspondence of Abraham Lincoln, 1833-1865. 3. Legal documents, 1834-1860. 4. Papers of William Henry Herndon, 1849-1891. 5. Papers of Jesse William Weik, 1830-1927. 6. Miscellany, circa 1824-1933.
4.1/4.2 ...	506	bb	‡a Collection open for research. Use of microfilm may be required when available.
4.2 ...	506	bb	‡a Collection stored offsite. Requests for containers in advance recommended.
3.1 ...	520	8b	‡a Collection composed of the papers of Lincoln, Herndon, and Weik, records (1933) of The Weik Manuscript Corporation, and miscellaneous material collected chiefly by Herndon and Weik for use in writing Herndon's *Lincoln: The True Story of a Great Life* (1889). Papers of Abraham Lincoln consist of correspondence (1833-1865); legal documents (1834-1860); scrapbooks (2 v., 1850-1860), one of which Lincoln allegedly prepared for use in his debates (1858) with Stephen Arnold Douglas; and other material. Subjects include national politics, chiefly the presidential campaigns of 1856 and 1860, and Lincoln's law practice in Springfield, Illinois. Lincoln's correspondents include John Bell, Mark W. Delahay, Joshua R. Giddings, and others. Papers (1849-1891) of William Henry Herndon include correspondence, manuscripts of writings on Lincoln, interviews, recollections, notes, and other material. Persons represented include Ninian Wirt Edwards (Lincoln's brother-in-law), Kate Roby Gentry (schoolmate), Mentor Graham (teacher), and others. Papers (1830-1927) of Jesse William Weik consist of correspondence, documents, interviews, and other papers.
6.2 ...	530	bb	‡a Microfilm edition of Groups I-V and of the card index available, ‡d no. 13,732.
4.4 ...	540	bb	‡a Copyright restrictions may apply.
5.2 ...	541	bb	‡a Gift and purchase, ‡d 1929-1982.
6.3 ...	544	bb	‡3 Broadside ‡e transferred to ‡a Library of Congress Rare Book and Special Collections Division.
6.3 ...	544	bb	‡3 Photographs and etchings ‡e transferred to ‡a Library of Congress Prints and Photographs Division.
4.6 ...	555	8b	‡a Finding aid available in the Library of Congress Manuscript Reading Room and on Internet.
4.6 ...	555	8b	‡a Calendar and index available in the Library of Congress Manuscript Reading Room and on Internet.
2.1 ...	590	bb	‡a MSS25791
	600	10	‡a Bell, John, ‡d 1797-1869 ‡v Correspondence.
	600	10	‡a Delahay, Mark W. ‡q (Mark William), ‡d 1818?-1864 ‡vCorrespondence.
	600	10	‡a Edwards, Ninian Wirt.
	600	10	‡a Gentry, Kate Roby.

	600	10	‡a Giddings, Joshua R. ‡q (Joshua Reed), ‡d 1795-1864 ‡vCorrespondence.
	600	10	‡a Graham, Mentor, ‡d 1800-1886.
	610	20	‡a Weik Manuscript Corporation.
	650	b0	‡a Practice of law ‡z Illinois ‡z Springfield.
	650	b0	‡a Presidents ‡z United States ‡x Election ‡y 1856.
	650	b0	‡a Presidents ‡z United States ‡x Election ‡y 1860.
	651	b0	‡a United States ‡x Politics and government ‡y 19th century.
	700	1b	‡a Herndon, William Henry, ‡d 1818-1891. ‡t Papers of William Henry Herndon, ‡f (1849-1891)
	700	1b	‡a Lincoln, Abraham, ‡d 1809-1865. ‡t Papers of Abraham Lincoln ‡f (1824-1865)
	700	1b	‡a Weik, Jesse William, ‡d 1857-1930. ‡t Papers of Jesse William Weik, ‡f (1830-1927)
2.2 ...	852	bb	‡a Library of Congress ‡b Manuscripts Division ‡e Washington, D.C.
4.6 ...	856	4b	‡3 Finding aid ‡u http://hdl.loc.gov/loc.mss/eadmss.ms001002

Field book of James C. Duane

2.1/4.5	008		810423s1858||||dcu | eng
2.1/8.1	040	bb	‡a DLC ‡e dacs ‡c DLC
2.6/12.1A	100	1b	‡a Duane, James C.
2.3/2.4	245	00	‡a Field book of James C. Duane, ‡f 1858.
2.5	300	bb	‡a 1 ‡f v. : 147 p.
4.1	506	bb	‡a Collection open for research.
3.1	520	8	‡a Field book (1858 May 17-Oct. 3) containing various observations during an expedition in Utah. Includes maps and other drawings, travel information, and observations on topography.
5.2	541	bb	‡c Purchase, ‡d 1940.
2.7/10.9	545	0b	‡a Army officer. Full name: James Chatham Duane. Born 1824, died 1897.
2.1	590	bb	‡a MSS21337
	651	b0	‡a Utah ‡x Discovery and exploration.
	655	b7	‡a Drawings ‡2 gmgpc
	655	b7	‡a Maps ‡2 gmgpc
	656	b7	‡a Army officers. ‡2 itoamc
2.2	852	bb	‡a Library of Congress ‡b Manuscript Division ‡e Washington, D.C.

Index

In this index, *DACS* stands for *Describing Archives: A Content Standard.*
Names of the data elements described in the text are capitalized in the index.
Numbers in parentheses are rule numbers for the elements.

AACR2. *see Anglo-American Cataloguing Rules,* 2nd ed.
abbreviations
    in birth and death dates, 97n41
    in estimated dates, 27n30
    in materials (4.5.3), 54
    in name segment (2.3.5), 18
    indicating incorporation (14.5C1), 171
    physical extent, 30n32
    before ships' names (14.5C4), 171
abstract of contents
    vs. Scope and Content Element (3.1), 35
    vs. supplied title, 17n21
academic degrees, honors, etc., added to personal names
        (12.19B), 150–51
access, conditions governing (4.1), 43–45
access points
    and authority files, 86
    creators (9.5), 89, 90
    custodians (5.1), 59
    definition, 201
    overview, xviii-xxi
    and Scope and Content Element (3.1), 35
access restrictions, 43-49
access tools
    application of *DACS* to, xvii
    definition, 201
accession numbers (5.2.5), 62
accrual, definition, 201
Accruals Element (5.4), 66–67
    and date ranges (2.4.8), 26
accumulation, definition, 202
Acquisition and Appraisal Elements, 59–67
    Accruals (5.4), 26, 66–67, 201
    Appraisal, Destruction, and Scheduling Information
        (5.3), 63–65
    Custodial History (5.1), 59–60
    Immediate Source of Acquisition (5.2), 61–62, 205
acronyms and initialisms in corporate names (14.1A,
        14.2B2), 159–60, 162
activities and functions
    access points, xxi
    in archival authority records, 87
    in biographical history (10.21), 99
    corporate bodies (10.30), 102
    in Scope and Content Element (3.1), 35
"added value" data elements, 7, 9, 11
addresses of contact information for originals (6.1.5), 69
administrative structure of corporate bodies (10.31), 102
Administrative/Biographical History Elements
        (2.7), 34, 93–104

administrative history of corporate bodies (10.25-
        10.36), 100–104
    and other creators (9.9), 91
    biographical history of individuals or families (10.14-
        10.24), 95–100
    in authority record (11.12), 108
    separate authority file (10.5-10.7), 94
    within description (10.8-10.12), 94–95
Afrikaans surnames with prefixes (12.5D1), 132-33
aggregations
    definition, 202
    system of arrangement (3.2), 40
aliases in biographical history (10.16), 96
alpha-numeric designations in notes (7.1.6), 78
alternative rules in *DACS,* use of, 4
amalgamations of corporate bodies (10.33), 103
ambiguous names. *see* Names not conveying the idea of ...
"and other material" in Title Element (2.3.20), 21
Anglo-American Cataloguing Rules, 2nd ed. (AACR2)
        (2.3.2), vi, vii, 17, 117–18, 209
antipopes (12.16B1), 147
APPM. see Archives, Personal Papers, and Manuscripts
appraisal decisions (5.3), 63–65
Appraisal, Destruction, and Scheduling Information
        Element (5.3), 63–65
approximations. *see* Estimations and approximations
Arabic script, names in (12.3C2), 128
        see also Romanization
archbishops. *see* Religious leaders and officials
architectural drawings, definition, 202
Archival Moving Image Materials, 209
archival series, definition, 202
archival unit, nature of (2.3.18-2.3.20), 20–21
archives, nature of, xi–xiii
Archives, Personal Papers, and Manuscripts (APPM), v-
        vii, 219
    crosswalk to *DACS,* 214-215
Archivist Element (8.1.5), 82
armed forces
    below national level (14.24B), 192
    entered subordinately (14.18), 184
    national level (14.24A), 191–92
arrangement
    and description, xii–xiii, xiv
    definition, 202
    levels of, *DACS vs. ISAD(G),* vii
    see also System of Arrangement Element (3.2)
Art & Architecture Thesaurus, xx-xxi, 210
articles (part of speech)
    initial articles in corporate names (14.5A), 170

in surnames with prefixes (12.5D1), 132–37
Asian languages, corporate names in (14.5C3), 171
associative relationships, 109
audiovisual materials, equipment required for, 48
    see also Physical Access Element (4.2)
Australian place names (13.4C), 155
authority files
    and Administrative/Biographical History Element (2.7,
        10.5-10.7), 34, 94
    archival *vs.* bibliographic, 86–87
    definition, 202
    see also Authority records
authority record identifier (11.19), 110
authority records, 105–14
    definition, 202
    description of the person, family, or corporate body
        (11.12), 108
    form of name (11.5-11.11), 106–8
    management of (11.18-11.27), 110–11
    related materials (11.28-11.31), 111–12
    related persons or bodies (11.13-11.17), 108–9
    see also Authority files
authorized name, definition, 202

biographical history. *see* Administrative/Biographical
    History Element (2.7, 10.5-10.7)
birth, date of. *see* Dates of birth, death, etc.
bishops. *see* Religious leaders and officials
Bistum (Holy Roman Empire) (14.27C3), 196
box lists. *see* Finding Aids Element (4.6)
branches
    armed forces (14.24), 191–92
    corporate bodies (10.28, 14.9, 14.13), 101, 175, 177
    government agencies (14.18), 182-84
brief title (2.3.3), 17–18
British Isles, place names (13.4D), 155–56
bulk dates, definition, 202
    see also Predominant dates

calendar, definition, 202
    see also Finding Aids Element (4.6)
Canada, place names (13.4C), 154–55
cardinals (ecclesiastical official). *see* Religious leaders and
    officials
Cartographic Materials, 209
cartographic materials, definition, 202
Cataloging Cultural Objects, 210
cataloging rules in authority record (11.20-11.21), 110
catalog, definition, 202
Categories for the Description of Works of Art, 210
Catholic Church
    councils (14.27A2), 194
    diplomatic missions (14.27D), 196–97
    Roman Curia (14.27C4), 196
    subordinate bodies (14.27C3), 196
    see also Popes
Channel Islands, place names (13.4D), 155–56
chapters of corporate bodies (14.9). *see* Branches
children of royal persons (12.16A4), 146

Chorepiscopus (12.16C), 147
church councils
    conventional names (14.3C2), 165n76
    headings for (14.27A), 194
churches, local (14.3G), 167–68
    see also Religious bodies; Worship, places of
citation information (7.1.5), 78
cities and towns added to place names (13.4F2), 156–57
civil courts (14.23A), 190
classification schemes. *see* Finding Aids Element (4.6)
"collection" in Title Element (2.3.18), 20–21
collection, definition, 203
collectors
    as creators, 89
    definition, 203
    information about, 93
    in name segment, 18–20
committees and commissions
    government agencies (14.18), 182
    joint committees (14.15), 180–81
    of legislative bodies (14.21B), 188–89
    subcommittees of U.S. Congress (14.21C), 189
    as subordinate corporate bodies (14.13), 177
completeness of records (3.1), 35
computer equipment requirements (4.3.6), 48–49
Conditions Governing Access Element (4.1), 43–45
Conditions Governing Reproduction and Use Element
    (4.4), 50–53
Conditions of Access and Use Elements, 43–58
    Conditions Governing Access (4.1), 43–45
    Conditions Governing Reproduction and Use (4.4), 50–
        53
    Finding Aids (4.6), 56–58
    Languages and Scripts of the Material (4.5), 54–55
    Physical Access (4.2), 46–47
    Technical Access (4.3), 48–49
conferences and congresses (14.7), 173–74
    ancient and international bodies (14.3C2), 165n76
    changes in place name of (13.3), 154
    delegations to (14.26), 193–94
    variant forms of names (14.3F), 166–67
conservation treatment notes (7.1.3), 77–78
consistency of creator names, 86
    see also Authority records
consorts of royal persons (12.16A3), 146
constitutional conventions, headings for (14.22), 189
consulates. *see* Embassies
containers, definition, 203
Content and Structure Elements, 35–42
    Scope and Content Element (3.1), 35–39
    System of Arrangement Element (3.2), 40–41
content dates
    definition, 203
    in Scope and Content Element (3.1), 35
    see also Dates of creation of materials
content element. *see* Scope and Content Element
contents, abstract of. *see* Abstract of contents
context of creation. *see* Administrative/Biographical
    History Element (2.7)

conventional names
    corporate bodies (14.3C), 164–65
    governments (14.3E), 166
copies
    existence and location of (6.2), 71–72
    see also Reproductions
copyright restrictions (4.4.6-4.4.10), 50–51
corporate bodies
    administrative history (10.25-10.36), 100–104
    chapters or branches of (10.28,14.9, 14.13), 101, 175, 177
    definition, 203
    in name segment (2.3.4, 2.3.16, 2.3.17), 18, 20
    predecessor and successor bodies (10.32), 102–3
    principles of description, xiv
    related corporate bodies (11.13-11.17), 108–9
corporate names, 159–97
    additions to names (14.4), 168–70
    changes in (10.34, 14.1C), 103, 161
    conventional names (14.3C), 164–65
    language (14.3A-14.3B), 163–64
    names not conveying the idea of a corporate body (14.4B), 168
    place names as distinguishing terms (14.4C2-14.4C4), 169–70
    place names in, changes in (13.3), 154
    variant names (14.2-14.3), 162–68
countries
    corporate names, distinguishing (14.4C2), 169
    place names, added to (13.4E), 156
country identifier code (2.1.5), 13, 15
courtesy titles. *see* Titles of nobility
courts (14.18A, 14.23), 184, 190
creators
    definition, 203
    description of, xv, 85–88
    finding aids prepared by (4.6.2), 56–57
    identification of, 85, 89–92
    in name segment of a title, 18–20
    more than one, 90–91
    Name of Creator(s) Element (2.6), 33
    see also Corporate names; Personal names; Provenance
creators, corporate
    administrative history (10.25-10.36), 100-104
    principles of description, xiv
creators, family
    biographical history (10.14-10.24), 95–100
    principles of description, xiv
creators, individual
    biographical history (10.14-10.24), 95–100
    principles of description, xiv
criminal courts (14.23A), 190
cross-references (11.10), 107
CUSTARD project, v–vi
Custodial History Element (5.1), 59–60
    see also Immediate Source of Acquisition Element (5.2)
custodians
    access points for, 59
    and creators, 89

    definition, 203
custody, changes in (3.1), 35
Czech surnames
    compound (12.5C5), 131
    with prefixes (12.5D1), 133

DACS. see Describing Archives: A Content Standard
Danish surnames, compound surname uncertain (12.5C6), 131–32
    see also Scandinavian surnames with prefixes
data elements in *DACS,* 3, 7
data structure standards, 212
    see also Encoded Archival Description Tag Library (EAD); MARC 21 Format for Bibliographic Data
Date Element (2.4), 24–28
date of archival description (8.1.5), 82
date ranges (2.4.7-2.4.12), 25–27
dates, estimated
    ranges (2.4.12), 27
    single dates (2.4.15), 27
dates, gaps in (2.4.11), 26
dates, multiple types of, 24
dates of appraisal/destruction actions (5.3.6), 64
dates of authority record creation (11.24), 111
dates of birth, death, etc.
    added to personal names (12.17), 148–49
    in biographical history (10.18), 97
    distinguishing personal names (12.19B), 150–51
dates of broadcast, 24
    definition, 203
dates of conferences (14.7A, 14.7B3), 173
dates of constitutional conventions (14.22A), 189
dates of creation of description (8.1.5), 82
dates of creation of materials, 24
    definition, 203
    see also Content dates
dates of dissolution (corporate bodies) (10.27), 101
dates of exhibitions (14.8B), 175
dates of founding (corporate bodies)
    in administrative history (10.27), 101
    distinguishing bodies (14.4C6), 170
dates of incumbency
    heads of government (14.20C1), 187
    heads of international intergovernmental organizations (14.20C2), 187
    heads of state (14.20B1), 186
    religious officials (14.27B1), 194–95
dates of jurisdiction (governments) (14.6D), 172
dates of military courts (14.23B), 190
dates of publication, distribution, etc., 24
    definition, 203
dates of record-keeping activity, 24
    definition, 203
dates of reign
    popes (14.27B2), 195
    sovereigns (14.20B1), 186
dates of related resources in authority records (11.31), 112

dates of relationship of related persons or bodies (11.16), 109
dates of reproduction (3.1.7), 38
    definition, 203
dates of revision of description (8.1.5), 82
dates, predominant or bulk (2.4.10-2.4.11), 26
dates, single (2.4.13-2.4.15), 27
dates, unknown (2.4.16), 28
death, date of. *see* Dates of birth, death, etc.
deeds of gift. *see* Transfer documents
defendants, courts-martial (14.23B), 190
delegations
    apostolic (Catholic Church) (14.27D), 196–97
    to international bodies (14.18, 14.26), 184, 193–94
departments (subordinate body)
    corporate bodies (14.13), 177
    government agencies (14.18), 182
dependent territories, governors of (14.20D), 187–88
Describing Archives: A Content Standard (DACS)
    background, v–viii
    data elements of, 7
    and other standards, vi–vii
    overview, viii
    purpose and scope, 3
describing archival materials, 3-84
describing creators, 85-104
description
    definition, 204
    overview, xvii–xxi
    principles of, xii–xv
Description Control Elements (8.1), 81–82
descriptions, multilevel, required data elements, 9–11
descriptions, single-level, required data elements, 8–9
descriptive outputs, 4-5, 88
descriptive record, definition, 204
descriptive unit, definition, 204
designations with names
    corporate names, distinguishing (14.4C7), 170
    corporate names not conveying the idea of a corporate body (14.4B), 168
    government names, distinguishing (14.6C), 172
    local church names (14.10B), 175
    personal names, distinguishing (12.19), 150–51
    personal names not conveying the idea of a person (12.11A), 142–43
    radio and television stations (14.11), 176
details, levels of, xiv
diacritical marks in personal names (12.1D), 121
Dictionary of Occupational Titles, xxi, 210
digitization (7.1.4), 78
    see also Existence and Location of Copies Element (6.2)
discrete items, definition, 204
distinguishing terms. *see* Designations with names
documentary forms
    access points, xx
    in Title Element (2.3.18-2.3.20), 20-21
    Scope and Content Element (3.1.6), 38
    see also Form and genre terms

document, definition, 204
donors (5.2.4), 61
    and access restrictions, 43
Dutch surnames with prefixes (12.5D1), 133–34, 135

EAD. *see Encoded Archival Description Tag Library (EAD)*
Eastern Church, autocephalous patriarchates of (14.3C3), 165
ecclesiastical principalities of the Holy Roman Empire (14.27C3), 196
education of creator in biographical history (10.20), 98–99
electronic records
    definition, 204
    equipment required for (4.3.6), 48. *see also* Physical Access Element (4.2)
    notes (7.1.4), 78
embassies (14.18, 14.25), 184, 192–93
emissaries, papal (14.27D), 197
Encoded Archival Description Tag Library (EAD), 212
    application of *DACS* to, xvii–xviii
    as output records, 7-9
    crosswalk from *DACS,* 220–21
    in examples, 5, 88
England, place names (13.4D), 155–56
English surnames
    compound surname uncertain (12.5C6), 131–32
    with prefixes (12.5D1), 134
entity, definition, 204
epithets in names of royalty (12.16A2), 145–46
    see also Words or phrases with names
estimations and approximations
    in Date Element (2.4.12, 2.4.15), 27
    in Extent Element (2.5.9), 31
events as corporate bodies. *see* Conferences and congresses; Exhibitions
examples in *DACS,* 5, 88
executive agencies of government, headings for (14.18), 183
exhibitions (14.8), 174–75
Existence and Location of Copies Element (6.2), 71–72
Existence and Location of Originals Element (6.1), 69–70
explanatory references in authority file for heads of state (14.20B2), 187
Extent Element (2.5)
    approximations (2.5.9), 31
    and equipment required for access, 48
    multiple statements (2.5.7-2.5.8), 31

facsimiles, published, 75
familial relationships (11.15), 109
families
    biographical history (10.14-10.24), 95–100
    information required (10.17), 96–97
    principles of description, xiv
    related families (11.13-11.17), 108–9
family names
    headings for (12.29), 152

name segment in Title Element (2.3.10-2.3.15), 18, 19–20

Faroese names, nature of surname uncertain (12.5C6), 132

FIAF Cataloguing Rules for Film Archives, 209

file, definition, 204

finding aid, definition, 204

Finding Aids Element (4.6), 56–58

Flemish surnames. *see* Dutch surnames with prefixes

fonds, definition, 204

    see also Respect des fonds

forenames. *see* Given names (forenames)

form and genre terms

    authorities for, 87

    definition, 21n26

    in Scope and Content Element (3.1), 35

    in Title Element (2.3.18-2.3.20), 21

    see also Documentary forms; Type of related resources
        in authority record

form, definition, 204

formal titles

    definition, 204

    transcription of (2.3.2), 17

fraternal orders (14.3C2), 165n76

French surnames

    compound (12.5C5), 131

    with prefixes (12.5D1), 134

fullness of names

    choice of (12.18), 149–50

    personal names (12.3A), 124–25

functions and activities. *see* Activities and functions

gaps in dates (2.4.11), 26

gaps in unit being described

    not resulting from appraisal decisions (3.1.5), 37–38

    resulting from appraisal decisions (3.1.2), 36

    see also Appraisal, Destruction, and Scheduling
        Information Element (5.3)

Gazetteer of the United States of America, xx

*General International Standard Archival Description
    (ISAD(G)),* v, vi–vii, 7, 9

    crosswalk to *DACS,* 216

generation of copy (6.2.4), 72

generically named subordinate bodies

    corporate bodies (14.13), 177–78

    government agencies (14.18), 182–83

genre terms. *see* Documentary forms; Form and genre
    terms

geographic areas of records (3.1), 35

geographic names. *see* Place names

geographic region of activity (corporate bodies) (10.28),
    101

Geomatic Data Sets, 209

GEOnet Names Server (GNS), xx

German surnames with prefixes (12.5D1), 134–35

Getty Thesaurus of Geographic Names, xx, 211

given names (forenames)

    as names in religion (12.16D), 147–48

    as part of phrases (12.11), 142–43

    bishops and other ecclesiastical officials (12.16C), 147

    distinguishing identical names (12.19A), 150

    entry under (12.8, 12.16), 139–40, 145–48

    hyphenated (12.1D2), 121

    in nonroman scripts (12.3C1), 126–27

    language of name (12.3B3), 126

    popes (12.16B), 146–47

    royalty (12.16A), 145–46

glosses to names. *see* Designations with names

government agencies (14.19), 181–86

    constitutional conventions (14.22), 189

    direct or indirect entry (14.19), 184–86

    embassies (14.25), 192–93

    entered subordinately (14.18-14.19), 182–86

    officials of (14.20E), 188

    references (14.19), 185–86

government officials (14.20), 186–88

governments

    changes in place names in (13.3), 154

    conventional names (14.3E), 166

    definition, 166n77

    identical names, distinguishing (14.6), 172

    see also Jurisdictions

governors

    of dependent or occupied territories (14.20D), 187–88

    as head of state (14.20B), 186–87

grandchildren of royal persons (12.16A4), 146

Graphic Materials, 209

graphic materials, definition, 204

Greek *vs.* vernacular form of personal names (12.3B2), 125

Guide to the Description of Architectural Drawings, 209

guide, definition, 205

    see also Finding Aids Element (4.6)

heading, definition, 205

heads of government (14.18, 14.20C1), 184, 187

heads of state (14.18, 14.20B), 184, 186–87

Hebrew names, 127n49

hierarchical relationships (11.15), 109

Holy Roman Empire ecclesiastical principalities (12.16C,
    14.27C3), 147, 196

honor, terms of. *see* Terms of honor

honors

    in biographical history (10.21), 99

    in corporate names (14.5B), 171

    in personal names (12.9B), 150–51

Hungarian surnames

    compound (12.5C5), 131

    women with né in name (12.15B2), 144

hyphenated personal names

    given names (12.1D), 121

    with place names (12.5C7), 132

    with prefixes (12.5E), 137

    surnames (12.5C3), 130–31

IASA Cataloguing Rules:...Sound Recordings, 210

Icelandic names (12.9B), 141

identical names, distinguishing

    corporate bodies (14.4C), 168–70

    governments (14.6), 172

    personal names (12.16-12.20), 145–51

place names (13.4F1, 13.5B), 156, 157
    saints (12.13B), 144
    terms for (12.19), 150–51
identifiers and identifying numbers
    and location of originals (6.1.6), 70
    authorized names (11.13), 109
    corporate bodies (11.11), 108
    Immediate Source of Acquisition Element (5.2), 62
    related materials (11.28), 111
    see also Alpha-numeric designations; Designations with
        names
Identity Elements, 13–34
    Administrative/biographical History (2.7), 34
    Date (2.4), 24–28
    Extent (2.5), 29–32
    Name And Location Of Repository (2.2), 16
    Name Of Creator(s) (2.6), 33
    Reference Code (2.1), 13–15
    Title (2.3), 17–23
Immediate Source of Acquisition Element (5.2), 61–62
    definition, 205
    see also Custodial History Element (5.1)
inclusive dates (2.4.7), 25–26
    definition, 205
incomplete units. *see* Gaps in unit being described
incorporation, terms indicating (corporate names) (14.5C),
    171
indexes. *see* Finding Aids Element (4.6)
initial articles. *see* Articles (part of speech)
initials
    and fuller form of name (12.18), 149–50
    and identifying compound surnames, 130n53
    as surnames (12.5A1, 12.10), 129, 141–42
    corporate bodies (14.1A), 159–60
    of academic degrees added to identical names (12.19B),
        150–51
    of Christian religious orders (12.16D1), 148
institution names
    added to chapters of corporate bodies (14.9), 175
    distinguishing corporate names instead of local place
        name (14.4C5), 170
intellectual characteristics of records. *see* Form and genre
    characteristics
intentionally assembled collections (2.3.18), viii, 20-21. *see
    also* Collection
international and intergovernmental bodies
    conventional names (14.3C2), 165
    delegations to (14.18, 14.26), 184, 193–94
    language of names (14.3B), 164
    officials of (14.20C2), 187
*International Standard Archival Authority Record for
    Corporate Bodies, Persons, and Families
    (ISAAR(CPF))*, v, vi, 86, 105
    crosswalk to *DACS*, 217-18
inventory, definition, 205
    see also Finding Aids Element (4.6)
Ireland, place names (13.4D), 155–56

ISAAR(CPF). *see International Standard Archival
    Authority Record for Corporate Bodies, Persons,
    and Families*
ISAD(G). *see General International Standard Archival
    Description*
Isle of Man, place names (13.4D), 155–56
ISO 3166-1 *(Codes for the representation of names of
    countries and their subdivisions)*, 15n20
ISO 15511 *(International standard identifier for libraries
    and related organizations)*, 14n19
Italian surnames
    compound (12.5C5), 131
    with prefixes (12.5D1), 135–36
item level description, 3
item, definition, 205

joint commissions and committees (14.15), 180–81
judges of Scottish Court of Session (12.6B2), 139
"junior" following surnames (12.5C8), 132
jurisdictions
    civil and criminal courts (14.23A), 190
    in disputed areas (14.6D), 172
    government names, distinguishing (14.6B), 172
    in place names (13.5), 157
    see also Governments
jurisdictions, religious and ecclesiastical
    added to names of local churches (14.10B), 175–76
    autocephalous religious bodies (14.3C3), 165
    in headings for religious officials (14.27B1), 194-95

knightly orders (14.3C2), 165n76

language
    corporate names (14.3A), 163–64
    international bodies (14.3B), 164
    of authority record (11.25), 111
    of name in name segment (2.3.5), 18
    parallel or variant names, 106–7
    personal names (12.3B), 125–26
    place names (13.2), 153–54
Languages and Scripts of the Material Element (4.5), 54–55
Latin *vs.* vernacular form of personal names (12.3B2), 125–
    26
legislation, enabling (corporate bodies) (10.29), 101–2
legislative bodies (14.18, 14.21), 184, 188–89
letters (alphabetic) as names (12.10), 141–42
level of detail in authority record (11.23), 110
levels of description, xiii, 7–11
    and creator names (9.10), 89, 91
    and levels of arrangement, xiv
Library of Congress Authorities, xviii, xx, 210
*Library of Congress Name Authority File. see Library of
    Congress Authorities*
Library of Congress Subject Headings (LCSH). *see Library
    of Congress Authorities*
local identifier code (2.1.3), 13, 14
locations
    changes in (3.1), 35
    chapters of corporate bodies (14.9), 175

conferences (14.7B4), 174
consulates (14.25), 192-93
copies (6.2), 71–72
exhibitions (14.8B), 175
local church names (14.10B), 175–76
offices of corporate bodies (10.28), 101
originals (6.1), 69–70
physical access limitations (4.2.6), 46–47
radio and television stations (14.11), 176
repository (2.2), 16
residences in biographical history (10.19), 97–98
see also Place names

maintenance information in authority record (11.27), 111
Malaysia, place names (13.4C), 155
mandate of corporate bodies (10.29), 101–2
MARC 21 Format for Bibliographic Data, 212
    as output records, 7-9
    crosswalk from *DACS,* 220–21
    in examples, 5, 88
    relationship of *DACS* to, vi-viii, xvii–xviii
married women
    compound surnames (12.5C5), 131
    given name in parentheses (12.2A1), 122
    Hungarian women with enclitic né (12.15B2), 144
    in biographical history (10.16), 96
    terms of address in name (12.1C, 12.15B), 120, 144
material types in Extent Element (2.5.5-2.5.6), 30
Medical Subject Headings, 210
medium of records
    and description, xiii–xiv
    definition, 205
meetings. *see* Conferences and congresses
memory requirements (4.3.6), 48–49
mergers of corporate bodies (10.33), 103
migration of electronic records (7.1.4), 78
military courts, ad hoc (14.23B), 190
"minimum" data elements, 7, 8, 10
ministries, government (14.18), 183
missions, papal diplomatic (14.27D), 196–97
more than one corporate body in the same unit (14.1C2), 161
more than one corporate body with the same or similar
    names. *see* Identical names, distinguishing
more than one creator, name segments for (2.3.7-2.3.9), 19
more than one person with the same name. *see* Identical
    names, distinguishing
Moving Image Genre-Form Guide, 210
moving images, definition, 205
multilevel description
    date ranges in (2.4.9), 26
    definition, 205
    extent of materials, 29
    inheritance of name segment, 18
    principle of, xiv, xv
    required elements for, 9-11
multimedia materials, description of, xiii–xiv

Name and Location of Repository Element (2.2), 16

Name of Creator(s) Element (2.6), 33
    see also Corporate names; Personal names
name of repository (2.2), 16
name segment in title (2.3.4-2.3.17, 9.8), 17–20, 90
names, access points for, xix
    see also Corporate names; Personal names; Place names
names, authorized form of
    under other rules (11.9), 107
names, authorized form of (11.5-11.6), xix, 106
names, changes in
    corporate bodies (10.34,14.1C), 103, 161
    personal names (12.2C), 124
    place names (13.3, 14.4C4), 154, 170
names in religion (12.16D), 147–48
    see also Religious leaders and officials
names not conveying the idea of ...
    church (14.10), 175–76
    corporate body (14.4B), 168
    government agency (14.18), 183
    person (12.11A), 142–43
    radio or television station (14.11), 176
    subordinate corporate body (14.13), 178
Names of Persons, 151n61
nature of the archival unit in Title Element (2.3.18-2.3.20), 20-21
nicknames (12.2A), 122
nominal access point, definition, 205
nonroman scripts. *see* Arabic script, names in;
    Romanization
Northern Ireland, place names (13.4D), 155–56
Norwegian surnames
    compound surname uncertain (12.5C6), 132
    with prefixes (12.5D1), 136
Notes Elements (7.1), 77–79
    dates in non-Gregorian or Julian calendars (2.4.5), 25
numbers
    in headings for armed forces (14.24A), 191–92
    in headings for conferences (14.7A, 14.7B2), 173
    in headings for exhibitions (14.8A,14.8B), 174, 175
    of legislatures (14.21D), 189
numerals as names (12.10), 141–42

occupations
    access points, xx–xxi
    in biographical history (10.21), 99
    in entry under given name (12.8A1), 139–40
occupied territories, governors (14.20D), 187–88
officers of corporate bodies (10.35), 103
operating systems (4.3.6), 48–49
"optimum" data elements, 7, 9, 11
optional rules in *DACS,* use of, 4
Oral History Cataloging Manual, 210
order of component files (3.2.3), 41
order of data elements, 3, 7
original order
    definition, 205
    maintenance/reconstitution of (3.2.4), 41
    in *respect des fonds,* xii

originals
    definition, 205
    destruction of (5.3.6, 6.1.2), 63–64, 69
    existence and location of (6.1), 69–70
    in same institution as copies (6.2.3-6.2.4), 71–72
output formats of descriptive information, 4–5
ownership, changes in, 35

"papers" in Title Element (2.3.18), 20–21
parallel name (11.7-11.8), 106–7
    definition, 205
patriarchates, autocephalous (14.3C3), 165
patronymics
    Icelandic names (12.9B), 141
    names including (12.8B), 140
    Romanian names (12.7), 139
peerage, Great Britain, 138n56, 143n57
periods in names of corporate bodies (14.1A), 159–60
peripherals, requirements for (4.3.6), 48–49
personal author, definition, 122n46
personal names, 119–52
    additions to (12.12-12.20), 143–51
    choice of different forms of the same name (12.3), 124–28
    choice of different names (12.2), 121–24
    identical names, distinguishing (12.17-12.20), 148–51
    in name segment of Title Element (2.3.4), 18
    initials, expansion of (12.18), 149–50
    initials, letters, or numerals as (12.10), 141–42
    language of (12.3B, 12.5D1), 125–26, 132
    nonroman scripts (12.3C), 126–28
    order of elements (12.4B), 128–29
    place names in (12.5C7), 132
    related persons (11.13-11.17), 108–9
    spelling variations (12.3D), 128
    titles of nobility (12.6, 12.12A), 138–39, 143
    words or phrases as names (12.11), 142–43
    see also Given names (forenames); Hyphenated personal names; Surnames
Physical Access Element (4.2), 46–47
physical carrier, definition, 205
physical characteristics
    affecting the use of the unit (4.2.5), 46–47
    definition, 206
physical condition of materials and physical access limitations (4.2), 46–47
place names, 153–57
    access points, xix–xx
    addition of larger places to (13.4A-13.4F), 154–57
    as government names (14.3E), 166
    changes of name (13.3, 14.4C4), 154, 170
    in corporate names, distinguishing (14.4C1 -14.4C4), 168–70
    in entry under given name (12.8A1), 139–40
    in Icelandic names (12.9B), 141
    in personal names (12.5C7), 132
    jurisdiction, type of (13.5), 157
    language (13.2), 153–54
    see also Territorial designations

place names, local
    corporate names, distinguishing (14.4C3), 169
place names in Scope and Content Element (3.1), 35
places. see Locations
places of worship (14.3G), 167-68
policies, institutional
    acquisitions information in public descriptive records, 61
    anomalous dates, 26n29
    choice of optional or alternative rules, 4
    Scope and Content Element (3.1), 35
political parties, American state and local units (14.16), 181
popes
    diplomatic missions (14.27D), 196–97
    entries for (12.16B), 146–47
    official communications (14.27B2), 195
Portuguese surnames
    compound (12.5C4), 131
    followed by words indicating relationship (12.5C8), 132
    with prefixes (12.5D1), 136
predecessor bodies (10.32), 102–3
    see also Temporal relationships
predominant dates (2.4.10-2.4.11), 26
    definition, 206
    see also Bulk dates, definition
predominant name (12.2A), 121–22
prefixes, surnames with (12.5D-12.5E), 132–37
prepositions in surnames with prefixes (12.5D1), 132
preservation and physical access limitations (4.2.7), 46, 47
Prince-Bishops and Prince-Archbishops (12.16C), 147
princes and princesses (children and grandchildren of royal persons) (12.16A4), 146
princes, ecclesiastical (Holy Roman Empire) (12.16C), 147
principalities, ecclesiastical (Holy Roman Empire) (14.27C3), 196
principles, statement of, xi–xv
professional judgment, use of, 4
provenance
    and related archival materials, 73-74
    definition, 206
    in description, xii
pseudonym
    definition, 206
    entry of (12.2B), 122–23
    names in biographical history (10.16), 96
pseudosurnames, entry under (12.11A), 142–43
public domain, materials in (4.4.10), 51
Publication Note Element (6.4), 75–76
publication
    conditions governing (4.4.13), 52
    definition, 206
    descriptions of materials (4.6.5), 57
    restrictions on (4.4.6), 50
    see also Finding Aids Element (4.6)
published descriptions of archival materials (4.6.5), 57
punctuation of heading, additions to place name (13.4A), 154

qualifiers to names. see Designations with names

RAD. see Rules for Archival Description
radio stations (14.11), 176
rank of royalty and nobility, 145n59
record, definition, 206
records destruction (5.3), 63-64
"records" in Title Element (2.3.18), 20–21
records management program, 63
records schedules, 63
Reference Code Element (2.1), 13–15
   definition, 206
   in Immediate Source of Acquisition Element (5.2.5), 62
reformatting of electronic records (7.1.4), 78
registers. *see* Finding Aids Element (4.6)
Related Archival Materials Element (6.3), 73–74
related corporate bodies (11.13-11.17), 108–9
related families (11.13-11.17), 108–9
related materials, in authority record, 111-12
Related Materials Elements, 69–76
   Existence and Location of Copies (6.2), 71–72
   Existence and Location of Originals (6.1), 69–70
   Publication Note (6.4), 75–76
   Related Archival Materials (6.3), 73–74
   see also Copies; Finding Aids Element (4.6)
related name, definition, 206
related persons in authority record (11.13-11.17), 108-09
related terms and authority files, 86
relationships between levels of description, xiv–xv
relationships between parts of corporate bodies (10.31), 102
relationships between successive creators, xv
relationships, nature of, in authority records (11.30), 112
relationships with other persons or organizations
   in biographical history (10.22), 99–100
   and entry of given names (12.11B), 143
   words indicating after surnames (12.5C8), 132
religious bodies
   conventional names (14.3C2), 165n76
   headings (14.27A), 194
religious leaders and officials
   headings for (12.16C), 147
   official communications of (14.27B), 194–95
   see also Names in religion; Popes
religious orders
   conventional names (14.3D), 165–66
   initials of in names (12.16D), 148
religious vocations, persons of (12.16D), 147–48
remote access and availability of copies (6.2.3), 71
repository as collector
   name segment in Title Element (2.3.6), 19
   description of, xv
   topical segment in title (2.3.22), 22
repository identifier code (2.1.4), 13, 14
   in authority record (11.18), 110
   see also Name and Location of Repository Element (2.2)
reproduction
   conditions governing (4.4.11-4.4.12), 51–52
   definition, 206

and restrictions on use of originals (4.2.7), 47
in Scope and Content Element (3.1.7), 38
see also Copies
Republic of Ireland, place names (13.4D), 155–56
respect des fonds
   definition, 206
   as principle, xii
restrictions on use
   nature of the information. *see* Conditions Governing Access Element (4.1)
   physical condition. *see* Physical Access Element (4.2)
   reproduction or publication. *see* Conditions Governing Reproduction and Use Element (4.4)
   technical requirements. *see* Technical Access Element (4.3)
retention schedules, 63
Revised Nomenclature for Museum Cataloging, 211
Roman Curia (14.27C4), 196
   see also Catholic Church
Roman names
   entry (12.9A), 141
   language of name (12.3B3), 126
roman numerals in names, 119
Romanian names
   patronymics (12.7), 139
   surnames with prefixes (12.5D1), 136
romanization
   corporate names (14.1B), 161, 161n70
   hyphenated personal names (12.1D), 121
   personal names (12.3C), 126–28
romanization tables, 126n48, 161n71
royalty
   additions to names (12.16A), 145–46
   entry of (12.8C), 140–41
   no longer reigning (12.5F), 137–38
   see also Titles of nobility
Rules for Archival Description (RAD), v–vi
rules for description (8.1.4), 81
rules or conventions in authority record (11.20-11.21), 110

saints (12.13), 143–44
Scandinavian surnames with prefixes (12.5D1), 136
schedules. *see* Records schedules
Scope and Content Element (3.1), 35–39
   multiple types of dates in, 25
   and Title Element (2.3.20), 21
Scotland, place names (13.4D), 155–56
Scottish Court of Session, law titles of judges of (12.6B2), 139
script of the material. *see* Languages and Scripts of the Material Element (4.5)
scripts, nonroman. *see* Romanization
"senior" following surnames (12.5C8), 132
separate identities, entry of (12.2B2), 122-23
series, definition, 206-07
sessions of legislatures (14.21D), 189
ships, abbreviations before names (14.5C4), 171
single-level description, requirements for, 8-9
Slovak surnames with prefixes (12.5D1), 133

software requirements (4.3.6), 48–49
sound recordings, definition, 207
sources used in description (8.1.3), 81
sources of information
    in authority record (11.26), 111
    choice of, 3–4
    corporate names (14.1A), 159
    variant corporate names (14.2B), 162
    see also specific elements, e.g., Reference Code
        Element
sovereigns. *see* Royalty
Spanish surnames
    compound (12.5C5), 131
    with prefixes (12.5D1), 136
spellings, variant. *see* Variant spellings
spirits (12.14), 144
states, names of
    added to place names (13.4C), 155
    distinguishing corporate names (14.4C2), 169
status of record in authority file (11.22), 110
subcommittees of U.S. Congress (14.21C), 189
subject headings
    access points, xx
    authorities for, 87
    in Scope and Content Element (3.1), 35
    standardized, xviii
    see also Authority files
subordinate bodies
    church councils (14.27A3), 194
    direct or indirect entry (14.14), 179–80
    entered directly (14.12), 176–77
    entered subordinately (14.13), 177–79
    government agencies (14.17-14.19), 181–86
    legislative bodies as (14.21), 188–89
    political parties (14.16), 181
    references (14.14), 180
    religious bodies (14.27C), 195–96
successor bodies (10.32), 102–3
    see also Temporal relationships
supplied title
    vs. abstract of contents, 17n21
supplied title
    definition, 207
    and identification of creator (9.8), 90
    rules for (2.3.3), 17–18
surnames
    distinguishing identical names (12.19B), 150–51
    elements functioning as (12.5B), 130
    entry under (12.5), 129–38
    in entry under title of nobility (12.6A), 138
    in nonroman scripts (12.3C2), 127–28
    of royalty (12.5F, 12.8C), 137–38, 140–41
    words and phrases added to (12.15), 144-45
    words indicating relationship following surnames
        (12.5C8), 132
    see also Personal names
surnames, compound (12.5C), 130–32
    hyphenated (12.5C3), 130–31
    married women (12.5C5), 131

nature uncertain (12.5C6), 131–32
    place names hyphenated with (12.5C7), 132
surnames, names without, designations added (12.1C), 120
    see also Given names (forenames)
Swedish names, compound surname uncertain (12.5C6),
    132
    see also Scandinavian surnames with prefixes
System of Arrangement Element (3.2), 40–41
system requirements (electronic records) (4.3.6), 48–49

Technical Access Element (4.3), 48–49
technical drawing, definition, 207
television stations (14.11), 176
temporal relationships, 109
    see also Predecessor bodies; Successor bodies
terms of address
    distinguishing identical names (12.19B), 150–51
    married women (12.1C, 12.15B), 120, 144
    as part of name (12.11B), 143
terms of honor
    distinguishing identical names (12.19B), 150–51
    in names without surnames (12.1C), 120
    see also Titles of nobility
territorial designations
    children and grandchildren of royal persons (12.16A),
        146
    in royal names (12.8C), 140–41
    in titles of nobility (12.6B1), 138–39
textual materials
    definition, 207
    use of term, 30n33
thesauri
    bibliography, 210–11
    use of, xviii
*Thesaurus for Graphic Materials I: Subject Terms (TGM
    I),* 211
*Thesaurus for Graphic Materials II: Genre and Physical
    Characteristics Terms (TGM II),* xx, 211
Title Element (2.3), 17–23
title proper, definition, 207
title, definition, 207
titles of nobility
    added to names (12.12A), 143
    change of personal name (12.2C), 124
    entry under (12.6), 138–39
    in biographical history (10.16), 96
    in Italian names (12.5D1), 136
    in names without surnames (12.1C), 120
    in United Kingdom, 138n56, 143n57
    not used by person (12.6B3), 139
    order of elements (12.4B4), 129
    see also Terms of honor
titles of position or office
    as personal name (12.11B), 143
    distinguishing identical names (12.19B), 150–51
topic of the archival unit in Title Element (2.3.21-2.3.22),
    18, 22
    see also Subject headings
transcriptions, published, 75

transfer documents, 59, 61
transfer lists, 56
type of related resources in authority record (11.29), 112
    see also Form and genre characteristics
typographic devices in names (12.10), 141–42

undated materials (2.4.16), 28
undifferentiated names, headings for (12.20), 151
Unesco Thesaurus, 211
uniform titles, authorities for, 87
Union List of Artists' Names, 211
uniqueness of archival records, xi–xii
uniqueness of creator names, 86
United States
    Congress, legislative subcommittees (14.21C), 189
    place names (13.4C), 155
    political parties, state and local elements (14.16), 181
unit being described, records of more than one corporate
    body in (14.1C2), 161
universities, subordinate bodies of (14.13), 178
unknown creator, assembler, or collector in name segments
    (2.3.6), 19
unknown location for originals (6.1.7), 70
USMARC Code List for Countries, 211
USMARC Code List for Languages, 211
USMARC Code List for Organizations, 211

variant forms of name
    corporate names (14.2-14.3), 162–68
    in authority record, 86, 106-07
    personal names (12.3), 124–28

variant name, definition, 207
variant names of corporate bodies (14.2-14.3), 162-68
    autocephalous patriarchates (14.3C3), 165
    conferences (14.3F), 166–67
    governments (14.3E), 166
    in reference sources (14.2C), 162
    in the records (14.2D), 163
    places of worship (14.3G), 167–68
    religious orders (14.3D), 165–66
variant spellings
    corporate names (14.2E), 163
    personal names (12.3D), 128
vernacular forms of personal names
    vs. English (12.3B3), 126
    vs. Greek or Latin (12.3B2), 125–26
vernacular forms of place names (13.2B), 154

Wales, place names (13.4D), 155–56
words or phrases as names (12.11), 142–43
words or phrases with names
    added to names without surnames (12.1C), 120
    government names, distinguishing (14.6C), 172
    in entry under given name (12.8A1), 139–40
    see also Designations with names; Epithets in names of
        royalty
worship, places of
    additions to names (14.10), 175–76
    variant forms of name (14.3G), 167–68

Yiddish names, 127n49